LIVING & WORKING ABROAD

GETTING A
JOB IN AMERICA

How and where to find the right employment opportunities and contacts

Roger Jones

4th edition

I'M HAVING MY DOUBTS ABOUT THIS ONE!

VISA APPLICATIONS

How To Books

By the same author

How to Emigrate
How to Manage Your Career
How to Get a Job Abroad
How to Teach Abroad
How to Master Languages
How to Retire Abroad
Obtaining Visas and Work Permits

British Library Cataloguing-in-Publication data
A catalogue record for this book is available from the British Library.

Cartoons by Mike Flanagan

© 1997 by Roger Alan Jones

Published by How To Books Ltd, 3 Newtec Place, Magdalen Road,
Oxford OX4 1RE, United Kingdom.
Tel: (01865) 793806. Fax: (01865) 248780

First edition 1992
Second edition 1994
Third edition 1995
Fourth edition 1997

Note: The material contained in this book is set out in good faith for general
guidance and no liability can be accepted for loss or expense incurred as a
result of relying in particular circumstances on statements made in ths book.
The laws and regulations are complex and liable to change, and readers
should check the current position with the relevant authorities before making
personal arrangements.

Roger Alan Jones hereby asserts his moral right to be identified as the author of this book.

Typeset by Kestrel Data, Exeter
Printed and bound in Great Britain by
The Cromwell Press, Broughton Gifford, Melksham, Wiltshire.

Contents

Illustrations

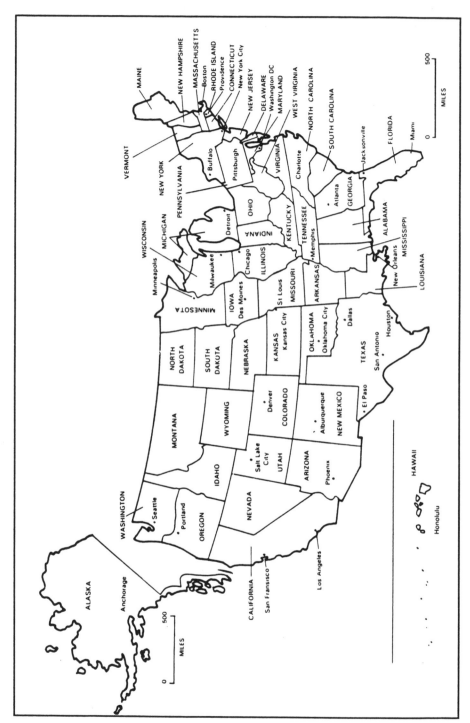

Fig. 1. Map of USA.

8

Preface
to the Fourth Edition

Each year thousands of people toy with the idea of working in the United States of America, but many are uncertain how to set about it. This book aims to provide some of the answers as well as some useful contacts for people who have never worked in the country before, whether they are applying for jobs from a foreign base or from inside America. I hope it will also be of benefit to employees who are being posted to the United States for the first time.

The US economy is looking more buoyant now, and so the number of employment opportunities for well-qualified people in a number of sectors is on the increase. However, such jobs are not open to all-comers and you need to be aware of the immigration restrictions that are placed on non-Americans. Rather than build up false hopes, you should first work your way through Chapter 2 to assess whether you are likely to qualify for the necessary visa. Even if you do, you could be subjected to a long wait.

In another book of mine, *How to Get a Job Abroad*, I place emphasis on the need for adequate preparation for a foreign posting in order to avoid such terrors as culture shock. While the cultural divide between the United States and Britain and Ireland is, happily, a narrow one, subtle differences do exist, and you need to be aware of these before you jet off.

Though every attempt has been made to ensure accuracy, information can go out of date, and I can only apologise for any inconvenience this may cause. I am, incidentally, always happy to receive suggestions and updated information from organisations which recruit for the United States, as well as from the recruited. It may be possible to include some of this material when the time comes for the book to be updated again.

For this the fourth edition of *How to Get a Job in America* I have undertaken a comprehensive revision of the text to reflect the many developments that have occurred since the last edition, not least the

9

Illegal Immigrant Reform and Immigrant Responsibility Act of 1996 (IIRIRA 96). I am particularly delighted to offer a more extensive list of UK based consultants who recruit for the USA and for the first time to explore the possibilities of the Internet in one's job search. The USA is way ahead of the rest of the world in using the Internet for recruitment purposes, and you may miss out if you ignore this medium. Fortunately the number of public access points to this network is growing (in the form of Internet cafés, for instance).

IIRIRA 96 appears to herald a tougher regulatory regime, and as a result people are going to need good advice on how to get through the red tape. So I have included a selection of US immigration lawyers and advisers in the UK Useful Addresses section. A more comprehensive worldwide listing is provided in *Obtaining Visas and Work Permits* also published by How To Books.

I trust that the book will continue to play a useful role in helping people to achieve their objectives and wish you successful job hunting.

Roger Jones

ACKNOWLEDGEMENTS

I am grateful to a number of people and organisations who have helped me in the preparation of this book by supplying me with information, allowing me to use their facilities or offering ideas and criticism. They include the American Community School, Hillingdon; the American School in London; the British Library; Cheltenham Public Library; the Central Bureau; the Department of Social Security; Expat Network; Sanwar Ali of BCL Immigration Services; Sarah Eykyn; Tommy Grant; Richard S. Goldstein; Ira Levy of US Visa Consultants; the National Association of Temporary Services; the New York State Office in London; Frederick Pearce; Peter Rushworth; the US Department of Labor; the US Customs Service, London; the US Information Service, London; the US–UK Educational Commission; the Visa Branch of the US Embassy, London as well as publishers, recruitment agencies and the staff of How To Books.

1
Land of Opportunity

THE USA PAST AND PRESENT

The past

The United States has always been regarded as the land of opportunity, and over the centuries millions of Europeans have crossed the Atlantic to seek their fortunes in the New World. The Spanish were the first to settle there in what is now Florida, and were followed by the French in Maine in 1604. The English were not far behind; the settlement of Jamestown in Virginia was founded in 1607. Dutch, Swedish and German communities were also established around this time.

For two centuries or so the English and the Irish predominated. In 1780, for instance, three out of four Americans could claim English or Irish ancestry. But over the past hundred years the population has become much more diverse, with mass immigration from eastern and southern Europe, and more recently from Asia. American blacks are a special case: they were unwilling immigrants.

Money was not always the motivating factor. The Pilgrim Fathers sailed to America in order to be able to worship as they pleased; during the years of the Potato Famine tens of thousands of Irish families went there to escape starvation; from 1880 onwards there was large scale emigration of Jews escaping the pogroms of Eastern Europe; and in our own time Cubans and South East Asians have sought asylum in America in large numbers.

For every one of these unfortunates, the United States meant hope and freedom, and many were doubtless inspired by the words on the base of the statue of Liberty in New York City harbour:

Give me your tired, your poor,
Your huddled masses yearning to breathe free,
The wretched refuse of your teeming shore.

Send these, the homeless tempest-tossed to me.
I lift my lamp beside the golden door.

The present

While the United States continues to open its door wide to refugees, the invitation does not extend to all comers. America, in common with most other countries, now places restrictions on immigration. The authorities are keen to protect the jobs of American citizens, and as a consequence employers are not allowed to offer jobs to outsiders ('aliens') if there is an American who can do the job just as well. So if you wish to take up employment you need to apply for a visa, and there is absolutely no guarantee that it will be granted.

Another change is that the US economy is not as buoyant as it was in the fifties and sixties, and while good opportunities undoubtedly exist you have to look harder for them and the competition is keen. Besides, if you wish to enjoy a good standard of living, Europe is as good a place as any in which to do so. We on this side of the Atlantic are no longer the poor relations of our American cousins.

Yet the United States continues to attract people from all over the world, for various reasons. Many of its industries are the leaders in their particular field and so are its academic institutions. It remains one of the world's leading economies, politically it is the most powerful country on earth and it is a trendsetter in many ways. American commercial interests span the globe and our business culture is strongly influenced by them.

For natives of the UK and Ireland there is a special benefit: it is a home from home—almost. Americans speak English—more or less —whatever George Bernard Shaw might say; American law has its roots in English law; Americans think in terms of pounds, miles, feet and inches; the food is familiar even if chips are called 'French fries'; the natives are hospitable and it is a 'swell' place to visit.

WHY WORK IN THE USA?

People hoping to work in the United States need to be clear from the start what they hope to gain from the experience. Your motives will often determine the kind of visa you apply for, and during the course of the application procedure you may well need to spell out your aims.

Here are some of the more usual reasons people give:

- To finance a stay in America. Students and young people in particular are almost invariably short of cash, so holidays or longer stays in the United States are only possible if they can find a means of financing themselves. What they do is immaterial: washing dishes, looking after children or waiting in restaurants are merely a means to an end. The important thing is to be there and to savour the country at first hand.

- To gain useful work experience. Some higher education courses require students to do a placement in a foreign country which could last from just a couple of months to over a year. Learning to work and survive in a different environment not only broadens one's outlook but could lead to excellent opportunities in the future in the international sphere.

- For career development. An increasing number of high level jobs nowadays call for people with international experience, who can work effectively in any part of the world and are equally at home in Birmingham, Bangkok or Bogota. Teachers and academics may also find that experience in a foreign country, apart from stimulating their ideas, also improves their status.

- To enjoy a better work environment. There are times when prospects at home look pretty bleak and people have an urge to look for greener pastures. In the sixties and seventies there was a considerable brain-drain from the British Isles to the United States, because R&D (research and development) facilities across the Atlantic were so much better funded. In certain areas, too, pay scales are much more generous.

- Because of family ties. If you have close relations in the United States, or you marry an American, you may have more compelling reasons than most to make your home there. You may also find that it is much easier for you to obtain the necessary documentation that will enable you to work.

- A company transfer. Some people do not specifically choose to go to the United States; they are asked to go there—to represent their company or their country, for instance, or to take control of a subsidiary firm. The move could represent a promotion and the prospect of higher earnings—in other words, you have an offer you can hardly refuse.

WHERE CAN I GO?

Clearly, people in the last category know precisely where they are to be located. Others may be in a position to choose, and for them a brief geography lesson is perhaps in order.

One mistake people tend to make is to think of America solely in terms of New York, Los Angeles and perhaps Washington, since these are the places that have the best media coverage. In fact, the United States is a semi-continent extending over 3.6 million square miles, which means it is almost twice the size of Europe. The scenery and climate are tremendously varied; and there are vast conurbations at one end of the spectrum and sparsely populated regions at the other.

In order to gain a better understanding of the country it is convenient to divide it into regions.

New England

Connecticut (CT): 4,872 sq m (area), 3.3 million (population), Hartford (capital)
Massachusetts (MA): 7,824 sq m, 6 million, Boston
Maine (ME): 30,995 sq m, 1.2 million, Augusta
New Hampshire (NH): 8,993 sq m, 1.1 million, Concord
Rhode Island (RI): 1,055 sq m, 1 million, Providence
Vermont (VT): 9,273 sq m, 570,000, Montpelier

Arguably the most English and historic part of the United States, some areas have experienced industrial decline in recent years. People here tend to be more formal and other Americans regard New Englanders as snobbish. The climate consists of cold winters (below freezing for three to four months of the year) and mild summers with rainfall on a par with the British Isles. The major centres of the area are Boston, Hartford (important for insurance) and New Haven (home to Yale University).

The Mid Atlantic Region

District of Columbia (DC): 63 sq m, 638,000
Delaware (DE): 1,932 sq m, 700,000, Dover
Maryland (MD): 9,837, 5 million, Annapolis
New Jersey (NJ): 7,468, 7.8 million, Trenton
New York (NY): 47,377 sq m, 18 million, Albany
Pennsylvania (PA): 44,888 sq m, 12 million, Harrisburg
Virginia (VA): 39,704 sq m, 6 million, Richmond
West Virginia (WV): 24,119 sq m, 2 million, Charleston

One of the major industrial centres of America and therefore a fruitful place for job hunting. New York State is the most populous state after California, and the New York Metropolitan area is home to 18 million. Both New York City and Washington have considerable expatriate British communities—50,000 in New York; 15,000 in Washington. Some 200 British firms have a Washington base. Other important centres are Baltimore, Philadelphia and Pittsburgh. In general the summers are warmer and the winters milder than those of New England, but inland you will encounter extremes.

The South
Alabama (AL): 50,767 sq m, 4.1 million, Montgomery
Arkansas (AR): 52,078 sq m, 2.4 million, Little Rock
Florida (FL): 54,153 sq m, 9.7 million, Tallahassee
Georgia (GA): 58,056 sq m, 6.7 million, Atlanta
Kentucky (KY): 39,669 sq m, 3.7 million, Frankfort
Louisiana (LA): 44,521 sq m, 4.2 million, Baton Rouge
Mississippi (MS): 47, 233 sq m, 2.5 million, Jackson
North Carolina (NC): 48,843 sq m, 6.8 million, Raleigh
South Carolina (SC): 30,203 sq m, 3.6 million, Columbia
Tennessee (TN): 41,155 sq m, 5 million, Nashville

This is *Gone with the Wind* country, where the pace of life tends to be slower, the cost of living lower and the climate warmer, though there can be plenty of snow inland in winter. Florida, which has a subtropical, somewhat humid climate, has expanded enormously in recent years and is perhaps the most promising place to seek work, particularly in the hotel and leisure industry. It has a large British community of more than 100,000 living principally in Tampa and Orlando, and its own newspaper the *Florida Brit*. The main centres are Atlanta, Kansas City, Miami, Nashville, New Orleans, Raleigh and Tampa.

The Mid West
Illinois (IL): 55,645 sq m, 11.4 million, Springfield
Indiana (IN): 35,932 sq m, 5.7 million, Indianapolis
Iowa* (IA): 55,965 sq m, 2.9 million, Des Moines
Kansas* (KS): 81,778 sq m, 2.4 million, Topeka
Michigan (MI): 56,954 sq m, 9.3 million, Lansing
Minnesota* (MN): 79,548 sq m, 4.5 million, St Paul
Missouri (MO) 68,945 sq m, 5.2 million, Jefferson City
Nebraska* (NE): 76,644 sq m, 1.6 million, Lincoln
North Dakota* (ND): 69,300 sq m, 650,000, Bismarck
Ohio (OH): 41,004 sq m, 11 million, Columbus
South Dakota* (SD): 75,952 sq m, 700,000, Pierre
*Great Plains agricultural states.

Wisconsin (WI): 54,426 sq m, 5 million, Madison

The hub of this vast area is Chicago, the nation's third largest city, and the region contains some of the country's richest farmland as well as many important mining industrial centres. However some of the activities of the area, notably the car industry in Detroit and agriculture on the Great Plains (the states marked with an asterisk), are in decline.

Other important centres are Cincinnati, Cleveland, Detroit, Milwaukee, Minneapolis St Paul, Omaha and St Louis. The temperatures are more extreme than in the UK and on the Great Plains winter temperatures of -40 degrees Celsius are not unusual.

The Rocky Mountains
Colorado (CO): 103,595 sq m, 3.5 million, Denver
Idaho (ID): 82,412 sq m, 1 million, Boise
Montana (MT): 145,388 sq m, 825,000, Helena
Utah (UT): 82,073 sq m, 1.8 million, Salt Lake City
Wyoming (WY): 96,989 sq m, 470,000, Cheyenne

Scenically stunning but sparsely populated, this is cowboy country. There may be job opportunities in some of the larger cities and in the National Parks. Colorado with its capital, Denver, is the fastest growing state of the Union. Salt Lake City is also an important centre.

The South West
Arizona (AZ): 113,508 sq m, 3.8 million, Phoenix
New Mexico (NM): 121, 335 sq m, 1.6 million, Santa Fe
Oklahoma (OK): 68,655 sq m, 3.2 million, Oklahoma City
Texas (TX): 262,017 sq m, 17.6 million, Austin

The oil industry gave this region a boost in the 1980s. Now the area is developing a substantial hi-tech industrial base and recruiting extensively from abroad. The main centres are Austin, Dallas-Fort Worth, Houston, Oklahoma City and Phoenix. Summers in the South West can be uncomfortably hot, but air conditioning makes life bearable.

The West
Alaska (AK): 570,833 sq m, 590,000, Juneau
California (CA): 156, 299 sq m, 31 million, Sacramento
Nevada (NV): 109,894 sq m, 1.4 million, Carson City
Oregon (OR): 96,184 sq m, 3 million, Salem

Washington (WA): 66,511 sq m, 5.1 million, Olympia

If California were a country it would rank among the top ten economies of the world. There is a large immigrant population in southern California since this is one of the largest industrial centres in the United States and is still expanding. The population of the Los Angeles Metropolitan Area numbers 13 million, and there is a sizeable British community here (consisting not only of film stars) which supports its own community newspaper, *The British Weekly* and TV channel. A monthly expatriate newspaper, *The Union Jack*, is also published in California and distributed nationwide. This is very much a home-from-home with British-style pubs and grocery shops.

Further north, in Washington State, is Seattle with its large aerospace industry. Apart from Los Angeles other important centres are Portland, San Diego, San Francisco, San Jose, Seattle, and—for gamblers and entertainers—Las Vegas. Alaska stands apart from the rest of the West; mining and oil are the mainstay of its economy and it has much of the old frontier atmosphere. It is also pretty cold in winter.

The Islands
Hawaii (HI) and various US Pacific and Caribbean territories (including Puerto Rico, Guam, American Samoa, Virgin Islands).
Hawaii (HI): 6,425 sq m, 1.1 million, Honolulu

One seldom associates these tropical islands with the United States. Employment opportunities here—apart from tourism—tend to be restricted.

So where should I make for?
In many cases the choice will be made for you; you go where you are sent or where you can get a good job. If the quality of life is an important consideration, the tables in Figures 2 and 3 will be of interest.

AM I ELIGIBLE TO WORK IN THE UNITED STATES?

One point you have to bear in mind throughout this book is that the United States has a well-educated population and is more or less self-sufficient in skilled people. The Federal Government therefore expects employers to recruit from this pool of talent wherever possible, rather than import staff from other countries. Not that the employers' choice is restricted to US citizens; nationals of other

Quality of Life Rankings

	*Education	Health Care	Cost of Living	Trans- portation	Overall Quality of Life
NEW ENGLAND					
Connecticut	14	3	2	32	4
Maine	18	17	45	17	24
Massachusetts	15	1	19	27	5
New Hampshire	32	4	33	14	17
Rhode Island	10	6	41	30	14
Vermont	9	10	49	9	19
MIDDLE ATLANTIC					
New Jersey	20	14	5	48	18
New York	26	12	35	42	31
Pennsylvania	22	13	27	25	20
EAST NORTH CENTRAL					
Illinois	33	20	9	29	23
Indiana	23	38	20	20	27
Michigan	30	27	17	33	28
Ohio	24	24	30	38	30
Wisconsin	3	8	34	23	8
WEST NORTH CENTRAL					
Iowa	4	11	37	4	3
Kansas	12	23	10	8	7
Minnesota	5	7	16	7	2
Missouri	36	19	8	40	25
Nebraska	7	16	24	12	6
North Dakota	6	2	38	3	1
South Dakota	17	26	31	1	9

*See Notes on page 20.

Fig. 2.   Quality of life rankings by region/state.

	Education	Health Care	Cost of Living	Trans- portation	Overall Quality of Life
SOUTH ATLANTIC					
Delaware	13	28	11	37	16
Florida	49	42	6	44	44
Georgia	47	45	15	43	47
Maryland	21	18	7	46	21
North Carolina	37	46	39	36	46
South Carolina	38	49	42	45	48
Virginia	27	29	12	34	26
West Virginia	34	30	44	18	38
EAST SOUTH CENTRAL					
Alabama	45	48	13	24	43
Kentucky	41	35	23	22	39
Mississippi	48	50	29	47	50
Tennessee	46	34	4	50	45
WEST SOUTH CENTRAL					
Arkansas	42	43	26	13	40
Louisiana	50	47	36	31	49
Oklahoma	39	39	25	15	37
Texas	43	44	14	26	42
MOUNTAIN					
Arizona	31	32	32	41	41
Colorado	16	9	28	16	12
Idaho	29	36	40	11	34
Montana	8	37	47	6	22
Nevada	40	31	18	10	29
New Mexico	25	33	22	35	33
Utah	28	22	43	21	32
Wyoming	1	41	50	2	13
PACIFIC					
Alaska	2	40	46	5	11
California	44	25	1	49	35
Hawaii	35	5	21	19	15
Oregon	11	21	48	39	36
Washington	19	15	3	28	10

Education index comprises: average teacher salaries as ratio or average pay of all workers; student teachers ratio (K 12); high school graduation rate; state expenditure per student for public education (K-12), per capita higher education state expenditures as a percentage of per capita income; and literacy rates.

Health care index comprises: the number of teaching hospitals; cancer treatment units and trauma units per 100,000 population; infant death rates; percentage of non-elderly population without health insurance; and physicians, registered nurses, and dentists per 100,000 population.

Cost of living index comprises: average costs for housing, food, and utilities as a percentage of average household income; and state income and property taxes as a percentage of total personal income.

Transportation index comprises: average urban commute time; percentage of state's budget dedicated to transportation; pavement condition of roadways; traffic-related fatalities and injuries per capita; per capita state transportation expenditures; and average daily traffic volume.

Overall quality of life is weighted composite of education, health care, cost of living, and transportation indices.

Source: Grant Thornton, Manufacturing Climates Study, June 1989.

countries who have permanent resident status (and are known in bureaucratic parlance as 'resident aliens') are eligible to apply for any jobs that are going.

However, you do not have to be a resident alien in possession of an **Alien Registration Receipt Card** (sometimes called the '**green card**') in order to work in the United States. A good many foreigners work for periods ranging from a few months to several years on temporary permits. There are certain restrictions: any employer wishing to recruit will normally have to demonstrate to the State authorities that he is unable to recruit the right kind of person locally. If he fails to convince them, they may well refuse his request for labour certification without which he cannot employ a non-US resident for a particular job.

The important matter of visas is treated at length in Chapter 2. It's a good idea to work through that chapter to find out what type of visa you will need in order to work in the United States. While it is now possible to move freely across borders within the European Union in search of a job, there is no open jobs market for British people—or indeed any non-American—in the United States, except for those with residential status.

Certain kinds of people are more welcome than others. You may have outstanding ability in your field or be able to offer skills that are much in demand. In the recent past certain areas of the United States have experienced a shortage of computer experts, electronics engineers, nurses and paramedics, and this shortage has been over-come by recruitment from abroad.

Your own connections can be crucial as well. You may be able to gain permanent residence on the strength of close family relationships; or you may be transferred to the United States by your firm or organisation. Entrepreneurial skills can also gain you access to the country: America welcomes investors.

WILL AMERICA SUIT ME?

Assuming there will be no problem in getting the necessary per-mission to work in the United States, you still need to consider whether a job on the other side of the Atlantic will really suit you. For, while most newcomers take to the United States like ducks to water, there are some who do not. They are irritated by the exuberance of many Americans, complain about the materialism they see around them, dislike the television programmes and the extremes of climate, and long for a pint of real ale and fish and chips.

Going to live and work in a strange location inevitably calls for adaptability; you must be prepared to meet the local people on their own terms. Fortunately, the American way of life is not as different from ours as that of, say, Mexico or Yemen, but even slight differences can irritate some people. You may dislike one part of the country and feel very much at home in another. There is, after all, considerable regional variety; if you dislike the formality of the east coast, you may feel more at home on the west coast where people are more casual.

It is unwise to take everything for granted. Public transport is a case in point: in much of the country public transport systems are rudimentary or completely non-existent. The car is king, and if you cannot drive you will be at something of a disadvantage. Another difference is that there is no government funded health service except for the old and handicapped; you will need to pay for medical treatment, or better, insure yourself against illness.

Though the language may sound reasonably familiar, it is perhaps wiser to regard the United States as a foreign country with different values and different customs. Even things which sound similar may be different: an American gallon, for instance, is less than the Imperial equivalent. Driving rules are different as well, with speed limits normally lower than those in Europe. The high-speed car chases you see in films are definitely not typical of the United States.

Average Monthly Temperature and Rainfall

T, temperature in Fahrenheit; P, precipitation in inches; L, less than 0.5 inch

Station	Jan T	Jan P	Feb T	Feb P	Mar T	Mar P	Apr T	Apr P	May T	May P	June T	June P	July T	July P	Aug T	Aug P	Sept T	Sept P	Oct T	Oct P	Nov T	Nov P	Dec T	Dec P
Albany	21	2.4	23	2.3	34	3.0	47	2.9	58	3.3	67	3.3	71	3.0	69	3.3	61	3.2	51	2.9	39	3.0	26	3.0
Albuquerque, N.M.	35	0.4	39	0.4	46	0.5	55	0.4	64	0.5	75	0.5	79	1.3	76	1.5	69	0.6	57	0.9	44	0.4	36	0.5
Anchorage, Alas.	13	0.8	18	0.9	24	0.7	35	0.7	46	0.6	54	1.1	58	2.0	56	2.1	48	2.5	35	1.7	22	1.1	14	1.1
Asheville, N.C.	37	3.5	39	3.6	46	5.1	56	3.8	63	4.2	70	4.2	73	4.4	73	4.8	73	3.2	56	3.3	46	3.3	39	3.5
Atlanta, Ga.	42	4.9	45	4.4	53	5.9	62	4.4	69	4.0	76	3.4	79	4.7	78	3.4	73	3.2	62	2.5	52	3.4	45	4.2
Atlantic City, N.J.	34	3.3	35	3.3	42	3.7	51	3.1	60	2.9	68	2.9	74	3.9	74	4.5	68	2.7	58	2.8	48	3.5	38	3.5
Baltimore, Md.	33	3.0	35	3.0	43	3.7	54	3.4	63	3.4	72	3.8	77	3.9	76	4.6	69	3.5	57	3.1	46	3.1	37	3.4
Barrow, Alas.	-14	0.2	-20	0.2	-16	0.2	-2	0.2	19	0.2	33	0.4	39	0.9	38	1.0	31	0.6	14	0.6	-1	0.3	-13	0.2
Birmingham, Ala.	42	5.2	46	4.7	54	6.6	63	5.0	70	4.5	77	3.7	80	5.4	80	3.9	74	4.3	62	2.7	52	3.6	45	5.0
Bismarck, N.D.	7	0.5	15	0.5	26	0.7	43	1.5	55	2.2	64	3.0	70	2.0	69	1.7	57	1.4	46	0.8	29	0.5	15	0.5
Boise, Ida.	30	1.5	36	1.1	41	1.0	49	1.2	57	1.2	66	1.0	75	0.3	72	0.4	63	0.6	52	0.8	40	1.3	32	1.3
Boston, Mass.	30	4.0	31	3.7	38	4.1	49	3.7	59	3.5	68	2.9	72	2.7	72	3.7	65	3.4	55	3.4	45	4.2	34	4.9
Buffalo, N.Y.	24	3.0	25	2.4	33	3.0	45	3.0	56	2.9	66	2.7	70	2.9	69	4.2	62	3.4	52	2.9	40	3.6	29	3.4
Burlington, Vt.	17	1.9	18	1.7	29	2.2	43	2.8	55	3.0	65	3.6	70	3.4	67	3.9	59	3.2	48	2.8	37	2.8	23	2.4
Caribou, Me.	11	2.4	13	2.1	24	2.4	37	2.6	50	2.9	60	3.2	65	4.0	63	4.0	54	3.5	43	3.1	31	3.2	16	3.1
Charleston, S.C.	49	3.3	51	3.4	57	4.4	66	2.6	73	4.4	79	6.5	82	7.3	81	6.5	77	4.9	68	2.9	59	2.2	52	3.1
Chicago, Ill.	21	1.6	26	1.3	36	2.6	49	3.7	59	3.2	68	3.5	73	3.6	72	3.5	65	3.4	54	2.3	40	2.1	28	2.1
Cleveland, Oh.	26	2.5	27	2.2	37	3.0	48	3.3	59	3.3	68	3.5	72	3.4	70	3.4	64	2.9	53	2.5	42	2.8	31	2.8
Columbus, Oh.	27	2.8	30	2.2	40	3.2	51	3.4	61	3.8	70	4.0	74	4.0	72	3.7	66	2.8	54	1.9	42	2.6	32	2.6
Dallas-Ft. Worth, Tex.	44	1.7	49	1.9	56	2.4	66	3.6	74	4.3	82	2.6	86	2.0	86	1.8	79	3.3	68	2.5	56	1.8	46	1.7
Denver, Col.	30	0.5	34	0.7	37	1.2	47	1.8	57	2.5	67	1.6	73	1.9	71	1.5	63	1.2	52	1.0	39	0.8	33	0.6
Des Moines, Ia.	19	1.0	25	1.1	35	2.2	51	3.2	62	4.0	72	4.2	76	3.2	74	4.1	65	3.1	54	2.2	39	1.5	26	1.5
Detroit, Mich.	23	1.9	26	1.7	35	2.5	47	3.2	58	2.8	68	3.4	72	3.1	70	3.2	63	1.9	52	2.1	40	2.3	29	2.5
Dodge City, Kan.	30	0.5	35	0.5	42	1.5	54	1.8	64	3.3	75	3.0	80	3.1	78	2.5	69	1.9	58	1.3	43	0.8	34	0.5
Duluth, Minn.	6	1.2	12	0.9	23	1.8	38	2.2	50	3.4	59	4.0	65	4.0	63	4.1	54	3.3	44	2.2	28	1.7	14	1.3
Eureka, Cal.	47	7.0	49	5.2	48	5.1	49	2.9	52	1.6	55	0.6	56	0.1	57	0.4	57	0.9	54	2.7	51	5.9	48	6.2
Fairbanks, Alas.	-13	0.5	-4	0.5	9	0.4	30	0.3	48	0.6	59	1.3	62	1.8	57	1.9	45	1.1	25	0.7	4	0.7	-10	0.7
Fresno, Cal.	46	2.0	51	1.9	54	1.6	60	1.2	68	0.3	75	0.1	81	L	79	L	74	0.2	65	0.4	53	1.2	45	1.6
Galveston, Tex.	54	3.0	56	2.3	62	2.1	69	2.6	76	3.3	81	3.5	83	4.3	83	4.4	80	5.8	73	2.6	63	3.2	57	3.6
Grand Junction, Col.	26	0.6	34	0.5	42	0.8	52	0.7	62	0.8	72	0.4	79	0.5	76	0.9	67	0.7	55	0.9	40	0.6	28	0.6
Gr. Rapids, Mich.	22	0.9	24	1.5	33	2.5	46	3.6	58	3.0	67	3.9	71	3.0	70	3.5	62	3.1	51	2.9	39	2.9	27	2.6
Hartford, Conn.	25	3.5	28	3.2	37	4.2	49	4.0	59	3.4	69	3.4	73	3.1	71	4.1	63	3.9	52	3.5	42	4.1	29	4.2
Helena, Mon.	18	0.7	26	0.4	32	0.7	42	1.0	52	1.7	60	2.0	68	1.0	66	1.2	56	0.8	45	0.7	31	0.5	23	0.6
Honolulu, Ha.	73	3.8	73	2.7	74	3.5	76	1.5	78	1.2	79	0.5	80	0.5	81	0.6	78	0.7	80	1.9	77	3.2	74	3.4
Houston, Tex.	51	3.2	55	3.3	61	2.7	69	4.2	75	4.7	81	4.0	83	3.3	83	3.7	78	4.9	70	3.7	60	3.4	54	3.7
Huron, S.D.	11	0.4	18	0.8	29	1.2	46	2.0	57	2.7	68	3.3	74	2.3	72	2.0	61	1.4	49	1.4	32	0.7	19	0.5
Indianapolis, Ind.	26	2.7	30	2.5	40	3.6	52	3.7	63	3.7	74	3.3	75	4.3	73	3.5	67	2.7	55	2.5	42	3.0	32	3.0
Jackson, Miss.	46	5.0	49	4.9	56	5.9	65	5.9	73	4.8	79	3.4	82	4.4	81	3.7	76	3.6	65	2.6	55	4.2	49	5.4
Jacksonville, Fla.	53	3.1	55	3.5	61	3.7	68	3.3	74	4.9	79	5.4	81	6.5	81	7.2	78	7.3	70	3.4	61	1.9	55	2.6
Juneau, Alas.	22	3.7	28	3.7	31	3.3	39	2.9	46	3.4	53	3.0	56	4.1	55	5.0	49	6.4	42	7.7	33	5.2	27	4.7
Kansas City, Mo.	26	1.0	32	1.0	42	2.1	55	2.7	65	4.4	76	4.1	79	3.5	77	3.2	68	3.3	58	2.5	43	1.2	32	1.1
Knoxville, Tenn.	38	4.7	42	4.2	50	5.5	60	3.9	67	3.7	74	4.0	78	4.3	77	3.0	72	3.0	60	2.7	49	3.8	41	4.6
Lander, Wyo.	20	0.5	26	0.6	32	1.1	42	2.2	53	2.7	62	1.5	71	0.7	69	0.5	58	0.9	47	1.2	31	0.8	23	0.5
Lexington, Ky.	32	3.6	35	3.3	44	4.8	55	4.0	64	4.2	72	4.2	76	5.0	75	4.0	69	3.3	57	2.3	45	3.3	36	3.8
Little Rock, Ark.	40	3.9	44	3.8	52	4.7	62	5.4	71	5.3	79	3.7	82	3.6	81	3.1	74	4.3	63	2.8	51	4.4	43	4.2

Fig. 3. Average monthly temperature and rainfall, based on a thirty-year period (National Climatic Data Center, US Department of Commerce).

Each cell gives average temperature (°F) and rainfall (in.). Columns run January–December.

City	Jan	Feb	Mar	Apr	May	Jun	Jul	Aug	Sep	Oct	Nov	Dec
Los Angeles, Ca.	57 3.7	59 3.0	60 2.4	62 1.2	66 0.2	69 L	74 L	75 0.1	73 0.3	69 0.2	63 1.9	58 2.0
Louisville, Ky.	33 3.4	36 3.2	45 4.7	57 4.1	65 4.2	74 3.6	78 4.1	76 3.3	70 3.6	58 2.6	48 3.5	37 3.5
Marquette, Mich.	12 2.0	14 1.9	23 2.8	37 3.3	50 4.0	60 3.6	65 3.2	63 3.3	54 3.9	44 3.6	30 2.9	18 2.4
Memphis, Tenn.	40 4.6	44 4.3	52 5.4	63 5.8	71 5.1	79 3.6	82 4.0	81 3.7	74 3.6	63 7.1	51 4.2	43 4.9
Miami, Fla.	67 2.1	68 2.1	72 1.9	75 3.1	79 6.5	81 9.2	83 6.0	83 7.0	82 8.1	78 7.1	73 2.7	69 1.9
Milwaukee, Wis.	11 1.6	23 1.3	32 2.6	45 3.4	55 2.6	65 3.6	71 3.5	69 3.1	62 2.5	50 2.6	33 1.3	25 2.0
Minneapolis, Minn.	20 0.8	18 0.9	29 1.7	46 2.1	59 3.2	68 4.1	73 3.5	71 3.6	61 2.5	50 1.9	37 1.0	19 0.9
Mobile, Ala.	51 4.6	54 4.9	60 6.5	68 5.4	75 5.5	81 5.1	82 7.7	82 6.8	78 6.6	69 2.6	59 3.7	53 5.4
Moline, Ill.	20 1.6	25 1.3	36 2.8	50 4.8	61 4.2	71 4.3	75 4.9	75 3.5	65 3.7	54 2.7	39 2.0	26 1.9
Nashville, Tenn.	37 4.5	40 4.0	49 5.6	60 4.8	68 4.6	76 3.7	79 3.8	78 3.5	72 3.7	60 2.6	49 3.5	41 4.6
Newark, N.J.	31 3.1	33 3.1	41 4.2	52 3.6	62 3.6	72 2.9	77 3.9	77 4.9	68 3.7	57 3.1	47 3.6	36 3.4
New Orleans, La.	52 5.0	55 5.2	61 4.7	69 4.5	75 5.1	80 4.6	82 6.7	82 6.0	79 5.9	69 2.7	60 4.1	55 5.3
New York, N.Y.	32 3.2	33 3.1	41 4.2	53 3.8	62 3.8	71 3.2	77 3.8	76 3.4	68 3.7	58 3.4	47 4.1	36 3.8
Nome, Alas.	9 0.8	3 0.5	7 0.6	18 0.6	36 0.5	45 1.2	51 2.2	50 3.1	42 2.3	28 1.3	16 0.9	4 0.7
Norfolk, Va.	40 3.7	41 3.3	49 3.9	58 2.9	67 3.8	76 3.5	78 5.2	78 5.3	72 4.4	61 3.4	52 2.9	44 3.2
Okla. City, Okla.	36 1.0	41 1.3	49 2.1	60 2.9	68 5.5	77 3.9	82 3.0	81 2.4	73 3.4	62 2.7	49 1.5	40 1.2
Omaha, Neb.	19 0.8	25 0.9	35 1.9	50 2.9	62 4.3	77 4.1	76 3.6	78 3.6	64 2.5	54 2.1	38 1.3	26 0.9
Pago Pago, Amer. Samoa	81 13	81 11	81 11	81 11	80 11	80 8.6	80 11	80 11	79 6.7	80 11	80 11	81 14
Philadelphia, Pa.	31 3.2	33 2.8	42 3.9	53 3.5	63 3.2	72 3.9	77 3.9	77 4.1	68 3.4	57 2.8	46 3.3	36 3.5
Phoenix, Ariz.	52 0.7	56 0.6	61 0.8	68 0.3	77 0.1	67 0.2	92 0.7	90 1.0	85 0.6	73 0.6	61 0.5	53 0.8
Pittsburgh, Pa.	27 2.9	29 2.4	39 3.6	50 3.3	62 3.1	67 2.8	72 3.8	71 3.3	64 2.8	53 2.5	42 2.3	31 2.6
Portland, Me.	22 3.8	23 3.6	32 4.0	43 3.9	63 3.3	63 1.5	68 2.8	67 2.8	59 3.3	49 3.8	38 4.7	26 4.5
Portland, Ore.	39 6.2	43 3.9	46 3.6	50 2.3	57 2.1	63 1.5	68 0.5	68 0.8	59 1.6	54 3.1	46 5.2	41 6.4
Providence, R.I.	28 4.1	29 3.7	37 4.3	48 4.0	64 3.5	67 2.8	73 3.0	73 1.5	64 3.5	53 3.8	43 4.2	32 4.5
Raleigh, N.C.	40 3.6	42 3.4	49 3.7	59 2.9	71 3.7	74 3.7	74 5.2	74 5.2	71 3.3	60 2.7	50 2.9	42 3.1
Rapid City, S.D.	21 0.4	26 0.6	33 1.0	45 2.0	62 2.6	65 3.3	73 2.1	73 1.5	61 1.0	50 0.8	35 0.5	26 0.5
Reno, Nev.	32 1.2	37 1.0	41 0.7	46 0.5	56 0.7	62 0.3	70 0.3	70 0.3	60 0.3	50 0.3	40 0.6	33 1.2
Richmond, Va.	37 3.2	39 3.1	47 3.6	58 3.6	66 3.6	74 3.6	78 5.1	78 5.1	70 3.5	59 3.7	49 3.3	40 3.4
St. Louis, Mo.	29 1.7	34 2.1	43 3.3	56 3.6	66 3.5	75 3.7	79 3.6	79 2.7	70 2.7	58 2.3	45 2.5	34 2.2
Salt Lake City, Ut.	29 1.4	34 1.3	41 1.7	49 2.2	59 1.5	68 1.0	78 0.7	78 0.9	65 0.9	53 1.1	40 1.2	30 1.4
San Antonio, Tex.	50 1.6	54 1.9	62 1.3	70 2.7	76 3.7	80 3.0	78 1.9	85 1.9	79 3.8	70 2.9	60 2.3	53 1.4
San Diego, Cal.	57 2.1	58 1.4	59 1.6	61 0.8	62 0.3	66 0.1	70 L	70 L	70 0.2	68 0.3	62 1.1	57 1.4
San Francisco, Cal.	49 4.7	52 3.2	53 2.6	55 1.5	58 0.3	61 0.1	62 L	62 L	64 0.2	61 1.1	55 2.4	49 3.6
San Juan, P.R.	77 3.0	77 3.0	78 2.3	80 3.6	79 5.6	80 4.7	82 4.9	82 6.0	82 6.0	81 5.9	80 5.6	78 4.7
Sault Ste. Marie, Mich.	13 2.2	14 1.7	24 2.0	38 2.4	58 3.6	58 3.3	64 3.0	64 2.9	55 3.9	45 2.9	33 3.2	20 2.6
Savannah, Ga.	49 3.1	52 3.2	58 3.8	66 2.4	73 4.6	79 5.7	81 7.4	81 6.7	77 5.2	67 2.3	58 1.9	51 2.8
Seattle, Wash.	39 6.0	43 4.2	44 3.6	49 2.4	55 1.6	60 1.4	65 1.3	64 0.7	60 2.0	52 3.4	45 5.6	41 6.3
Spokane, Wash.	26 2.5	32 1.6	38 1.4	46 1.1	55 1.4	62 1.2	68 0.7	64 1.3	60 0.7	48 1.1	35 2.1	29 2.5
Springfield, Mo.	32 1.6	36 2.1	45 3.4	56 4.0	65 4.3	73 4.7	78 3.6	77 3.2	70 4.2	58 3.2	45 2.9	36 2.6
Syracuse, N.Y.	23 2.6	24 2.7	33 3.1	46 3.3	57 3.2	66 3.6	71 3.8	71 3.8	62 3.3	51 3.1	45 3.5	28 3.2
Tampa, Fla.	60 2.2	61 3.0	66 3.5	72 1.8	77 7.4	81 5.3	82 7.4	82 7.6	81 6.2	74 2.3	67 1.9	61 2.1
Washington, D.C.	31 2.8	34 2.6	42 3.4	53 3.1	62 3.4	71 4.2	76 3.8	76 4.2	74 4.2	55 3.0	45 3.0	35 3.3
Wilmington, Dal.	31 3.1	33 3.0	42 3.9	52 3.4	62 3.2	71 3.5	76 3.9	75 4.0	68 3.6	56 2.9	48 3.3	36 3.5

Will my family like living there?

If you have a family, you need to consider the implications of a move to the United States with care. What may be an exciting challenge for you could turn out to be a mild form of torture for them.

Your spouse

This is most frequently a wife, but sometimes the wife is the main breadwinner and the accompanying spouse is male.

Problems can arise when both partners want to pursue their own careers. You need to discuss whether your spouse is prepared to give up his or her job in order to accompany you to the United States, or whether you should settle for a bachelor existence with holidays and the occasional weekend spent together.

There are also financial considerations. If your spouse gives up her/his job you are probably faced with the matter of living on one income instead of two. There is no guarantee that your spouse will be granted the type of visa that will enable him/her to work in America.

Some spouses may relish a life away from the workplace, but for others who are used to a busy existence time may hang heavy. While you may have plenty of colleagues with whom to socialise at work, your spouse has to go out and make his/her own social contacts. If they cannot drive or do not have the use of a car, this can be a problem in suburbia and in remote areas.

Fortunately, in most areas there are clubs to join and adult education classes to attend. Organisations such as the Women's

Computer Science	$32,769	Hotel, Restaurant Mgt.	$23,885
Nursing	$30,078	Education	$22,898
Geology	$28,689	Social Science	$22,606
Chemistry	$28,551	Retailing	$22,195
Accounting	$28,002	Advertising	$21,870
Physics	$27,330	Communications	$21,860
Financial Admin.	$26,838	Home Economics	$21,353
Mathematics	$26,630	Liberal Arts	$21,124
Marketing/Sales	$24,782	Journalism	$20,637
Business Admin.	$23,950	Telecommunications	$20,820

Fig. 4.   Starting salaries for new graduates (Collegiate Employment Research Institute).

| | Median weekly earnings ($) | | | |
	1993 Men	1993 Women	1994 Men	1994 Women
Managerial and professional specialty	791	576	802	594
Executive, administrative, and managerial	790	523	792	550
Professional specialty	792	603	811	624
Technical, sales, and administrative support	529	377	522	376
Technicians and related support	585	473	588	472
Sales occupations	543	328	564	323
Administrative support, including clerical	492	374	462	372
Service occupations	349	255	332	258
Private household	(1)	183	(1)	183
Protective service	540	431	534	380
Service, except private household and protective	291	258	284	257
Precision production, craft, and repair	514	354	513	385
Mechanics and repairers	513	579	524	512
Construction trades	500	(1)	487	(1)
Other precision production, craft, and repair	539	320	546	366
Operators, fabricators, and laborers	402	293	404	300
Machine operators, assemblers, and inspectors	410	291	414	300
Transportation and material moving occupations	463	351	471	340
Handlers, equipment cleaners, helpers, and laborers	316	280	314	292
Farming, forestry, and fishing	269	239	294	226

(1) *Data not shown where base is less than 100,000*

Fig. 5. Median usual weekly earnings (in dollars) of full-time wage and salary workers (Bureau of Labor Statistics, US Department of Labor).

State	Average annual pay 1993	1994	Percent change 1993-4	State	Average annual pay 1993	1994	Percent change 1993-4
United States	**26,361**	**26,939**	**2.2**	Missouri	23,898	24,628	3.1
Alabama	22,786	23,616	3.6	Montana	19,932	20,218	1.4
Alaska	32,336	32,657	1.0	Nebraska	20,815	21,500	3.3
Arizona	23,501	24,276	3.3	Nevada	25,461	25,700	0.9
Arkansas	20,337	20,898	2.8	New Hampshire	24,962	25,555	2.4
California	29,470	29,878	1.4	New Jersey	32,722	33,439	2.2
Colorado	25,682	26,155	1.8	New Mexico	21,731	22,351	2.9
Connecticut	33,169	33,811	1.9	New York	32,919	33,439	1.6
Delaware	27,144	27,952	3.0	North Carolina	22,773	23,460	3.0
D.C.	39,199	40,919	4.4	North Dakota	19,382	19,893	2.6
Florida	23,571	23,918	1.5	Ohio	25,338	26,134	3.1
Georgia	24,865	25,313	1.8	Oklahoma	22,001	22,293	1.3
Hawaii	26,325	26,746	1.6	Oregon	24,093	24,780	2.9
Idaho	21,188	21,938	3.5	Pennsylvania	26,274	26,950	2.6
Illinois	28,425	29,107	2.4	Rhode Island	24,889	25,454	2.3
Indiana	24,109	24,908	3.3	South Carolina	21,933	22,477	2.5
Iowa	21,441	22,189	3.5	South Dakota	18,613	19,255	3.4
Kansas	22,430	22,907	2.1	Tennessee	23,368	24,106	3.2
Kentucky	22,170	22,747	2.6	Texas	25,523	25,959	1.7
Louisiana	22,633	23,178	2.4	Utah	22,250	22,811	2.5
Maine	22,026	22,389	1.6	Vermont	22,704	22,964	1.1
Maryland	27,686	28,416	2.6	Virginia	25,504	26,035	2.1
Massachusetts	30,229	31,024	2.6	Washington	25,760	26,362	2.3
Michigan	28,260	29,541	4.5	West Virginia	22,373	22,959	2.6
Minnesota	25,710	26,422	2.8	Wisconsin	23,610	24,324	3.0
Mississippi	19,693	20,382	3.5	Wyoming	21,745	22,054	1.4

Fig. 6. Average annual pay by state (US Bureau of Labor Statistics).

Median Sales Price of Existing One-Family Homes, by Selected Metropolitan Area: 1990 to 1995
(in thousands of dollars)

Metropolitan area	1990	1993	1994	1995
US all areas	95.5	106.8	109.8	112.9
Albany-Schenectady-Troy, NY	106.9	112.3	112.0	105.9
Annaheim-Santa Ana, CA MSA	242.4	217.2	211.0	208.8
Atlanta, GA	(NA)	91.8	93.6	97.5
Baltimore, MD	105.9	115.7	115.4	111.3
Birmingham, AL	80.8	96.5	100.2	103.6
Boston, MA PMSA	174.1	173.2	179.3	179.0
Buffalo-Niagara Falls, NY CMSA	77.2	83.5	82.3	81.3
Charlotte-Gastonia-Rock Hill, NC-SC	93.1	106.1	106.5	107.8
Chicago, IL PMSA	116.8	142.0	144.1	147.9
Cincinnati, OH-KY-IN PMSA	79.8	91.4	96.5	100.4
Cleveland, OH PMSA	80.6	95.0	98.5	104.7
Columbus, OH	81.6	91.8	94.8	99.1
Dallas, TX PMSA	89.5	94.5	95.0	96.4
Denver, CO PMSA	86.4	104.7	116.8	127.3
Detroit, MI PMSA	76.7	86.0	87.0	98.2
Ft. Lauderdale-Hollywood-Pompano Beach, FL PMSA	92.6	103.1	103.1	105.9
Ft. Worth-Arlington, TX PMSA	76.7	82.9	82.5	83.7
Hartford, CT PMSA	157.3	135.3	133.4	133.4
Honolulu, HI	352.0	358.5	360.0	349.0
Houston, TX PMSA	70.7	80.9	80.5	79.2
Indianapolis, IN	74.8	86.6	90.7	94.6
Jacksonville, FL	72.4	77.1	81.9	83.1
Kansas City, MO-KS	74.1	83.6	87.1	91.7
Las Vegas, NV	93.0	108.2	110.5	113.5
Los Angeles-Long Beach, CA PMSA	212.1	195.4	189.1	179.9
Louisville, KY-IN	60.8	74.5	80.5	86.4
Memphis, TN-AR-MS	78.1	87.0	86.3	86.5
Miami-Hialeah, FL PMSA	89.3	98.8	103.2	107.1
Milwaukee, WI PMSA	84.4	104.1	109.0	114.7
Minneapolis-St Paul, MN-WI	88.7	98.2	101.5	106.8
Nashville, TN	81.8	90.4	96.5	107.3
New Orleans, LA	67.8	76.8	76.9	78.0
New York-Northern New Jersey-Long Island, NY-NJ-CT CMSA	174.9	173.2	173.2	169.7
Oklahoma City, OK	53.2	64.9	66.7	70.4
Orlando, FL	82.8	90.1	90.7	89.2
Philadelphia, PA-NJ PMSA	108.7	118.0	119.5	118.7
Phoenix, AZ	84.0	89.1	91.4	96.8
Pittsburgh, PA PMSA	70.1	82.2	80.7	82.1
Portland, OR PMSA	79.5	106.0	116.9	128.4
Richmond-Petersburg, VA	87.5	94.1	95.4	103.1
Riverside/San Bernardino, CA PMSA	132.1	134.4	129.1	120.9
Rochester, NY	79.8	84.8	85.6	85.0
St. Louis, MO-IL	76.7	84.8	85.0	87.7
Sacramento, CA	137.5	129.2	124.5	120.2
Salt Lake City-Ogden, UT	69.4	84.9	98.0	113.7
San Antonio, TX	63.6	77.0	78.2	80.8
San Diego, CA	183.2	176.9	176.0	171.6
San Francisco, CA PMSA	259.3	254.4	255.6	254.4
Seattle-Tacoma, WA CMSA	142.0	150.2	155.9	159.0
Tampa-St. Petersburg-Clearwater, FL	71.4	75.0	76.2	78.3
Washington, DC-MD-VA	150.5	158.3	157.9	156.5
West Palm Beach-Boca Raton-Delray Beach, FL	108.0	114.6	117.6	121.3

Fig. 7.   Median sales price of houses (National Association of Realtors, Washtington, DC).

Average House Prices and Mortgages

	Median-priced existing home ($)	Average mortgage rate (%)	Monthly principal and interest payment ($)	Payment as percentage of median income (%)
1981	66,400	15.12	677	36.3
1982	67,800	15.38	702	35.9
1983	70,300	12,85	616	30.1
1984	72,400	12.49	618	28.2
1985	75,500	11.74	609	26.2
1986	80,300	10.25	563	23.0
1987	85,600	9.28	565	21.9
1988	90,600	9.31	591	22.0
1989	93,100	10.11	660	23.1
1990	97,500	10.04	673	22.7
1991	99,700	9.51	671	22.3
1992	100,900	8.48	620	20.0

Fig. 8. Housing affordability (National Association of Realtors).

Corona Society and Christians Abroad may also be able to find a contact to look after your spouse in the initial stages.

Your children

If you are planning to live in the United States for several years, or possibly for ever, you will doubtless want to take your children with you. However, if they are into their teens consideration has to be given to their education. The American education system differs fundamentally from the British system, and if crucial examinations are looming up and you want them to go on to further or higher education in the UK, you need to consider their future carefully.

There are various options:

- enable them to continue at their present school
- put them into a UK boarding school
- enrol them in a school in the United States
- enrol them in a school in America which offers a British style curriculum.

Schools in the last category, which prepare pupils for British examinations or the International Baccalaureate, tend to be few and far between, and generally only in those centres where there is a sizeable British community (see also Chapter 5).

THE FINANCIAL AND OTHER REWARDS

Will I earn more money in the United States? Will my salary go as far as it would at home? These are the questions that are often uppermost in people's minds when they consider taking up a posting in the United States. Unfortunately, there is no simple answer.

The table of Earnings by Occupation and Sex in Figure 4 may provide some clue, though the earnings quoted relate to US residents rather than expatriates. If you are recruited in the UK for a short-term contract you may well earn more than the average for a particular job. The same will doubtless be true if you are sent to the United States by your firm when all the perks and other inducements are taken into account. Others may not be so lucky; resident aliens, for instance, may have to settle for pay rates that are closer to the local norms.

When it comes to the actual cost of living, one can only generalise. Household goods are often cheaper than in the UK and so are cars. The cost of accommodation varies considerably. New York City is expensive to live in, but probably no more so than London; and renting an apartment in Manhattan could well set you back the same amount as its equivalent in Mayfair. However, if you are living in Manhattan the chances are that your employer is paying your rent anyway.

There are, of course, cheaper areas where you can live reasonably well, just as there are in Greater London, and if you have to pay your own rent you will doubtless head for these. Boston, Los Angeles, San Francisco and Washington DC are other cities where accommodation tends to be on the expensive side, as the table in Figure 7 shows, but elsewhere housing is relatively cheap. For instance, in Houston it is possible to find a modest, three-bedroomed house for around $60,000, or an apartment to rent for $600 per month or less. (To calculate annual rents approximately, divide the figures for house prices in the table by ten.)

However, you should not count your chickens before they are hatched, since there are various obstacles to be negotiated. One of the most difficult is the immigration hurdle. The next chapter is devoted to this.

2
Getting Into the United States: The Red Tape

This book is primarily about getting a job in the United States, not about the United States immigration laws. However, an understanding of these laws is vital in order to ensure a trouble free entry into the United States. Your working intentions will determine and be determined by the type of visa you apply for.

A few myths need to be dispelled first:

- You don't need a visa in order to take up casual work in the United States.
  Wrong. If you are employed in the United States in any capacity you need a work visa; anybody without one is classified as an illegal immigrant and is breaking the law. Nonetheless, there are plenty of people who are willing to take the risk regardless of the consequences.

- In order to work in the United States you need first to obtain a 'green card'.
  Wrong. The **Alien Registration Receipt Card,** to give it its official title, is for people with permanent resident status, and not everybody needs this. Most newcomers to the United States enter on non-immigrant (temporary) visas which permit them to work and can often be extended or adjusted.

- It is essential to use a lawyer to obtain a work permit.
  Wrong. United States immigration laws may be complicated, but many people and employers manage quite happily without a legal adviser. Besides if you do not qualify for a visa, using a lawyer will not change anything. However, if your situation is complicated or you have doubts about your eligibility it is prudent to seek advice

THE NEED FOR A VISA

As you saw in the first chapter, the United States no longer has an open door policy with respect to immigration. The country's population has grown enormously, so partly to protect the interests of its workforce it now imposes limits on immigrants. For instance, a maximum of 675,000 immigrants are allowed in annually. Whether you seek temporary employment or permanent residence you have to apply for a visa before you go.

The only exceptions to the rule are citizens of certain countries (including Britain) who are making a holiday or business trip of 90 days or less, and are in possession of a return ticket. People who can claim American citizenship by reason of birth or parentage are also exempt. Anybody else needs to get an appropriate visa, whether they are involved in an exchange or a course of study, or whether they are planning to settle permanently.

Be warned. If you enter the country without an appropriate visa and take up employment, you and your employer are breaking the law. While you may manage to get away with it for a time—and quite a lot of people do—you are running a considerable risk. You will be regarded as an illegal immigrant, and if you are found out you could be deported and prohibited from entering the United States again. The longer you stay, the greater the danger of being found out.

There are ways out of the dilemma.

- You may be able to legalise your status with the Immigration and Naturalisation Service. But if you have been unlawfully present for over six months you will be barred from legalising your status for three years. For anyone who has outstayed his welcome in this way for over a year the bar is for ten years. There are few exceptions to this rule.

- You can marry a United States citizen, and file a petition for a green card.

- The Federal Government has offered an amnesty to illegal immigrants in the past, but you cannot count on it happening in the future.

If you are hoping to enter the United States job market by the back door, you had better forget it. Immigration officials (particularly those at major ports of entry, such as New York and Los Angeles) can be very strict. If they suspect you are a job seeker posing as a tourist, they have powers to search you and your luggage. Should they find a job offer or job advertisements among your belongings, or discover that you have not enough cash to finance your visit, they could well refuse you entry.

That is why I recommend you try to get things right from the start. By wading through this chapter you should gain an insight into US immigration practices and what type of visa you should aim for.

THE 1990 IMMIGRATION LAW (IMMACT 90)

United States immigration law underwent a complete overhaul in 1990. You therefore need to make sure that any advice or information you get is completely up to date, otherwise you may find yourself setting off on completely the wrong track.

The information given below should serve as a guide, but do not regard it as the last word. If your position is a complicated one, you or any firm that wants to employ you will need to obtain advice from the nearest United States consulate (for applicants outside the United States), or the nearest Immigration and Naturalisation Service (INS) office (for applicants within the United States). Alternatively, you could refer to manuals such as *Applying for a United States Visa* or call on the services of an immigration lawyer or consultant.

If you decide to use a lawyer, the US Embassy can supply you with a list of American immigration lawyers operating in the UK and you will find several listed in Appendix F. *Obtaining Visas and Work Permits* has a more extensive list covering several countries. I would recommend you deal with specialists who practise within your own country, and whose reputation you can check up on. Also, be prepared to shop around.

First, though, you need to decide how long you intend to be in the United States. If you do not intend to stay in the country permanently, but just for a matter of months or years, you will need a non-immigrant (temporary) visa of some kind, which in many cases can be extended.

Even if your long-term aim is permanent residence, there is no reason why you should not start off with a non-immigrant visa. For one thing, these are normally easier to obtain. There is nothing to prevent you from petitioning for adjustment of status to that of permanent resident at a later date once you are in the country.

NON-IMMIGRANT (TEMPORARY) VISAS

To determine what kind of visa you require you should ask yourself the following questions:

- Are you going purely for a holiday or for a business trip?
  Under the Visa Waiver Pilot Program (VWPP) citizens of Western Europe, Japan and New Zealand do not need a visa, if their visit is for less than 90 days and they are in possession of a return ticket. However, it is impossible to extend your stay or change your immigrant status.

  If you plan to stay longer, travel by a non-participating carrier or if you are a citizen of another country, you will need to obtain a business visitor visa (B-1) or a tourist visa (B-2).

- Are you planning to undertake temporary vacation employment?
  or
  Do you want to undertake a paid traineeship (internship) or academic exchange?
  or
  Do you want to work as an au pair for a year?
  You will probably be eligible for exchange visitor status which is a fairly quick and straightforward process. It involves approaching a sponsoring organisation, such as BUNAC, Camp America, CIEE and certain au pair agencies, which are authorised to issue you with Form IAP-66. This enables you to obtain a category **J-1 visa**. Chapter 3 deals with exchanges in detail.

- Are you involved in an approved cultural exchange programme?
  If you are at least 18 years old and providing practical training, employment and the sharing of the history, culture and traditions of your home country you should apply for a **Q** visa which enables you to take paid employment. Normally the prospective employer or agent will submit the application to INS.

- Do you plan to work in the United States on a temporary basis but do not qualify for an exchange visitor visa?
  You will need an **H-2 temporary worker visa**. However, first of all your prospective employer will need to apply to the state department of labor for labor certification and demonstrate that he has not been able to recruit a US resident for the post. In the case of non-graduates this can take time as the employer may be required to advertise the post locally first.
  If the job requires a graduate, and you have a degree or equivalent, you might be eligible for an **H-1B visa**. A professional nurse qualifies for an **H-1A visa**.

- Are you planning to do a traineeship not covered by the exchange visitor visa?
  Your employer has to submit an application for an **H-3 industrial trainee visa** to the local office of the Immigration and Naturalisation Service (INS).

- Are you planning to study in the United States and work during the vacation?
  If you enter the United States on an **F visa** you are not normally entitled to take a job in your first year, though on-campus employment is permitted provided it does not displace a United States resident. If you want to undertake employment off-campus (for instance, during the vacation), you will need to apply to the Immigration and Naturalisation Service (INS) for permission.

- Do you have specialist knowledge to first degree level or beyond, equivalent experience, or a licence to practise and does the job require these qualifications?
  You are eligible to apply for a **H-1B visa** which will allow you to stay up to six years (with renewals). There is a quota of 65,000 H-1B visas annually, and once the quota is used up no further visas can be issued until the start of the next fiscal year (in October).
  First your prospective employer has to submit an attestation to the United States Department of Labor documenting the salary, working conditions and absence of a strike or lockout, and this process can take a little time. In the case of nurses and other professionals in great demand some of the red tape may be waived.

- Are you a person considered outstanding in your particular field (*eg* as a scientist, artist or entertainer)?
  You are eligible for an **O-1** for which labor certification is not required.

- Are you a recognised athlete, entertainer or artist going to compete or perform in the US?
  You should apply for a **P-1** visa.

- Are you being sent to the United States by your company?
  You should be eligible for an **L-1 Intra Company Transferee visa**, provided you have worked for the company for one year during the three years preceding your application for a visa. The

PLEASE TYPE OR PRINT YOUR ANSWERS IN THE SPACE PROVIDED BELOW EACH ITEM

1. SURNAMES OR FAMILY NAMES (Exactly as in Passport)

DO NOT WRITE IN THIS SPACE

2. FIRST NAME AND MIDDLE NAME (Exactly as in Passport)

3. OTHER NAMES (Maiden, Religious, Professional, Aliases)

4. DATE OF BIRTH (Day, Month, Year)

8. PASSPORT NUMBER

5. PLACE OF BIRTH
City, Province   Country

DATE PASSPORT ISSUED
(Day, Month, Year)

6. NATIONALITY

7. SEX
☐ Male
☐ Female

DATE PASSPORT EXPIRES
(Day, Month, Year)

9. HOME ADDRESS (include apartment no., street, city, province and postal zone)

10. NAME AND STREET ADDRESS OF PRESENT EMPLOYER OR SCHOOL
(Postal Box number unacceptable)

11. HOME TELEPHONE NO.

12. BUSINESS TELEPHONE NO.

13. COLOR OF HAIR

14. COLOR OF EYES

15. COMPLEXION

16. HEIGHT

17. MARKS OF IDENTIFICATION

24. PRESENT OCCUPATION (If retired state past occupation)

18. MARITAL STATUS
☐ Married   ☐ Single   ☐ Widowed   ☐ Divorced   ☐ Separated
If married, give name and nationality of spouse

25. WHO WILL FURNISH FINANCIAL SUPPORT, INCLUDING TICKETS ?

19. NAMES AND RELATIONSHIPS OF PERSONS TRAVELING WITH YOU
(NOTE: A separate application must be made for each visa traveler, regardless of age.)

26. AT WHAT ADDRESS WILL YOU STAY IN THE USA ?

20. HAVE YOU EVER APPLIED FOR A U.S. VISA BEFORE, WHETHER IMMIGRANT OR NON-IMMIGRANT?
☐ No
☐ Yes
When ? _____ Where ? _____
Type of Visa ? _____
☐ Visa was issued   ☐ Visa was refused

27. WHAT IS THE PURPOSE OF YOUR TRIP ?

21. HAS YOUR U.S. VISA EVER BEEN CANCELED?
☐ No
☐ Yes
When ? _____ Where ? _____
By Whom ? _____

28. WHEN DO YOU INTEND TO ARRIVE IN THE USA ?

22. Bearers of visitors visas may generally not work or study in the U.S.
DO YOU INTEND TO WORK IN THE U.S.?   ☐ No ☐ Yes
If YES, explain

29. HOW LONG DO YOU PLAN TO STAY IN THE USA ?

23. DO YOU INTEND TO STUDY IN THE U.S. ?   ☐ No ☐ Yes
If YES, write name and address of school as it appears on form I-20.

30. HAVE YOU EVER BEEN IN THE USA ?
☐ No
☐ Yes   When? _____
For How long ? _____

NONIMMIGRANT VISA APPLICATION

COMPLETE ALL QUESTIONS ON REVERSE OF FORM

OPTIONAL FORM 156 (Rev 4-91) PAGE 1   50156-108
Department of State

NSN 7540-00-139-0053

Fig. 9. Non-immigrant visa application.

31. (a) HAVE YOU OR ANYONE ACTING FOR YOU EVER INDICATED TO A U.S. CONSULAR OR IMMIGRATION EMPLOYEE A DESIRE TO IMMIGRATE TO THE U.S.? (b) HAS ANYONE EVER FILED AN IMMIGRANT VISA PETITION ON YOUR BEHALF? (C) HAS LABOR CERTIFICATION FOR EMPLOYMENT IN THE U.S. EVER BEEN REQUESTED BY YOU OR ON YOUR BEHALF?

(a) ☐No ☐Yes   (b) ☐No ☐Yes   (c) ☐No ☐Yes

32. ARE ANY OF THE FOLLOWING IN THE U.S.? (If YES, circle appropriate relationship and indicate that person's status in the U.S., ie. studying, working, U.S. permanent resident, U.S. citizen, etc.)

HUSBAND/WIFE _____   FIANCE/FIANCEE _____   BROTHER/SISTER _____

FATHER/MOTHER _____   SON/DAUGHTER _____

33. PLEASE LIST THE COUNTRIES WHERE YOU HAVE LIVED FOR MORE THAN 6 MONTHS DURING THE PAST 5 YEARS. BEGIN WITH YOUR PRESENT RESIDENCE.

Countries	Cities	Approximate Dates

34. IMPORTANT: ALL APPLICANTS MUST READ AND CHECK THE APPROPRIATE BOX FOR EACH ITEM:

A visa may not be issued to persons who are within specific categories defined by law as inadmissable to the United States (except when a waiver is obtained in advance). Are any of the following applicable to you?

— Have you ever been afflicted with a communicable disease of public health significance, a dangerous physical or mental disorder, or been a drug abuser or addict? .... ☐Yes ☐No

— Have you ever been arrested or convicted for any offense or crime, even through subject of a pardon, amnesty, or other such legal action? .... ☐Yes ☐No

— Have you ever been a controlled substance (drug) trafficker, or a prostitute or procurer? .... ☐Yes ☐No

— Have you ever sought to obtain, or assist others to obtain a visa, entry into the U.S., or any U.S. immigration benefit by fraud or willful misrepresentation? .... ☐Yes ☐No

— Were you deported from the U.S.A. within the last 5 years? .... ☐Yes ☐No

— Do you seek to enter the United States to engage in export control violations, subversive or terrorist activities or any unlawful purpose? .... ☐Yes ☐No

— Have you ever ordered, incited, assisted, or otherwise participated in the persecution of any person because of race, religion, national origin, or political opinion under the control, direct or indirect, of the Nazi Government of Germany, or of the government of any area occupied by, or allied with, the Nazi Government of Germany, or have you ever participated in genocide?........... ☐Yes ☐No

A YES answer does not automatically signify ineligibility for a visa, but if you answered YES to any of the above, or if you have any question in this regard, personal appearance at this office is recommended. If appearance is not possible at this time, attach a statement of facts in your case to this application.

35. I certify that I have read and understood all the questions set forth in this application and the answers I have furnished on this form are true and correct to the best of my knowledge and belief. I understand that any false or misleading statement may result in the permanent refusal of a visa or denial of entry into the United States. I understand that possession of a visa does not entitle the bearer to enter the United States of America upon arrival at port of entry if he or she is found inadmissable.

DATE OF APPLICATION _____

APPLICANT'S SIGNATURE _____

If this application has been prepared by a travel agency or another person on your behalf, the agent should indicate name and address of agency or person with appropriate signature of individual preparing form.

SIGNATURE OF PERSON PREPARING FORM _____
(If other than the applicant)

DO NOT WRITE IN THIS SPACE

37mm x 37mm

PHOTO

Glue or Staple
photo here

Optional Form 156 (Rev. 4-91) PAGE 2
Department of State

Fig. 9. – continued.

stay is limited to seven years for executives and managers and five years for individuals with specialist knowledge. There are usually few, if any, problems in obtaining visas for high-ranking executives.

- Are you seeking temporary admission to the United States to manage substantial trade between the United States and your own country?
  If so, you are eligible to apply for an **E-1 Treaty Trader visa**. However, you must be an individual trader or an executive or be performing services that are essential to the company's operation in the United States. The company must also show that it is engaged in continuous trade of a substantial nature between the United States and a country with which the United States has a Treaty of Commerce and Navigation. (See also Chapter 9).

- Are you seeking temporary admission in order to develop and/or direct a substantial investment in the United States?
  You are eligible to apply for **E-2 Treaty Investor** status based on the following criteria:
  —investment of substantial funds
  —the enterprise is up and running
  —the investment is more than marginal
  —you are in a position to develop and direct the enterprise.
  Employees of a Treaty Investor are also eligible if they are executives, highly trained staff or essential to the operation by reason of their qualifications.
  For anyone in the E category the initial period of a stay is one year, but this can be extended almost indefinitely. (See also Chapter 9.)

Other types of visa
There are various other categories of non-immigrant visa, such as for diplomats and for the staff of international organisations, but in most cases the employer is responsible for getting the visa, and this procedure presents no real problems. A person working for a religious organisation, for instance, would just need a letter from the employing organisation certifying his credentials to support his application.

If you intend to study in the United States it is also necessary to obtain a visa, and the institution where you plan to study will provide you with the appropriate form (I-20A). However, bear in mind that a study visa does not automatically grant you the right to work on a part-time or seasonal basis. If you wish to do so, you should apply for permission to accept employment on Form I-538. This form also needs to be completed if you want to extend your stay or transfer to another academic institution.

Applying for a non-immigrant (temporary) visa

1. The first step
This will normally be to get in touch with the nearest United States consulate or INS office to find out which procedures you must go through.

- Exchange visitors must complete **Form OF-156** obtainable from the nearest US Consulate. J-1 applicants must also submit **Form IAP-66** and Q-1 applicants **Form I-129** prepared by the sponsoring organisation (*eg* CIEE, BUNAC).
- For H, L, O and P visas, your prospective employer or agent must first submit **Form I-129** (Petition for a Nonimmigrant Worker) to the INS.
- For E-1 and E-2 visas you may need to complete a supplemental form in addition to **Form OF-156** and submit it to the nearest US consular office.

2. Approval of the application
If the application is approved the INS issues the **Notice of Approval of Non-Immigrant Visa** petition **(Form I-797)** to the consulate that is dealing with your application.

Should you have not yet submitted Form **OF-156** (application form), this is the time to do so together with your passport, a passport-sized photograph and any other documentation you are asked for.

If your application is turned down, you may appeal to the regional commissioner in control of the INS or the consulate to which you have applied.

3. Immigration procedures on arrival in the United States.
On arrival at the port of entry make sure you look reasonably presentable. Immigration officers have been known to refuse entry to people whose appearance is bohemian or unkempt, as well as those with the wrong kind of visa. If entry is refused unjustly, you have no right of appeal, unless you are seeking asylum.

The length of time you are permitted to stay in the United States is entered on your **INS Arrival/Departure Record (Form I-94)**. This is an important document which will play a part in any subsequent immigration procedures and you should take good care of it.

4. Extension or change of status

Once in the United States you can apply for an adjustment of non-immigrant status or for an extension to your stay. With **Form I-539** this will normally be done through the regional office of the Immigration and Naturalization Service—the addresses of which are in Appendix G.

If your application is not granted you can ask for a review—a 'motion to reopen and reconsider' in officialese.

The main types of Non-Immigrant (Temporary) Visa
(with numerical limits where applicable)

B-1	Business visitor
B-2	Tourist
F-1	Student taking academic course
E-1	Treaty Trader
E-2	Treaty Investor
L-1	Intra-Company transferee
H-1A	Professional nurse
H-1B	Specialist occupation (65,000)
H-2A	Agricultural worker (temporary or seasonal)
H-2B	Other worker category
H-3	Trainee (not medical or academic) (50)
J-1	Exchange visitor
M-1	Full-time vocational student
O-1	Person with extraordinary ability in the sciences, arts, education, business and athletics
P-1	Recognised athlete, entertainer or artist (25,000)
Q	Cultural programme participant
R-1	Person in religious occupation

IMMIGRANT VISAS

The chances are that you will be able to skip the second half of this chapter. Immigrant visas are generally more difficult to obtain, and in any case the majority of people from the UK who go to work in the United States do so on non-immigrant (temporary) visas, which have already been dealt with.

However, if at some time in the future you decide to settle permanently in the United States you will need to apply for immigrant status and an Alien Registration Receipt Card (the 'green card'). (Later on you may decide to go the whole hog and become a naturalised United States citizen, but that will not be discussed in this book.)

Full immigrant status can be granted on the basis of:

● family relationships
● your trade or profession (employment based preferences)
● other criteria (*eg* the Diversity Immigrants Scheme).

Family relationships
If you have close relatives living in the United States this can generally facilitate matters. The level of family sponsored immigration is currently set at 480,000.

Immediate relatives
● Are you the spouse or child of a United States citizen?
● Are you the parents of United States citizens who are 21 years old or more?

In both the above cases numerical limits do not apply and you should therefore experience no difficulty in getting an immigrant visa.

Family sponsored preferences
Here you have to stand in the queue to take up places that have not been taken up by immediate relatives. The annual numerical limit is determined by subtracting the previous year's immediate relative total from the specified world-wide level of family sponsored immigrants (*ie* 480,000). The following questions will help you work out whether you qualify:

● Are you the unmarried son or daughter of a United States citizen? You come under **FSP 1** for which there is a quota of 23,400.

● Are you the spouse or child of a permanent resident? You come under **FSP 2A** for which there is a minimum quota of 87,394.

● Are you the unmarried son or daughter of a permanent resident and over 21? You come under **FSP 2B** for which there is a minimum quota of 26,266.

● Are you the married son or daughter of a citizen? You come under **FSP 3** for which there is a quota of 23,400.

● Are you the brother or sister of a citizen aged 21 years or over?

You come under **FSP 4** for which there is a quota of 65,000 a year.

Employment Based Preferences

If you have no family connections in the United States you may be able to enter the country on the strength of your employment or entrepreneurial skills. Under the new Immigration Act the number of employment based immigrants has been increased substantially from 54,000 to 140,000. Work out whether you qualify by asking:

- Are you an individual with .extraordinary ability in the arts, sciences, education, business or athletics?
- Are you a professor or researcher recognised internationally as outstanding in your field and with three years' experience, entering the United States for a tenured or tenure track position?
- Are you a multinational executive or manager employed with the sponsoring employer or affiliate for at least one year in the three years preceding your application for residence in or entry to the United States?
- Are you working in a religious occupation?

Anyone who fits the above criteria is regarded as a **Priority Worker** and falls into **Employment-Based Preference Category One** (E1) for which the annual quota is 40,000. No labour certification is required, but for people in the last three categories the prospective employer must provide a job offer and apply to the INS.

- Do you possess advanced qualifications in a professional field?
- Are you a person of exceptional ability in the arts, sciences or business?

If so, you could be considered for **Employment-Based Preference Category Two** (E2), **Members of the Professions**, for which the quota is 40,000 plus any unused visas from Category One. Labor certification is required **or** Schedule A designation (nurses and physiotherapists, *etc*) **or** you have to be in a shortage occupation defined in the Labor Market Information Pilot Program. This means that employers need to obtain a certificate from the Department of Labor demonstrating that there are not sufficient United States workers who are able, willing, qualified and available for the position in which they are seeking to recruit an alien.

- Are you a skilled worker with a minimum of two years' training or experience?
- Are you a professional with a Bachelor's degree?
- Do you have less than two years training and experience?

You may fall into **Employment-Based Preference Category Three** (E3), **Professionals, Skilled and Unskilled Workers,** for which the quota is 40,000 plus any unused visas from Categories One and Two. However, no more than 10,000 visas are available to Unskilled Workers. You are subject to the same restrictions (labor certification, *etc*) as Category Two.

- Are you employed in a professional capacity by a religious organisation?
- Are you an overseas employee of the US Government?
- Are you a retired employee of an international organisation?
- Are you a current or former employee of the United States Armed Forces?

You fall into **Employment-Based Preference Category Four— Special Immigrants** (E4), which also includes Panama Canal employees and others. The quota is 10,000.

- Are you an investor in a new commercial enterprise that will create full-time employment for at least ten persons who are not members of your immediate family?

Employment Based Preference Category Five (E5) sets aside 10,000 visas for foreign investors, of which not less than 3,000 are reserved for investors in rural or high unemployment areas. The minimum investment is normally $1 million but $500,000 in a targeted area of high employment or a rural area.

Other categories of immigrant visa

Diversity Immigrants
In October 1994 a new category of visa came into effect under which applicants from certain countries are selected in random order. Applicants are required to have either a high school education or at least two years' work experience in an occupation that requires two years' training or experience. Only one petition may be submitted each year and there is a quota of 55,000 visas.

Currently people born in Ireland (Eire and Ulster) and various other countries are eligible to participate in the Diversity Immigrant Visa Lottery. However, anyone born elsewhere in the UK is not eligible for this scheme. (Natives of Canada, China, Mexico, the Philippines, Taiwan, Vietnam, *etc* are not eligible either.) But this could change in future years. In recent years there have been more than 100 applicants for each place under the scheme. The initial application is straightforward and you will not need to use the services of a lawyer.

Fiancé(e)s of American citizens
A person who plans to get married to a US citizen needs a K visa to enter the United States, and the US citizen needs to file a petition (Form I-129K) with the appropriate regional office of the INS. The marriage has to take place within 90 days of entry, and a petition then has to be lodged with the INS for adjustment of status to legal permanent residence.

Refugees and asylum seekers
Registration for classification as a refugee requires the completion of Form I-590, and for an asylum seeker Form I-589.

Immigrant visas: how to apply

1. The first step

- For a family sponsored immigrant visa your relative should normally file a petition (Form I-130) with the regional office of the Immigration and Naturalisation Service (INS) in the United States.

- For an employment based immigrant visa, Form I-140 must be filed with the INS.

- Where labor certification is necessary the applicant must complete Department of Labor Form ETA-750B (Statement of Qualifications) and send it to the prospective employer who completes Form ETA-750A (Application for Certification) and forward it to the local office of the State Employment Service. For Schedule A the employer submits a completed, uncertified Form ETA-750 and I-140 petition to the INS. For current information on the Labor Market Information Pilot Program you should contact INS.

- Special immigrants (E4) must file a Form I-360 petition with an INS office.

- Investors (E5) should file a Form I-360 petition with the INS.

- Information regarding the Diversity Immigrant Visa Lottery can be obtained from US Embassies and Consulates and the application has to be sent to the National Visa Centre, Portsmouth, New Hampshire.

2. Preliminary application
In most cases the consulate will send you two forms: the **Preliminary Questionnaire for Residence (OF-169)** and the **Biographic Data for Visa Purposes Form (OF-179)**.

3. Interview
Eventually you will be called for an interview and need to submit an **Application of Immigrant Visa and Alien Registration (Form 230)**. The consular officer will inform visa applicants of the documents required to support the application (*eg* passport, birth certificate, police certificates).

4. Medical Examination
You will need to undergo a medical examination conducted by a doctor designated by the consular officer, and for which a fee is payable.

5. Visa fees
A fee is payable for the visa which is not refundable.

6. Issue of a visa
Immigrant visas are issued in the chronological order in which the petitions were filed, and you should not rely on being issued with a visa very promptly. If you fall into a category which is over-subscribed there may be a waiting period of some years. A visa is valid for four months from the date of issue.

7. Arrival in the United States
On arrival the immigration authorities will stamp a temporary 'green card' stamp in your passport. Your alien registration receipt card will be sent to you in the post several months later.

Applying for immigrant status in the United States

If you decide to apply for permanent residence once you are in the country, you will normally need to contact the INS office closest to your place of residence. Applications are usually sent by post, but some offices can deal with you in person.

Note that it is not a case of 'once an immigrant always an immigrant'. If you leave the United States you could lose your immigrant status. To avoid this, you should obtain a re-entry permit if you plan to stay outside the United States for more than a year. This involves completing **Form I-130 Application for Issuance or Extension of Permit to Re-enter the United States**. If you take out citizenship, this formality is no longer necessary.

PEOPLE NOT ELIGIBLE FOR VISAS

Certain visa applicants are considered statutorily ineligible. The main categories are:

- sufferers of communicable diseases (*eg* tuberculosis)
- people with a dangerous physical or mental disorder
- people who have committed serious criminal acts
- terrorists, subversives, members of a totalitarian party
- people likely to become public charges in the United States
- anyone who has used fraud or other illegal means to enter the United States
- anyone with convictions for domestic violence and stalking
- anyone without proof of vaccination against certain diseases (including measles, polio, hepatitis B).

It may however be possible to get a waiver of ineligibility, which would permit a visa to be issued.

If you have been an exchange visitor in the past you may have to live outside the United States for two years before you can apply for another visa, while physicians who plan to practise medicine must pass a qualifying exam before they can get a work visa.

You need to bear in mind that immigration policy and procedures are subject to modification and some of the information in this chapter may be rendered invalid by future legislation.

The monthly newspaper *Going USA* publishes details of the latest immigration rules and there are a number of websites on the Internet which answer frequently asked questions (FAQs) regarding immigration (e.g. www.uslawyer.com). The US Visa Office in London operates a general information line.

3
Vacation Jobs and Exchanges

This book draws a distinction between people who are interested in spending a substantial part of their careers or lives in the United States and those whose aims are short-term. Young people, for instance, want to experience the country at first hand and are prepared to undertake a variety of vacation jobs in order to finance their trip. Others, both young and old, are keen to go to America in order to develop skills in their particular fields.

While anyone wishing to undertake employment needs to obtain a visa, if you are participating in a recognised exchange programme this process is usually little more than a formality. There are a number of agencies based in Britain and Ireland which are authorised by the US Government to issue the necessary documentation (the IAP-66 form) for obtaining the **J-1 Exchange Visitor Visa**, though for some programmes different arrangements may be necessary. The most significant of these are listed towards the end of the chapter.

You must bear in mind that you may only work under the terms of the exchange programme and are not eligible to seek other employment while you are in the United States. Nor will you normally be allowed to take up employment there within two years of the exchange. On the brighter side you are automatically exempt from paying US social security and income tax, and the visa is issued free.

Unfortunately for most of these exchange programmes a limit is placed on numbers of participants and eligibility criteria are often restrictive. If you find that you do not qualify for any of the programmes mentioned in this chapter, you will have to look into the possibility of obtaining a different kind of visa, and this can take time. For an **H-2 Temporary Worker Visa** or an **H-3 Industrial Trainee Worker** the prospective employer has to obtain the necessary labor certification first, and you will be subject to social security tax.

THE OPPORTUNITIES AVAILABLE

Working in children's camps

A great many American youngsters—some seven million—spend their summer holidays in camps run by organisations such as the YMCA, the scouting organisations, religious or philanthropic agencies as well as by private individuals. There are over 12,000 camps in all; some are fully residential and in areas of natural beauty, while others are in effect day centres providing recreational facilities during the hours of daylight.

There are broadly two types of post available.

Camp counsellors

These are camp leaders or organisers who put together a programme of activities and encourage their protegees to participate. This can be challenging work, since American youngsters can be lively and precocious, and you may well be expected to demonstrate that you have experience of dealing with children.

As the ICCP brochure points out:

'Spending a summer as a camp counsellor in an American camp may not be for everyone; it can mean long days, hard work and little privacy and spare time. Working as a camp counsellor can also mean a lot of adjustments while living in a simple and often isolated setting. Participation in ICCP is not a low-cost ticket to "see the USA" or a money-making summer job.'

Ancillary staff

These are the backroom boys and girls—the cooks, the cleaners, the people who maintain the campsite. This can turn out to be tiring work involving long hours, especially at the beginning of the camp season when there can be much to prepare. Flexibility and a capacity for hard work are essential.

The *Parents' Guide to Accredited Camps* published by the American Camping Association lists around 2,500 summer camps and includes a section on the camp job market. See also BUNAC, AIFS, Camp America, Camp Counsellors USA and YMCA entries in this chapter.

Other vacation jobs in the United States

There are a number of seasonal jobs available, especially during the summer in resorts around the country. If you are still a student it may well be possible to enter the US on an Exchange Visitor visa

For counsellors

0700	Wake up call
0745	Flag raising
0800-0830	Breakfast
0830-0900	Clean-up
0900-1200	Activities
1200-1230	Lunch
1230-1330	Rest hour
1330-1700	Activities
1730-1830	Dinner service
1800-1830	Dinner
1900-2100	Evening activities
2100-2200	Lights out
2400-0100	Curfew—All staff back in cabins

For ancillary staff

0630	Kitchen duties begin
0730-0800	Breakfast service and auxiliary duties begin
0800-0830	Office duties begin
0830-1200	General duties
1130-1230	Lunch service duties
	(1-2 hours off midday)
1230-1700	Resume duties
1800-2030	Resume auxiliary duties
	(Evenings usually off duty)
2400-0100	Curfew—All staff back in cabins

Fig. 10. A typical Camp America Schedule.

provided you set about things the right way. The jobs do not have to be related to your course subjects or your intended profession, and may well pay better than jobs in summer camps.

The current *Summer Employment Directory of the United States* will give you an idea of the types of jobs available. Many of the jobs are seasonal ones in summer resorts, notably in the hotel and catering industry. The National Park Service has openings virtually everywhere, and in states such as Colorado guiding jobs are available.

There are also behind the scenes jobs with summer theatres, in amusement and theme parks and on ranches. In the bigger conurbations temporary office work may be available. If you are particularly enterprising and lucky, you may find more unusual employment. BUNAC reports that three participants on its programmes have worked as a masseuse, an oyster digger and a private detective!

There are two ways of setting about getting a job under the exchange visitor scheme:

● You arrange your job in advance and apply to an agency such as BUNAC or Camp America that can issue an **IAP-66** form. Many people do this through personal contacts in the United States or by applying to organisations mentioned in handbooks such as the *Summer Employment Directory of the United States.*

● You try your luck at getting a job on arrival. However, in order to qualify for an Exchange Visitor Visa, you will need to find a private sponsor in the United States who is acceptable to the authorities. You can either contact employers direct or try an employment agency specialising in temporary work. **The National Association of Temporary Services** is the trade body for these. (See also Chapter 6.)

Au pair work

It is now possible, if you are aged between 18 and 26, to spend a year working as an au pair on an Exchange Visitor Visa. There are two programmes:

● **Au Pair in America** administered by the American Institute for Foreign Study (AIFS)
● **Au Pair Homestay USA** organised by EIL (Experiment in International Living) Ltd.

Both schemes are recognised by the Federal Government.

For jobs in the United States you will normally be expected to have some experience of looking after children, and also to be a car driver and a non-smoker. You will be required to look after the children and undertake light household duties for around 40 hours a week. In return you receive:

● pocket money of around $125 a week
● your board and lodging
● your travel expenses
● up to six hours a week of classes in a subject of your choosing.

If you would prefer to work as an au pair just for the summer, Camp America runs the **Family Companion** programme under which you will be expected to work for ten weeks, in return for which your air fares will be paid and you will receive board and lodging and an allowance of $300. One perk is that you may be required to accompany your host family on holiday.

A number of people enter America as tourists in order to take up positions as au pairs and nannies, but this is a risky business these days. For instance, you could be turned back by immigration officials at your port of entry; or your employers could be fined for illegally employing an alien.

An excellent reference book for would-be au pairs is *The Au Pair and Nanny's Guide* by Susan Griffith and Sharon Legg (Vacation Work).

Internships

An internship is not a prison sentence but an opportunity to gain work experience, normally in one's chosen career field. Students on vocationally based courses in Britain tend to get placements in the British Isles, but if you wish to gain international experience, why not try for a placement in the United States? Among the organisations that can facilitate such a move are **AIESEC** (business sector), the **Central Bureau** (hotel and catering sector), **IAESTE** (technical and scientific placements), the **Mountbatten Internship Programme** and **CIEE** (most sectors). If your college or employer can arrange an internship for a US national in the UK on a reciprocal basis, so much the better.

While an internship may last up to 18 months, many are much shorter, and are confined to vacations. To get an idea of the range of internships available, you should browse through a copy of the directory *Internships* (Writers' Digest). A significant proportion of internships in the directory are open to non-Americans, provided they have the necessary documentation, including federal government jobs in Washington. Some offer salaries; others do not.

Professional exchanges

These exchanges should be seen not so much as a chance to earn money as a form of professional development. Sometimes these exchanges are organised by professional organisations. Teachers and academics need to look to either the Central Bureau or the Fulbright Commission.

Post-to-post exchanges are available for teachers and lecturers with at least five years' experience. Although posts can be exchanged for a term, it is more usual for people to spend a complete academic year abroad. Under the Central Bureau scheme, teachers from the UK are seconded on full salary and receive a grant to offset the increased cost of living and travel expenses.

Other exchange programmes exist for nurses and young farmers and are arranged by their national organisations, and for youth workers with the American Youth Work Center. There are also opportunities for artists, librarians, policemen, screenwriters and others with the Fulbright Commission. If you belong to a professional organisation it would be worthwhile enquiring whether it operates any exchange scheme.

THE PRINCIPAL AGENCIES

AIESEC (Association Internationale des Etudiants en Sciences Economiques).

29–31 Cowper Street
London EC2A 4AP
Tel: (0171) 336 7939
Fax: (0171) 336 7971
E-mail: aiesec@cityscape.co.uk
Website: http:www.aisec.org/uk/index.htm

An international organisation specialising in exchanges for students of business (*eg* accountancy, finance, marketing, business administration, computing). There are local branches throughout the UK in higher education institutions, and students apply through, or are nominated by their local branches. Normally AIESEC arranges very few placements in the United States.

American Institute for Foreign Study (UK) Ltd

See Au Pair in America or Camp America on pages 52 and 53.

American Youth Work Center

1751 N Street NW, Suite 302
Washington, DC 20036

AYWC's Children and Youth Practical Training Exchange Program enables foreign youth workers in the early stages of their careers (usually under 30) to receive 12-18 months' practical training with American youth service agencies. You will receive similar wage and fringe benefits to American youth workers.

Whereas in the British Isles youth service is an education-based service, in the United States it involves dealing with young people with problems, including young offenders, runaways and drug addicts. Experience in social work, drug counselling, mental health as well as youth and community work would be of relevance. Over 50 placements are made annually.

Au Pair in America
37 Queen's Gate
London SW7 5HR
Tel: (0171) 581 7322. Fax: (0171) 581 7355.
Freephone: 0800 413116. E-mail: info@aupairamerica.co.uk
This AIFS programme places over 4,000 young people annually with American host families for twelve months. It offers an orientation course in New York on arrival, accommodation and free air travel from London to your destination, a weekly allowance of $125 plus a study allowance. Follow-up is provided by a network of community counsellors in cities throughout the USA. A deposit is payable which is refunded on successful completion of the contract.

British Universities North America Club (BUNAC)
16 Bowling Green Lane
London EC1R 0BD
Tel: (0171) 251 3472. Fax: (0171) 251 0215.
E-mail: BUNAC@easynet.co.uk
Website: http://www.latoile.com.BUNAC/
This is a non-profit, non-political educational student club with branches on many university campuses throughout the UK. Current membership fees are £3 annually.

Since 1962 BUNAC has operated general student work exchange programmes and is recognised by the appropriate government agencies in Britain and the United States. It runs similar schemes in Canada, Australia and Jamaica, and works in conjunction with the travel bureau of:

The Union of Students in Ireland (USIT)
19 Aston Quay
Dublin 2
Tel: (Dublin) 778117.

In a normal year it handles up to 8,500 placements.

For all three of its programmes, in return for an administration fee BUNAC deals with the paperwork and arranges orientations, insurance and cheap flights to the United States. The programmes are:

BUNACAMP Counsellor Programme
This involves working as a camp counsellor (leader) in a children's holiday camp. To be eligible for this programme you need to be aged 19½ to 35, but not necessarily a student. You need to have experience of working with children, or medical or secretarial skills. If you are interested, you need to apply for an interview. Interviewing starts in November and carries on until early May, but it is a case of the early bird catching the worm: the sooner you apply, the better your chance of getting a placement.

Kitchen and Maintenance Programme (KAMP)
This programme also involves working at children's summer camps in an ancillary capacity, doing a variety of jobs such as cooking, laundry, cleaning, site maintenance and driving. You need to be a full-time student and a member of BUNAC, and also to attend an orientation session during the Easter vacation. You apply through BUNAC for positions listed in the KAMP directory ranking them in order of choice.

Work America
This is a more flexible programme sponsored by the Council on International Educational Exchange which enables you to take up any summer job, but quota restrictions are imposed—currently around 4,500. In order to qualify you need to demonstrate you can support yourself in one of three ways:

1. You have a definite job offer for the summer months.
2. You have a private American sponsor who could take financial responsibility for you.
3. You have an indefinite or vague offer of a job or private sponsorship backed up by substantial funds.

Many people find their jobs through the *Work America Job Directory* obtainable from BUNAC, but there is no reason why you should not make your own employment arrangements. If you can find a private sponsor, you will be able to go to the United States on spec.

Camp America
37 Queen's Gate
London SW7 5HR
Tel: (0171) 581 7373

Camp America Family Companion Summer Programme
This offers a placement of from ten to 13 weeks as an au pair starting
in early June. Some experience of baby-minding is required and
possession of a driving licence is desirable. The age limit is 18 to 24.
Normally you will have two weeks' paid holiday and one-and-a-half
days off per week.

Camp America Camp Counsellor Programme
This programme has been in operation since 1969 and places around
7,000 people a year in over 1,000 camps. It is open to suitable people
aged between 18 and 35. The commitment is for nine to ten weeks
and participants must be able to start in June.

Camp America Campower Programme
This is for people who do not qualify for counsellor positions, though
in this case participants have to be full-time students. Many of the
jobs are kitchen jobs, but people with secretarial and technical skills
are also needed as are janitors, groundsmen and nightwatchmen.

Camp Counsellors USA

6 Richmond Hill	27 Woodside Gardens
Richmond on Thames	Musselburgh
Surrey TW109QX	Edinburgh EH21 7LJ
Tel: (0181) 332 2952	Tel: (0131) 665 5843

E-mail: 100744.1754@compuserve.com
Website: http://www.campcounselors.com
This programme operates along similar lines to BUNACAMP and
Camp America and is for people between the ages of 18 and 30
(including teachers and nurses). Applications are accepted between
October and March for the coming summer. The organisation
arranges orientations in Britain and in New York and provides free
insurance and air fares. The minimum commitment is for nine weeks.
International Headquarters is at:

420 Florence Street
Palo Alto
CA 94301.

Central Bureau for Educational Visits and Exchanges
The British Council
10 Spring Gardens
London SW1A 2BN
Tel: (0171) 389 4733

Fax: (0171) 389 4426
E-mail: 101472.2264@compuserve.com

3 Bruntsfield Crescent
Edinburgh
EH10 4HD
Tel: (0131) 447 8024.

1 Chlorine Gardens
Belfast BT9 5DJ
Tel: (01232) 664418.

The Bureau organises post-to-post exchanges for teachers and lecturers. More than 100 British educators exchange their jobs with American partners each year. The American side of the exchange is handled by the United States Information Agency (USIA).

Council on International Educational Exchange (CIEE)
52 Poland Street
London W1V 4JQ
Tel: (0171) 478 2006
Fax: (0171) 734 7322
E-mail: infouk@ciee.org

CIEE is the UK affiliate of a private, non-profit organisation in the USA which promotes educational exchanges between the US and other countries. It works in cooperation with organisations such as BUNAC and the Central Bureau.

General Career Development Programme
This programme enables qualified professionals to work in an American company for up to 18 months. The position contains a training component and has to be related to a person's previous experience. Participants are responsible for finding their own placements, and every year the Central Bureau assists 150 people on average to gain entry to the US. For this programme the Central Bureau also assists students from Ireland.

Hospitality and Tourism Exchange Programme
This is for students and graduates of hotel and catering management and on average 100 placements are made each year. Nine out of ten participants arrange their own placements, but a placement service is available.

Both programmes are administered in the USA by the Association for Practical Training (AIPT), Park View Building, Suite 320,

10400 Little Patuxent Parkway, Columbia, MD 21044 (Tel: 301 997 2200).

Internship Programme
This enables students and recent graduates to undertake a period of course-related practical training in the USA lasting up to 18 months. Participants are responsible for finding their own work placements, but CIEE handles all the paperwork, offers insurance cover and can provide various support services in the USA, including an orientation day. If the proposed internship is for longer than six months, a letter must be provided from a British employer offering an internship to a qualified American during the same calendar year.

Experiment in International Living (EIL Ltd)
287 Worcester Road
Malvern
Worcs WR14 1AB
Tel: (01684) 562577
Fax: (01684) 562212

Courthouse Chambers
27/29 Washington Street
Cork
Ireland
Tel: (00 353 21) 275101
This organisation operates in much the same way as AIFS (see above), except that interviews are conducted in Worcestershire (or Dublin) and there is a one-day orientation before departure, as well as a two-day orientation on arrival in the United States. If things do not work out, transfer to another family is possible during the first month. A refundable deposit is payable plus an administration charge.

The Fulbright Commission
US-UK Educational Commission
62 Doughty Street
London WC1N 2LS
Tel: (0171) 404 6880
Fax: (0171) 404 6834
Website: http://www.fulbright.co.uk
The Commission organises a programme of educational and cultural exchanges enabling people in some 130 countries to travel to the United States for advanced study, teaching or research. Among

the awards are **Faculty Exchange Fellowships** which enable a British academic to exchange posts with an American academic for a limited period.

There are also awards for academic administrators, artists, fashion designers, film and TV practitioners, librarians, police, screenwriters —and crime writers.

International Agricultural Exchange Programme
National Agricultural Centre
Kenilworth
Warwickshire CV8 2LG
Tel: (01203) 696578
Fax: (01203) 696684

A work exchange programme of up to nine months for young people aged between 18 and 28 with at least one year's agricultural experience.

The National Federation of Young Farmers' Clubs runs a programme along similar lines—the International Farm Experience Programme—and is based at the same address. Tel: (01203) 695584.

International Association for the Exchange of Students for Technical Experience (IAESTE)
Central Bureau
The British Council
10 Spring Gardens
London SW1A 2BN
Tel: (0171) 389 4774
Fax: (0171) 389 4426
E-mail: iaeste@centralbureau.org.uk

Founded at Imperial College London in 1948, this is a world-wide organisation represented in over 50 countries. It offers short-term, course-related work experience in three broad categories: scientific (*eg* in a company laboratory or research institute), professional (work designed to improve your professional capabilities) and manual (with little technical content but offering an insight into foreign work patterns and conditions).

The scheme is open to full-time students between 19 and 30 who must normally be nominated by an educational institution or sponsored by a company in the UK. IASTE welcomes reciprocal placements for incoming foreign trainees. Placements in the United States tend to be of several months' duration. The organisation works closely with AIPT in the US. E-mail: iaeste@aipt.org

Mountbatten Internship Programme
13 Moffats Lane
Brookmans Park
Hatfield
Herts AL6 7RX
Tel: (01707) 661870
Fax: (01707) 660083

This is a personal development programme started in 1984 which offers work experience in New York City to young people aged 19 + (including graduates) with qualifications in book-keeping, secretarial studies, management and business studies. A year's internship can lead to the award of a Certificate in International Business Practice (Oxford University Local Examinations Syndicate). A monthly living allowance is payable.

Winant-Clayton Volunteer Association
38 Newark Street
London E1 2AA
Tel: (0171) 375 0547.

There are opportunities for up to 20 volunteers a year to undertake work on various community projects in New York or on the East Coast for around two months. The projects include residential and day centres for the physically and mentally handicapped, psychiatric rehabilitation centres, play schemes for inner city children and luncheon clubs for the elderly.

Volunteers receive board, lodging and pocket money during their placement, but are normally expected to pay the air fare. However, a few bursaries are available. Applications need to be submitted by early January.

John Winant, incidentally, was the US Ambassador to Britain during the Second World War who brought groups of Americans over to Britain to do voluntary social work in association with Rev 'Tubby' Clayton, the founder of Toc H.

YMCA International Camp Counsellor Programme (ICCP)
71 W 23rd Street
Suite 1904
New York, NY 10010
Tel: 001 212 727 8800 ext. 122
Fax: 001 212 727 8814

This is another programme which recruits staff for more than 400 children's summer camps. These are organised not only by the

YMCA itself, but also by scouting organisations and individuals. Some camps cater for disadvantaged and handicapped people or concentrate on teaching special skills.

The age range for applicants is between 20 and 30, though camp staff usually range in age from 18-23. Camps vary in size and some may have as many as 100 staff working in different capacities. The main need is for

- **General counsellors** who live with and supervise groups of six to ten campers, care for camper health and safety, organise camp activities and assist in specific programme areas.
- **Skill specialists** who organise and teach specific activities, such as swimming, sports or crafts.
- **YMAK participants**, ancillary staff involved in cooking, office work and general maintenance.

In some camps staff may perform more than one of these roles.

A placement lasts nine to ten weeks, and you will be provided with air fares, medical insurance, pocket money and support services.

Other organisations
  Christian Movement for Peace
  Bethnal Green United Reformed Church
  Pott Street
  London E2 0EF
  Tel: (0171) 729 1877

International Voluntary Service
162 Upper New Walk
Leicester LE1 7QA
Tel: (0116) 2549430.

United Nations Association
International Youth Service
Welsh Centre for International Affairs
Temple of Peace
Cathays Park
Cardiff CF1 3AP
Tel: (01222) 223088.

These organisations organise placements of up to one month's duration, often at international workcamps in the United States.

FURTHER READING

Working Holidays (Central Bureau).
Summer Employment Directory of the United States (Writer's Digest Books).
Internships (Writer's Digest Books).
Volunteer Work (Central Bureau).
Directory of International Internships (Office of Overseas Study, Michigan State University, East Lansing, MI 48824, USA).
Advisory List of International Travel and Exchange Programs (Council on Standards for International Educational Travel, 1906 Association Drive, Reston, VA 22091, USA).
How to Find Temporary Work Abroad (How To Books, 1994).
How to Spend a Year Abroad (How To Books, 2nd edition 1995).
How to Do Voluntary Work Abroad (How To Books, 1995).
Summer Jobs USA (Peterson's Guides).

4
Arranging a Job Before You Leave

Much of the rest of this book concentrates on the needs of people who are planning to work in the United States for a period of years rather than months. Chapter 6 will be of more interest to people who are already in possession of a work permit, stand a good chance of getting one or qualify for permanent residence because of close family ties. If you do not fall into this category, your search starts here.

As stressed before in this book, you normally need an offer of employment before you can obtain a visa entitling you to work in the United States. Unfortunately, even if you are offered a position there, you cannot always count on a visa being forthcoming. You stand a good chance, however, if you possess good qualifications and you have skills that are in short supply in the locality of the employer.

This, though, is putting the cart before the horse. Finding a job is the initial step, so first take a look at ways and means of accomplishing it.

REPLYING TO ADVERTISEMENTS

If you see a job advertised, it is reasonable to assume that there is a genuine vacancy to be filled. Sometimes the advertiser is the employer himself; but increasingly employers are using intermediaries (recruitment consultants and employment agencies) to find their staff.

Advertisements in British or Irish newspapers and journals
If the advertisement appears in a publication in a country outside the United States it means that the job is open to non-Americans and that the employer is reasonably confident that he can obtain the necessary authorisation for the issue of a work permit.

Many job advertisements tend to be placed not by the companies or organisations themselves but by intermediaries working on their behalf based in the UK or Ireland. These intermediaries will be familiar with British procedures and terminology, and you will normally need to send your application with a British style CV to an address in the British Isles. No fee should be charged.

If you have to apply to an address in the United States, you should not assume that the recipient is completely au fait with British qualifications and working practice. If you are a member of a professional association, write out your designation in full and explain what it means; the same goes for qualifications such as A-Level and City and Guilds. You may also need to draft an American style résumé in preference to a British style CV in order to comply with local labour laws.

Virtually every national daily or Sunday newspaper carries advertisements for jobs in America from time to time. You should also peruse professional journals for vacancies, such as *Computer Weekly* in the case of IT experts, and *Nursing Times* for nurses.

Advertisements in international job papers

The overwhelming number of advertisements in newspapers and journals tend to be for posts within the UK (or Eire, in the case of Irish publications), but there are a number of publications that concentrate on the would-be expatriate.

Publications which may include jobs in the United States are: *Overseas Jobs Express, Nexus, Job Finder* and *Home and Away*. Their addresses are listed in Appendix D. There are also job listings which reproduce advertisements from other periodicals, but these may not be completely up to date.

Advertisements in the American press

While some American employers may welcome applications from overseas, the majority will be looking for someone who is already resident in the country. Working on the principle that a bird in the hand is always worth two in a bush, employers will prefer to hire someone who is on the spot, not several thousand miles away.

Unless the employer is recruiting for a senior or highly specialised post, or has a number of vacancies, it will probably not be worth the time, effort and cost to set up an interview abroad and go through a lot of red tape with the Immigration and Naturalisation Service (INS). Only if the organisation cannot find the candidates it wants will its personnel department look further afield.

This is not to say that there is no point at all in looking through the adverts in US journals and magazines or on the Internet. These may not lead you to a specific position, but they will give you an idea of the opportunities available and the salary you could expect. Such information will come in extremely useful if you decide to try speculative approaches to find a job. But on the whole you would need to be very lucky to land a position this way.

The disadvantages

Advertisements, of course, have one major disadvantage: they often elicit a large number of applicants, the majority of whom never reach the shortlist.

In order to avoid being screened out in the early stages of the sifting process, you need to make a special effort and tailor your application to fit the specifications laid down in the advertisement, either by adapting your CV accordingly or by writing a carefully worded letter. Appendix E should give you a few ideas.

There is a school of thought that advises would-be candidates to get ahead of the competition. This means adopting a speculative approach to finding a job, seeking out vacancies before they are advertised. How does one do it?

SPECULATIVE APPLICATIONS

Recruitment consultants in the UK

The role of intermediaries in the recruitment process has already been mentioned. Firms in the United States, like those in the UK, very often delegate their recruitment. So rather than send off applications to individual firms it is more sensible to contact an agency which recruits for positions in your field for a range of companies.

You need, however, to do your homework carefully before putting pen to paper. The majority of recruitment consultants recruit only for positions within the British Isles; and those that do undertake international recruitment are more likely to recruit for the Middle East, Europe or the Far East. Even if you track down an agency that recruits for the United States, it may not offer jobs in your particular field. Many international consultancies specialise in particular job sectors.

How do you find out who does what?
You get an idea by referring to *The Yearbook of Recruitment and Employment Services, The CEPEC Recruitment Guide,* or *The Executive Grapevine*. Alternatively, you can turn to Appendix B in this book which lists a select group of consultancies and agencies that recruit for the United States to a greater or lesser extent. The list is by no means complete but includes organisations that supplied details of their current needs when this book was in progress.

Alas, circumstances change and no reference book can claim to be completely up-to-date. Employment markets tend to be volatile and recruitment requirements can change over a period of just a few months. The best plan is to peruse the advertisement columns of newspapers, international job lists and trade journals, and take note of the agencies recruiting for the United States which seem to handle your type of job. Send them your CV (British style) with a covering letter and ask them to put your details on file.

Do not necessarily expect an acknowledgement of your speculative letter; some organisations are inundated with speculative applications—often from people who have not done their homework properly and have applied to a firm that is not remotely interested in their skills. If you have selected the agency with care, you are more likely to get noticed.

Recruitment consultants in the United States

The chances of landing an appointment through a speculative approach to a recruitment consultant in the United States from abroad are slim, unless you are an exceptionally well-qualified person with much sought after expertise. As Intercristo, the Christian Placement Agency, explains:

'. . . Communication between the potential employer and applicant is time-consuming and cumbersome. This places the applicant at a severe disadvantage compared to candidates who are more accessible to potential employers.'

On the other hand, if you happen to be visiting America there is no harm in knocking on the doors of recruitment agencies to find out what kinds of jobs are on offer and leaving your particulars. Remember, though, that no job can be yours unless you can secure the required work visa. Note that you may have to pay a fee if the agency succeeds in placing you; more of this in Chapter 6.

Since a number of US consultancies have branches in the UK, it may be more sensible to contact these first of all to find out if there is any point in your applying to their office in, say, New York or San Francisco. If you have skills that are much in demand, the branch over here might be prepared to forward your details to their transatlantic colleagues.

Personal contacts

Have you a cousin three times removed living in Wyoming? Does your brother-in-law have connections with a firm in Omaha? Is your uncle on the board of a British plc with a subsidiary in Des Moines? Does a pal of yours know a chap who runs an engineering outfit in San Diego?

If you do not know the answers, perhaps it is time to remedy the situation by asking around. Networking, or what used to be called 'the old boy network', continues to flourish in the 1990s. I would be surprised if at least half the people in the UK and Ireland did not know someone who lives in the United States, possibly a relative. If you have no acquaintances across the Atlantic, then you could try contacting the relevant user group on the Internet.

Do not expect your American contacts (once you have tracked them down) to find you a job from out of the blue. However, they might be able to give you an idea of the lie of the land, and suggest employers in their immediate area that might be worth trying. They might also be willing to keep an eye open for job openings in your particular field.

Transfer or secondment

If you are in employment, have you explored the possibility of going to the United States with your firm or organisation? Some multinationals like to second key staff to overseas affiliates, while smaller organisations may exchange employees for short periods with companies abroad.

If you make it known that you are keen to work in the United States, you may well find that opportunities do arise. Your very keenness could be a point in your favour. You may find it surprising, but some key employees do not relish the prospect of a posting abroad, particularly if they have family commitments, and your employer may prefer to send someone who is enthusiastic and committed rather than a reluctant expatriate who needs various inducements before he will budge.

If you are sent abroad by your employer you will enjoy the best of all worlds including a generous relocation allowance, continuity of employment and possibly an enhanced salary.

Companies in the UK

There are numerous companies and organisations which function on both sides of the Atlantic, and if you join one of these and prove your worth, there is a possibility that you might be posted to the United States in the course of time.

Two categories of company are worth considering:

- British, Irish or other European companies with business interests in the United States
- American companies with subsidiaries in UK and Ireland.

The first category is more likely to offer you the opportunity of a US posting, particularly if you have prior experience or special knowledge of the country. Careful research will pay dividends; and in order to be in the right place at the right time you should watch out for companies that are aiming to expand their operations in the United States. Some British hotel companies, for instance, have acquired US hotel chains in recent years.

A good business reference library will have information on the leading firms in both the UK and the United States. You need to go and search out books such as the *Directory of US Subsidiaries of British Companies, Dun and Bradstreet's Million Dollar Directory, Dun and Bradstreet's Middle Market Directory* and *Thomas Register of American Manufacturers*. The business, trade and professional press is also required reading. (See Bibliography.)

Firms in the United States

Speculative applications from afar are unlikely to yield positive results; you may not even receive an acknowledgement. There are, of course, exceptions. If you are an acknowledged expert in your particular field or have skills that are in short supply, you could be successful in landing a position. However, do not count on it.

If you are planning a trip to America, the position is different. You can send off a copy of your résumé with a covering letter that mentions you will be passing through the city where the employer is based on such-and-such a date, and you would welcome an opportunity to visit him. While there is no guarantee that this approach will open doors, you may arouse the recipient's curiosity sufficiently to gain an invitation.

This approach could prove expensive, since your fare across the Atlantic is unlikely to be reimbursed by the people you see. However, if you target a number of companies and organisations effectively, your chances of gaining a hearing—and ultimately a position—will be enhanced.

A useful reference book for people planning direct applications is Dun's *Employment Opportunities Directory (The Career Guide)* which lists 5,000 employers and their employment needs. Unhappily, few, if any, reference libraries in this country seem to have it on their shelves and the tome is extremely expensive. There are plenty of reference books (see Bibliography) which list American companies, and you would be able to consult some of them in a large public reference library, such as:

The City Business Library
1 Brewers Hall Garden
London Wall
London EC2V 5BY.
Tel: (0171) 638 8215.

If you cannot locate the book you need, then the US Information Service Library at the US Embassy has an extensive selection of reference books. Visits are by appointment only.

'Situation wanted' advertisements

Invididuals sometimes advertise their availability in British publications that circulate in the United States (*eg The Economist*), but you could also try American newspapers and journals or the Internet. Some of the main newspapers are listed in Appendix G and a few, but by no means all, have UK agents who can handle your advertisement.

It is difficult to judge how successful self-advertising really is. You are more likely to achieve success if you include a US address or fax numbers for replies, mention that you will be visiting America in the near future and indicate that you either have, or are able to obtain, the necessary permits.

Miscellaneous organisations

Leeson's Employment and Accommodation Service (LEADS) and International Jobsearch offer advice and assistance to people planning to work in the United States, including:

- lists of companies employing your particular trade or profession together with all employment bureaux and consultants in any area of your choice
- help in assessing employability
- advice on all your approaches to personnel officers and employers
- interviews in the UK on behalf of US companies
- CV preparation.

Expat Network operates Joblink which forwards its members' CVs to overseas employers.

Walker & Walker publish Emigration Packs which include lists of employers and employment agencies.

WHAT ARE THE POTENTIAL PROBLEMS?

One problem you encounter when applying for a job in the United States from another country is that the process takes time. In most cases your details have to be sent across the Atlantic, and before the employer can take you on he has to obtain permission to employ you (labor certification) from the authorities. Once this comes through your nearest US consulate has to be informed, and even then some time may elapse before you are granted the appropriate visa. You may, for instance, have to be interviewed by the US consul or undergo a medical, so it could take months before you get the go-ahead. On the other hand, all the formalities might be completed in just three weeks.

Another major problem with applying for a job from the UK is that more often than not you do not get a chance to visit your prospective employer and see the working environment for yourself at first hand. Normally only senior (and well-paid) executives of some years' standing with their company are given the chance to see their workplace in advance. If you do not like what you see on arrival, it is too late to do anything about it.

This is less of a problem for people who already know the United States as a result of having visited the country or, better still, lived there. If you have not, you need to be given a thorough briefing before you commit yourself irrevocably. Do not rely on Hollywood films to give you sufficient insight into everyday American life.

Most organisations brief their staff as a matter of course or enlist the help of outside agencies, such as the Centre for International Briefing at Farnham Castle. (Others are listed in Appendix F.) If no orientation is mentioned you could contact organisations such as the Women's Corona Society (even if you are a man), Christians Abroad, which can put you in touch with people who have returned from the US, or Employment Conditions Abroad which produces a self-assessment package *Planning to work abroad*.

Even with the best of briefings you have to take certain things on trust and rely on the impressions of other people whose tastes and inclinations may diverge quite markedly from your own. What may seem like the next best thing to a holiday for some people can turn out to be a damp squib for others.

In order to avoid disappointment, you must make every effort to understand what you are letting yourself in for. Talk to people who have lived and worked in the US; make sure that you understand the differences in working practice and life style that you will encounter. Read up about the place where you will be.

The **Visit USA Association** may have useful free information on the place you are making for, albeit with something of a tourist gloss, and the **US Information Service** (at the US Embassy) can provide an information pack. *The Economist Business Travel Guide: US* is worth consulting and *Inside Tracks* offers short, regularly updated destination profiles of a number of US cities including Chicago, Houston, Los Angeles, San Francisco, New Orleans and Washington DC. The monthly journal *Going USA* contains useful reports on living in the US. Expat Network publishes *Location Reports* and ECA *Country Profiles for Expatriates.*

YOUR CONTRACT

Before you leave the country you should be asked to sign a contract. If you are being sent abroad by your company a contract may not be deemed necessary, but you should have a memorandum which details your responsibilities and entitlements.

A contract is just as much for your benefit as that of your employer, and you should read it through carefully and query matters which are unclear. It is also sensible to ask a solicitor or an expatriate service organisation to read it through and offer their comments.

These are some of the details you need to look out for:

- the name and address of your employer
- your job title and responsibilities
- staff member you are answerable to
- the location of your employment
- your net salary and dates of payment
- the commencement date and duration of your employment
- working hours.

Some items may need to be gone into in greater detail, such as:

- Paid leave. Don't take this for granted, particularly if you are employed on contract terms. In any case, leave entitlements are far from generous—often only one or two weeks per year.

- Sick leave. Often there is no open-ended entitlement but a fixed number of days when sickness pay can be claimed. (See Chapter 7.)

- Medical insurance. Make sure this is provided and will be adequate for your needs. (See also Chapters 5 and 7.)

- Accommodation. Contract workers may get a per diem allowance to cover accommodation costs, which will be similar to those enjoyed by American employees working outside their home states. Sometimes accommodation is provided, particularly a hotel on arrival.

- Hardship allowance. This may be payable if you take up employment in Alaska.

- Married allowance. Normally contract employees would not be eligible for extra allowances if accompanied by their spouse and family. If you are being transferred to the United States by your employer such a perk is more likely to be forthcoming.

- Pension. Contract posts, particularly short-term ones, do not always have a pension provision. Some employers, however, may offer a 401K transferable pension scheme. (See also Chapter 5.)

- Termination bonus. This is not usually offered with US postings.

- Fares to and from your destination. With company transfers it is normal for fares to be paid for the employee and his dependants. If you are a contract employee, the chances are that only your fare will be paid. Only in very exceptional circumstances should you pay your own fare.

- Baggage allowance. Transferees are likely to have more generous entitlements than a contract employee.

- Premature termination of contract. There should be a clause that covers procedures in such an eventuality.

- Restrictions. There may be restrictions on your working for other organisations.

No contract will be able to deal with every eventuality, and you need to familiarise yourself with working conditions in the US before you leave. (See Chapter 7.) Adequate preparation is, of course, vital and you should read the following chapter with care.

5
Preparations Before Departure

Any trip abroad, even just a week's holiday, involves a certain amount of preparation. If you are planning to be away for an extended period—whether months, years or forever—preparing for the move needs to be done thoroughly and systematically.

WHAT SPECIFIC ARRANGEMENTS DO I NEED TO MAKE?

This chapter is a checklist of things that you need to think about. Not all the items will be of concern to you—particularly if your stay will be a short one or you are single and unencumbered—but the longer you are planning to stay in the United States the more matters there will be to attend to. I therefore suggest you look through the list and note down what is of importance to you.

The topics covered in this chapter in alphabetical order are:

- arrival arrangements
- banking
- car
- credit and charge cards
- customs and prohibited articles
- doctor and dentist
- driving licence
- educational arrangements (for your children)
- financial advice
- your flat or house
- health
- insurance
- investments
- journals
- kin

- library
- luggage and personal effects
- moving
- National Insurance
- orientation
- passports
- pension
- pets
- professional advisers
- qualification certificates
- redirection of mail
- rental agreements
- subscriptions
- tax
- travel
- utilities—electricity, gas, telephone, water
- visas
- voting rights.

Arrival arrangements

It is sensible to inform your prospective employer when you plan to arrive. The chances are you will be travelling to the United States by air, in which case you should state the flight number in addition to the estimated arrival time. Long haul flights are sometimes delayed.

Find out what arrangements have been made for meeting you and accommodating you on arrival; and make sure you have one or two contact telephone numbers in case arrangements go awry.

Banking

You need to inform your UK bank of your imminent change of address and discuss arrangements for the administration of your account during your absence (eg how you plan to top up your account to service regular payments).

Since the bank may not have a branch at your destination (some British and Irish banks have affiliates or representatives in the United States), you could also ask if it can recommend a bank in the locality and provide a letter of introduction. This will facilitate opening a bank account in the United States in case your employer has no procedures to help you in this respect.

Even if you are planning to leave the UK for good, it is sensible to keep your account open and topped up—for the time being at least—as there may be occasions in the future when it is more convenient to make or receive payments in sterling.

You will also need to arrange for money to tide you over the first month or so in the United States. This involves purchasing foreign exchange in the form of dollars and dollar travellers cheques (other denominations are not readily accepted) and perhaps arranging for a bank transfer. Note that you will also be able to withdraw cash with a credit or charge card.

Car

In many parts of the United States public transport is fairly rudimentary, and you will find that some means of private transport is essential. There is, however, little point in shipping your car to the country—unless it happens to be a very distinguished one—since automobiles are much cheaper over there. In any case, it will probably not meet US safety, bumper and emission standards, which are very tough; modification can work out prohibitively expensive.

For more information on emission standards contact:

The US Environmental Protection Agency
Manufacturer Operations Division (EN-340F)
Investigation/Imports Section
401 M Street SW
Washington DC 20460
USA
Tel: 202 382 2504
Fax: 202 245 4089

Note that in order to import a car you will need prior written approval from the EPA or a manufacturer's label affixed to the vehicle stating it meets all US emission requirements.

For information on bumper and safety requirements you should get in touch with:

The US Department of Transportation
National Highway Traffic Safety Administration
Director of the Office of Vehicle Safety Compliance (NEF-32)
400 Seventh Street SW
Washington DC 20590
USA
Tel: 202 366 5313.

As a non-resident you may import a vehicle duty-free into the United States, but duty is payable if the car is sold within a year of importation. Employees of foreign governments and international organisations on assignment in the United States may be exempt from the compliance regulations; and the same is true for non-residents who import the car for one year and then export it.

If you are going to America for a number of years it will make sense to sell your vehicle and rely on car hire for visits to the UK. Do not forget to inform the Driver Vehicle Licensing Centre and your insurance company when the car is sold and claim a refund on your insurance if appropriate.

If your stay in the United States is for a shortish period, you could put your vehicle in storage or entrust it to a friend or relation. Whatever you do, make sure you inform your insurance company of your plans.

The US Customs Service publishes a useful leaflet entitled *Importing A Car* which is obtainable either from:

The US Customs Service
Department of the Treasury
Washington
DC 20229
USA
or the Customs Attaché of the US Embassy.

Credit and charge cards

Before you leave, you ought to inform your card company of your new address for statements. You should also ask if it has a list of banks that accept your particular card in the United States. Credit and charge cards are used widely in America, and are a most convenient method of payment and obtaining cash. If you need to hire a car, for instance, the deposit is often waived if you produce a credit or charge card.

In view of the widespread use of these cards in the United States, you might find yourself at a disadvantage if you do not own one. It is therefore worth looking into the possibility of obtaining either type of card, ideally by approaching a bank or building society that does not charge for their issue.

If your credit limit is fairly low, this might be a good time to have it raised, to enable you to cope with the extra expenses you will incur in settling in. Note that you will continue to be billed in sterling.

Ultimately you may well decide to open a credit card account in the United States which will bill you in dollars. However, as in the UK, it may take a little time before the account is operational.

Customs and prohibited articles

You will normally be allowed to import personal and household effects free of duty. One litre of alcohol may be brought in duty free provided this does not conflict with the laws of the state in which you arrive. Two hundred cigarettes or the equivalent can also be imported free of duty. The leaflet *US Customs Hints*, available from the Customs Attaché of the US Embassy, offers further information.

Restrictions are imposed on the import of firearms, narcotics and certain foodstuffs, notably meat. For further information on the import of foodstuffs contact:

The Import/Export and Emergency Planning Staff
US Department of Agriculture
APHIS
VS 6505
Belcrest Road
Hyattsville
MD 20782
USA.

The Customs Attaché at the US Embassy may also be able to advise.

During your flight or voyage to the United States you will be given a customs declaration (Form 6059B) to fill in, which is designed to expedite customs clearance on arrival. Failure to declare a prohibited item can lead to an on the spot fine.

Doctor and dentist

Visit your dentist before you leave and ask him to make sure your teeth are in good shape, since dental care in the United States can be extremely expensive and is not always covered by medical insurance.

A visit to your doctor is also in order to tell him of your plans and perhaps have a check-up. You may in any case have to have a medical examination prior to confirmation of your appointment or in order to satisfy immigration requirements. If you have a particular medical condition that requires you to take prescription drugs, you should ask the doctor for a letter that you can take to a medical practitioner in the United States. You may also need to show the letter to customs officials at your port of entry.

If you are likely to be out of the country for a lengthy period of time you should surrender your NHS card to the local Family Practitioner Committee, or hand it to the immigration officer at your point of departure.

Driving licence
You could acquire an International Driving Licence from the AA or
RAC but it is really not necessary to do so, since you will be able to
drive on your own licence for a year. When the year is up you will
need to take a US driving test.

The ability to drive is a great asset in the United States since public
transport is not available everywhere. If you do not drive already,
sooner or later you will probably need to learn, simply in order to
survive. Although US driving tests are reckoned to be easier than
UK ones, you may prefer to pass your test in more familiar home
surroundings.

The rules of the road in the United States differ in some respects
from the British Highway Code, and you should take steps to
familiarise yourself with them.

Educational arrangements
If your children are of secondary school age, you need to decide
whether they are likely to re-enter the British educational system later
in their lives. If so, they really need to be enrolled at a school which
adheres to the British system or prepares them for the **International
Baccalaureate** (IB)—a highly regarded qualification which is recognised by all universities.

There are various options:

- A boarding school in Britain. Private schools can be costly, unless
  your employer can be persuaded to meet most or part of the bill,
  but a number of local authorities also run schools for children
  whose parents are abroad, and you could discuss the problem
  with your local education authority. Further information is
  available from Dean Associates, the Independent Schools
  Information Service (ISIS), Gabbitas Educational Consultants,
  and SFIA.

- A school offering a British style or IB curriculum in the USA,
  such as:

  Anglo-American School
  18 West 89 Street
  New York
  NY 10024.

  Armand Hammer United World College of the American West
  PO Box 248

Montezuma
NM 87731.

United Nations International School
24-50 East River Drive
New York
NY 10010.

Washington International School
3100 Macomb Street NW
Washington
DC 20008.

There are also French schools in Los Angeles, San Francisco and Houston. If you wish to enrol your children in one of the above mentioned schools, do not leave it until the last moment, otherwise you will find there are no places available.

- A correspondence course. Mercer's College provides a complete tuition service by correspondence for children living abroad with their parents up to the age of 18, while the Worldwide Educational Service offers an educational programme for the under-13s which enables parents with no teaching experience to educate their children.

Bear in mind that the residential status of your children could be crucial when the authorities in the UK come to deciding whether they are to be treated as British students or foreign students with respect to fees and grants. It would be wise to explore the financial implications of moving your children to the United States if they are approaching college age.

If, on the other hand, you are likely to be living in the United States indefinitely, there is everything to be said for enrolling your child(ren) in an American school. If you opt for **public** (*ie* **state) education** (which is free), you can find out about local schools by contacting the Department of Education of the state in which you will be living (addresses in Appendix G) or the School Board of the district where you plan to reside. Alternatively, you may decide to opt for a **parochial school** (run by a religious denomination) or a **private (independent) school.** *The Handbook of Private Schools* or *Independent and Boarding Schools World Yearbook* can provide details of the latter.

Ultimately your offspring may well want to attend a college in the United States, though this can prove an expensive business since grants are not as readily available as they are in the UK. For more information on higher education I suggest one of the following:

- *Lovejoy's College Guide*, C.E. Lovejoy (Simon & Schuster).
- *Comparative Guide to American Colleges* J. Cass and M. Birnbaum (Harper & Row).
- *Profiles of American Colleges* (Barron's Educational Series).
- *Study in the USA* (Study in the USA Inc, 119 S Main St, Suite 220, Seattle, WA 98104).

Financial advice

If you are planning to be in the United States for some time it will pay you to find a reputable adviser who can help you understand the tax and other financial implications of the move and give you advice on such matters as insurance, pensions, *etc*. Your bank may be able to offer advice through one of its specialist branches, or you could turn to one of the specialist advisers that advertise in expatriate journals. Some of these are included under Useful Addresses (Appendix F).

Your flat or house in the UK

If you own a house or flat there are various options open to you, depending on how long you will be away.

Leave the accommodation empty

This is fine provided you live in a part of the country that is reasonably secure, your absence is likely to be short and there is no risk of squatters moving in. However, your insurance company may increase the premium, and if you have a mortgage, your bank or building society might have qualms. In any case, both organisations should be informed.

Ask someone to look after it for you

This is quite a sensible option provided the person lives quite close. If you are unable to find a neighbour, friend or relative who will take on the responsibility, you could contact an organisation that offers houseminding services, such as Animal Aunts or Homesitters Ltd. People participating on exchange programmes often allow their exchange partners use of the house.

Let it

This is a way of paying for the upkeep of the property and helps pay off the mortgage, if you have one, but you need to check first whether the lender approves. It is always best if you can find a tenant whom you know and trust, as not every tenant turns out to be reliable. Failing that, you can either advertise for a tenant yourself or appoint a letting agent to do the work for you. A good agent will

- advertise for tenants
- interview prospective tenants
- take up references
- draw up a leasing agreement and serve relevant notices
- draw up inventories
- visit properties and attend to any complaints or queries
- collect rent
- serve notice to quit and attend court
- attend to building repairs and any major building work
- account to clients by way of statements and payment of rents
- pay water rates and other charges
- negotiate rent increases
- deal with insurance claims.

If you plan to return during your vacations, contact the accommodation office of local colleges and universities to see if they have staff or students who need to rent accommodation during term time only.

Sell it
This is a sensible option if you are planning to stay in the US for several years, but you will need to set the process in train some time before you leave. In recent years houses have taken ages to sell.

There is no need to deal with such matters here, since there are several excellent books on buying and selling houses and flats, *eg*: *Which? Way to Buy, Sell and Move House* (Consumers' Association).

You may well decide to use some of the proceeds to finance the purchase of property in the US. Initially you should find a safe and profitable haven for your cash.

And if your accommodation is rented
Make sure that you give your landlord plenty of notice.

Health
There are no special vaccinations that you need to have before going to the United States, since you are unlikely to encounter any particular health hazards there. However, in view of the costs of health care in America it makes sense to ensure you are in the best of health before

you go. Visits to your doctor and dentist have already been suggested; it would also be a good idea to go to the optician for an eye test or for a spare pair of spectacles.

The Department of Health produces two useful booklets: *Before You Go* (SA40) and *While You're Away* (SA41). See also the note on medical insurance.

Insurance

Medical and accident insurance
The United States does not have the equivalent of the British National Health Service, and what government health provision there is tends to be limited to only a small sector of the population, particularly the destitute and the elderly.

It is therefore up to the individual to ensure that he is properly insured against illness. Many employers assume this responsibility, and if you are fortunate you may well find that medical insurance is one of the perks of the job. If this is not the case, you will need to make your own arrangements, though this could work out expensive.

None of the medical expenses you incur in the United States can be refunded by the NHS, but you will continue to be eligible for free treatment in Britain when you return or when visiting, provided you have not taken up permanent residence in the United States.

There are a number of insurance companies and brokers in the UK that will insure you for a short visit to America, including BUPA, Expat Network and PPP. Not all will be prepared to do so for the longer term, and you may find it is easier to insure yourself with an American insurer, such as Blue Cross, when you arrive.

The Health Insurance Association of America will be able to answer any queries. The organisation produces a number of useful leaflets, such as *What You Should Know About Health Insurance* and *How to Use Private Health Insurance with Medicare*.

When looking at a health plan, whether it is to be provided by your employer or financed by yourself, it is vital to make sure you have adequate cover. Here are a few of the questions you need to ask.

- What percentage of the cost of treatment do I have to pay, if any?
- What kinds of treatment (*eg* dental, psychiatric) are excluded?
- How soon do benefits start?
- Am I covered for existing medical conditions?
- Does the policy cover prescription drugs?
- Is there a ceiling on the amount I can claim each year?

Life insurance
You need to notify your insurance company of your impending move. This might be a good time to review your needs.

Insurance of personal effects
This is a matter that you should look into. If you employ removers they should be able to advise you; otherwise you may be able to arrange an insurance package which includes medical, accident, loss and damage provisions.

Investments

If you have any investments, you need to inform the organisations concerned (*eg* unit trust managers, the Premium Bond office, your stockbroker) of your change of address. You may also wish to appoint someone to look after them in your absence (*eg* your bank or solicitor).

This may be a timely moment, if you are planning to be away an appreciable length of time, to review your investment strategy in the light of your new circumstances, in order to make your investments as tax efficient as possible. Bear in mind that if you become a permanent US resident, the Internal Revenue Service will tax you on your total worldwide income.

In the past many expatriates have found it profitable to move their investments into an offshore haven such as the Channel Islands or the Isle of Man, but you could run into legal difficulties if you try to do this with any US earnings. So you would be wise to take advice from a financial expert who is au fait with expatriate financial matters.

Journals and newspapers

If you subscribe to journals you need to weigh up whether to continue your subscription or not. If not, you need to cancel; if you wish to continue, you should notify the publisher of your change of address.

If you are going to a part of the United States where British publications are hard to come by, you might consider taking out a subscription to a publication such as *The Guardian Weekly* or *The Economist* in order to keep abreast of developments in the UK and elsewhere. Only a minority of US newspapers provide extensive coverage of international news. There are, incidentally, some British newspapers in the United States: the *British Weekly* serves the British community in California, the *Florida Brit* circulates in Florida, while the monthly *Union Jack* has a national circulation. (See under California, Appendix G.)

Another way of keeping in touch is to listen in to the BBC World Service, in which case you may wish to take out a subscription to its monthly programme bulletin *London Calling* or *BBC World-Wide*. The BBC also has an international TV service and is extending its satellite TV coverage. (See Appendix F.)

There are a number of journals which cater especially for expatriates to which you might consider subscribing, *eg*: *Expatriate Today, The International, Resident Abroad* (see Appendix D for details).

Kin (next of)

Make sure that your employers and professional advisers know the name and address of your next of kin in case of accidents. Details of your next of kin should also be noted in your diary and passport.

Library

Your local public library will probably have some useful books on the United States, and you should endeavour to read or, at least, browse through some of them before you go, in order to familiarise yourself with the prospect before you. The **Centre for International Briefing** has an excellent library, geared to expatriate needs, which can be used for a fee.

Do not forget to return any library books you have borrowed otherwise you could incur a steep fine in the future.

Luggage and personal effects

If you are only planning to be in America for a matter of months, the best plan is to travel light. If you are planning to be there for some years you will want to take a lot of your possessions with you, if at all possible. However, due to cost constraints you will not be able to take everything, so you need to work out what you really need and what you can do without.

For instance, if you are going to be in furnished accommodation there is clearly no need to take much furniture with you, except perhaps for a few choice items. It can either stay in your home or, if you are selling the house, you could put it in storage. Bulky electrical goods are best left behind since they are relatively cheap in the United States. Besides, the current in the US is different (110V 60Hz against 240V 50Hz in the UK), the TV transmission system is different, and you would need transformers and adaptors for two-pin sockets.

Household items (such as cutlery, sheets, blankets, kitchen utensils) are quite sensible items to take along; curtains are not, since you won't know the size of your windows. Books are weighty items, and you will need to think twice about shipping out your whole library, unless it happens to be very valuable.

There is little point in indulging in a shopping spree before you leave, since items are often available more cheaply in the United States. Instead save your cash until you arrive and discover exactly what you need.

Airlines are more generous these days than they used to be with regard to accompanied luggage, with dimensions a more important consideration than weight. Check whether your employer is prepared to pay for a modest amount of extra accompanied luggage, and whether there are allowances for items sent by sea or unaccompanied air freight.

Moving

If you have a large number of items to ship, the best plan is to enlist the aid of an experienced and reputable international removal contractor and leave him to do the packing, make all the transport arrangements and sort out the paperwork. Normally, if your employer is paying for the move, he will expect you to get a number of quotes before giving the go-ahead.

There are a number of removal firms that can handle international removals, a few of which are listed in Appendix F. If no firm near you is mentioned contact the British Association of Removers (Overseas Group) or the Institute of Freight Forwarders Ltd.

National Insurance

There is a **Social Security Agreement** between the UK and the United States to ensure that you do not have liability for contributions in both countries at the same time.

If you work in America for a UK employer for not more than five years you will remain insured under the UK National Insurance scheme and normal Class 1 contributions will be paid. Contributions will not be payable to the US scheme. Self employed people ordinarily resident in the UK also remain insured in the UK when working in the United States.

On the other hand, if you go to America to work for a US or other non-UK employer you may have to contribute to the US social security scheme. It is sensible to contact the US authorities on arrival to find out about your obligations.

You should let your local social security office know of your date of departure and address in the US. Further information is available from:

Benefits Agency or Contributions Agency
Department of Social Security

Overseas Branch
Newcastle upon Tyne NE98 1YX.
Tel: (0191) 213 5000 or
(0191) 228 7777 (Benefits)
(0191) 215 4811 (Contributions)

Residents of Northern Ireland should contact:

The Overseas Branch of the Social Services Agency
Castle Court
Royal Avenue
Belfast
Tel: (01232) 336000

For information on the US social security scheme contact:

Federal Benefits Unit
United States Embassy
24 Grosvenor Square
London W1A 2LQ.

The relevant authorities in the United States are:

Social Security Administration Office of International Policy
PO Box 17741
Baltimore
MD 21235 (contribution enquiries).

Social Security Administration Office of International Policy
PO Box 17049
Baltimore
MD 21303 (other enquiries).

Orientation
In order to get off to a good start it is vital to be briefed thoroughly
not only about the job, but also about living conditions. There are
subtle differences between the way of life in the United States and
life on this side of the Atlantic which could catch you unawares, so
you need to be aware of these differences and prepare for them.

A number of organisations conduct their own orientation programmes; others use the expertise of briefing centres, such as the
Centre for International Briefing at Farnham Castle, Going Places

and Employment Conditions Abroad. Christians Abroad may also be able to help, as can the Women's Corona Society, which publishes a useful series of booklets entitled *Notes for Newcomers*. Finally, Howell & Associates offer courses designed by the Institute for Training in Intercultural Management.

There are a number of useful publications you could consult, such as *Going USA, How to Live and Work in America, Living in the USA, Long Stays in America* and *Coping with America*. (See Bibliography.) However, a person-to-person briefing is infinitely preferable, since you have the opportunity to ask your own questions.

Passports
One year Visitor's Passports are no longer issued and you will need to obtain a full passport from a passport office; you can get a passport application form from your Post Office. If your passport is about to expire, you would be wise to renew it.

UK Passport Office addresses
Clive House
70 Petty France
London SW1H 9HD
Tel: (0171) 213 3434 (personal callers only).

Olympia House
Upper Dock Street
Newport
Gwent NP1 1XA
Tel: (01633) 244500 (for Wales and the West of England).

Aragon Court
Northminster Road
Peterborough PE1 1QG
Tel: (01733) 895555 (for the Midlands and Eastern England).

5th Floor
India Buildings
Water Street
Liverpool L2 0QZ
Tel: (0151) 237 3010 (for the North of England and North Wales).

3 Northgate
96 Milton Street

Cowcaddens
Glasgow G4 0BT
Tel: (0141) 332 0271 (Scotland, London and Middlesex).

Hampton House
47–53 High Street
Belfast BT1 2QS
Tel: (01232) 232371 (Northern Ireland).

Pension

If you are taking up a contract appointment, the chances are that you
will not be covered by any pension scheme, and it would be worth
your while to explore the possibility of contributing to a personal
pension scheme. If you are already working for a company based in
the UK or Ireland, you need to clarify whether the company pension
scheme covers postings abroad. The Society of Pensions Consultants
or Company Pensions Information Centre, both in London, may be
able to advise or put you in touch with someone who can.

Pets

It is normally possible to take your pets with you to the United States,
but you need to be aware of certain restrictions, such as quarantine
periods in certain states. The leaflet *Pets, Wildlife, US Customs* gives
full details of the restrictions.

However, you ought to consider whether your pet will necessarily
relish the change. Your local branch of the RSPCA, Cats Protection
League, Canine Defence League or other animal charities should be
able to advise you on this and on the transport of animals abroad.

If you are off on a short-term assignment it may be more convenient
to find your pet a home with friends or relations during your absence;
or you could enlist the aid of a pet-minding service, such as Animal
Aunts. (See Useful Addresses.)

Professional advisers

It is important to inform professional advisers, such as solicitors
and accountants, of your new address. In addition, you may have to
make arrangements with at least one of them for the day to day
management of your affairs while you are away. By granting him
power of attorney, for instance, he will be able to sign documents on
your behalf. If you have not yet made a will, this could be a good
time to do so.

On the other hand, you may feel you are quite able to handle your
affairs yourself from the other side of the Atlantic.

Qualification certificates

It is advisible to take all your diplomas and certificates—and those of your dependants—with you, as prospective employers and the authorities may need to inspect them. Photocopies alone may not suffice.

Redirection of mail

While you may make a Herculean effort to inform all and sundry of your move, you will inevitably miss out someone or some organisation, such as a long-lost aunt in Australia who decides to get in touch after 20 years. You therefore need to arrange to have your mail redirected. If you have tenants, you may be able to prevail on them to do the honours; or the Post Office will redirect your mail—for a fee. Forms are available at any Post Office.

Rental agreements

If you have rental agreements remember to cancel them in good time. If buying on credit or hire purchase, you should inform the finance company in question of your movements.

Subscriptions

Subscriptions to associations should either be cancelled or the organisation concerned be informed of your new address. See also under Journals.

Tax

You need to inform both the Inland Revenue and the Treasurer of your local district or borough council so that they can assess your liability to income tax and local taxes (*ie* council charge, community charge or rates). You might even get a rebate! If you are self-employed and subject to VAT, you will have to tell the local VAT inspector as well.

The Inland Revenue produces a number of booklets that will guide you, including IR 25 which sets out the rules governing the taxation of income from overseas. As a rule of thumb, if the Inland Revenue regards you as non-resident in the UK for tax purposes you will not be liable to UK income tax, though you may well have to pay it to the United States authorities. You should not, however, have to pay income tax twice over since there is a double taxation agreement between the UK and the United States. US taxation is dealt with in the next chapter but you can obtain advance information from the Internal Revenue Service c/o the US Embassy.

There are a number of expatriate tax advisers (some of them listed in Appendix F) and if your tax affairs are complicated you may wish to seek advice in order to minimise tax liability both in the UK and United States. Books such as the *Allied Dunbar Expatriate Tax Guide* and *Working Abroad* are also worth dipping into.

Travel arrangements

It is normal for your employer to pay your fares, and if not, you should enquire why not. Expect to travel by air rather than on the QE2, and if you are on contract do not rely on getting free air travel for your dependants. Allow yourself plenty of time to get to the airport.

Utilities—electricity, gas, telephone, water

Inform the respective companies of the date of your departure and arrange for the payment of outstanding bills and disconnection, if appropriate. Also cancel milk and newspaper deliveries.

Visas

The different visa categories are explained in Chapter 2. If you have any doubts or your situation is complicated, you may need to seek help from a lawyer or consultant specialising in US immigration law. The Embassy can supply you with a list of these.

Voting rights

British people who live abroad now have the right to vote in elections, thanks to the **Representation of the People Act 1989**, and you can receive information on this from the Electoral Registration Officer of the district in which you reside.

If you wish to receive election literature you should inform the offices of the different parties in the constituency in which you reside, since this is the place where you have your vote. On arrival in the United States you need to contact the nearest British Consulate for the appropriate voting registration forms and an explanatory leaflet.

6
Looking for a Job on Arrival

Making contact with potential employers who are thousands of miles away is not an easy matter. Conducting your job search from within the United States itself can work out more satisfactory. You then have a chance to see what conditions are like, assess job prospects and employers, and understand what you are letting yourself in for.

However—and I cannot stress this point too much—in order to be able to work in the United States you need to be in possession of the appropriate kind of visa. If you are not, before you take up a position you must seek to regularise your status with the Immigration and Naturalisation Service. (The local offices are listed in Appendix G.) This is no mere formality, and there is no guarantee that you will be granted the necessary permission.

If you possess an Alien Registration Receipt Card (the 'green card') there is no problem. This document indicates that you have been granted permanent residence, and allows you to get a job anywhere without restriction. In most other situations, the employer will have to obtain permission to employ you, and since it can take months to get the necessary go-ahead, many firms will think twice before taking you on. The subject of visas has been dealt with in Chapter 2.

This chapter is aimed mainly at people who have the necessary permission to work in the United States. However, it will also be of interest to anyone who decides to visit America for a holiday or business trip and carry out a job reconnaissance at the same time. You may be fortunate enough to come across an employer who offers you a job on the spot, but it is just as valuable to glean information about the jobs market that will be useful to you in the future.

As in the UK there is no one golden way of finding a job, and you will achieve success sooner if you try a variety of approaches. Where you base yourself is also crucial. Generally speaking, you need to position yourself in an area where there are plenty of opportunities in your particular field. This will normally mean in or near a large and expanding commercial or industrial centre. In this respect

California, New York and parts of Texas are better bets than Wyoming or South Dakota.

SHOULD I APPROACH AN EMPLOYER DIRECT?

The direct approach can be very productive, especially if you research the jobs market thoroughly beforehand. You need to identify employers who could make use of your expertise, and in particular ones that appear to be expanding and taking on extra staff. Among the useful sources of information are:

- Commercial and professional directories (see Bibliography). Dun's *Employment Opportunities Directory* is particularly useful because it gives details of the recruitment practices and requirements of different companies.

- Reports and articles in newspapers and journals, on radio and TV, particularly the business news.

- Professional associations, careers counsellors, friends and acquaintances.

- The Internet. Many companies have their own web sites.

You then need to see if you can identify individuals within the organisation who might be interested in your expertise and have the authority to recruit personnel. In small outfits this could well turn out to be the managing director himself. Otherwise, contact the personnel officer, who in larger firms is likely to have the title Vice President of Human Resources.

This step involves one of the following procedures:

A personal visit
If the organisation is in the locality where you are staying, you could call in and ask about current and future recruitment needs. If things look promising, see if you can make an appointment with the relevant person and leave a copy of your résumé (American style CV). If the firm is a small one you may be lucky enough to see someone straight away, but normally you will have to make an appointment for a later date.

Be prepared to ask questions about the organisation itself and how a person with your experience and qualifications would fit in. Before leaving, see if you can pick up brochures about the organisation. Such information could prove useful at some future meeting.

A letter

On the whole speculative letters are less effective than personal visits, but unless you are prepared to spend an enormous amount on your job hunting it is not feasible to visit organisations throughout the United States purely 'on spec'. Distances are greater than you think: for instance, Istanbul is much closer to London than Los Angeles is to Boston.

If the organisation is within a few hundred miles of your base, you could increase the effectiveness of your application by indicating that you will be in the vicinity during the course of the next few weeks and asking for an appointment. For positions further afield you should consider targeting a number of employers in just a few, well-chosen states. Then, if some interest is shown, you can back the application up with a visit in which you kill several birds with one stone.

In the case of more distant employers you need to stress your mobility and willingness to relocate. Your initial base in the United States, after all, is (or should be) essentially a temporary one.

(For a sample of a speculative application letter turn to Appendix E.)

A telephone call

If you have a confident telephone manner, you could try canvassing for job leads by telephone. In this way you can cover a lot of ground in a short period of time. John Truitt's book *Telesearch: Direct Dial the Best Job of Your Life* describes this technique in some detail.

Do not expect every phone call to result in a job interview. Some organisations may dislike this type of approach and will ask you to apply in writing; others will give you details of their needs and send you an application form; others will state that they have no recruitment plans. But if you do get an encouraging reaction, be prepared to describe briefly your skills and job objectives.

You may achieve greater success if you adopt a more subtle approach. Instead of asking for a job, why not mention that you are visiting the area and would like to have a look at the company or organisation? Americans are usually very welcoming to foreign visitors and might be flattered by your interest. You may not land a job as a result of your enquiry, but you will doubtless pick up useful information and possibly some job leads.

PRIVATE RECRUITMENT AGENCIES

As in the UK there are many recruitment organisations that find staff for their clients, some of which are household names on this side of the Atlantic, too. The main difference is that firms operating in the United States have the right to charge job seekers a fee—normally a percentage of the first month's or year's salary—if they, achieve a placement. Not all do so, and generally speaking the more reputable agencies don't. In some states there are laws that place a limit on how much an agency can charge.

Just as in the UK, too, there are agencies which cover the whole range of jobs and others that specialise in certain sectors. Catering for the top of the market are the executive search firms (sometimes known as 'headhunters') which recruit for high level positions. The vacancies they handle are not always advertised, and the firms approach candidates they deem suitable for the positions. There is no harm at all in sending your résumé to a consultancy with a good track record in your particular field and asking to be put on their files.

There is often an overlap between executive search firms and those that deal with jobs at middle management and other levels. Some firms operate under one roof, using a number of different names according to job level and specialisation.

One very good way of finding an employment agency is by personal recommendation. There are, alas, cowboy outfits that are more intent on earning a fast buck than on making satisfactory placements, and these are to be avoided. Otherwise you can find the names by looking through the job advertisement columns of newspapers and journals or in telephone directories (*Yellow Pages*). In some directories employment agencies are classified according to their specialisation.

Many recruitment consultancies belong to one of the following organisations that publish directories of their members: Association of Executive Search Consultants, National Association of Executive Recruiters, National Association of Personnel Services and the National Association of Corporate and Professional Recruiters. (Addresses: see Appendix G.)

Temporary help agencies

There are some 3,500 national, regional and independent companies operating in this field, including some names familiar in UK high streets (*eg* Manpower). Normally such companies recruit their own employees and assign them to clients for limited periods as needed.

The breakdown of jobs in the industry is as follows:

63 per cent office/clerical positions

15 per cent industrial work; *eg* assembly line workers and janitors

11 per cent technical and professional jobs; *eg* engineers, accountants, lawyers, computer programmers, draughtsmen, managers

10 per cent medical; *eg* nurses, therapists, nursing orderlies, lab
technicians

(Source: National Association of Temporary Services)

Temporary employment is a growth area, and the technical and
medical sectors appear to be growing faster than the others. This
trend is expected to continue. It is particularly attractive to people in
search of flexible working hours, additional income or a way back
into the job market. In some cases a temporary job can lead to a
permanent engagement.

This is probably only an option for people in possession of a 'green
card', since non-immigrant visas are not normally issued to people
engaged by a temporary help agency. If you are a student with
permission to work or have exchange visitor status (see Chapter 3)
you might well contact such a firm in your quest for vacation
employment.

The National Association of Temporary Services is the national
trade organisation for the temporary help industry and publishes a
directory of its members. (See also Appendix C.)

JOB ADVERTISEMENTS

In the United States there is no national press as we know it. Virtually
all newspapers serve a particular locality, and even a national newspaper such as the *Wall Street Journal* appears in regional editions.

This means that when looking for a job you will need to look in
the newspapers published in the region where you plan to work. If
you are living in New York and want to work in San Francisco, there
is little point in looking through the classified ads of the *New York
Times*. You need to get hold of a San Francisco paper.

In Appendix D and Appendix G the names and addresses of the
leading newspapers are listed state by state. If you are living outside
the state concerned you may have to arrange for copies to be sent to
you. Find out which are the best days for job advertisements; the
Sunday editions are usually a good bet.

Professional and trade journals normally have national distribution, and would therefore include job advertisements for all areas
in the United States. *The National Business Employment Weekly*—
a weekly supplement of the *Wall Street Journal*—and other

more specialised job listings are also worth looking at. (See Appendix
D.)

The Internet is growing in popularity as a medium for advertising
vacancies, and you can make contact with an extensive number of
agencies and employers by accessing websites such as cweb.com,
careermosaic.com and adamsonline.com.

As you saw in Chapter 4, the trouble with job advertisements is
that they normally generate a lot of replies. You are probably up
against stiff competition and therefore need to prepare your application as expertly as possible. (See Appendix E for ideas on how to do
this.) Furthermore, it is no use replying to just one or two job ads;
you need to reply to several in order to increase your chances of
success.

PUBLIC SECTOR AND OTHER EMPLOYMENT SERVICES

The state employment services, sometimes called **Job Service**,
operate in conjunction with the US Department of Labor Employment Service and have some 2000 local offices, whch are listed
on the Internet under jobcenter.com. They are similar to Job Centres
in the UK, do not charge a placement fee, and recruit for both white
collar and blue collar positions, though not usually for senior and
middle ranking ones.

Most states have computerised job banks which provide daily
listings of job openings in the area of public and private sector
vacancies. In addition there is a network of **Federal Job Information Centers** throughout the country. The addresses of the
departments handling the employment service are listed state by state
in Appendix G. The website for Jobbank is www.ajb.dni.us.

There are various other non-commercial recruitment organisations operated by voluntary organisations. **Intercristo,** for instance,
is a Christian placement network which finds personnel for Christian
organisations within the United States. For the older job seeker there
are **40+ Clubs.**

College placement offices are another source of information
about jobs, more specifically for graduates. Of course, their main pre-
occupation is finding jobs for their own graduates, but if you are
lucky, you may find a placement officer who can spend a little time
with you. For addresses you should consult the *Directory of Career
Planning & Placement Officers* obtainable from:

College Placement Council Inc.
Box 2263
Bethlehem
PA 18001
USA.

NETWORKING

Making use of one's contacts is one of the most successful methods of landing a job in the United States—for US residents, at least—but as a newcomer you may feel at a disadvantage. You arrive knowing virtually nobody and need time to build up a network of contacts in a strange land.

How can you overcome this difficulty? The best solution is to begin to develop your network before your departure for the New World. You should have plenty of contacts at home—relatives, business colleagues, people you socialise with, professional contacts, *etc*—so why not ask them to suggest people whom you might look up on your visit? There is also scope for making contacts on the Internet.

Do not overlook the services of organisations to which you belong—your trade union, professional association, local church, the local Rotary Club, for instance. Many such associations have counterparts in the United States, and some of the professional ones are listed in the appropriate job sector of Appendix A. Find out the names and addresses of local representatives in the area(s) where you will be staying and either get a letter of introduction or drop them a line to announce your visit. Chambers of Commerce in the United States are also worth approaching.

WHAT ARE THE PROS AND CONS OF JOB HUNTING FROM A US BASE?

There are obvious advantages to conducting your job search within the United States. You have a chance to meet potential employers and their staff face to face and to see working conditions in different companies at first hand. You also have access to much more information on job opportunities in the form of press advertisements, reference books, job guides and advisers.

On the other hand, if you do not have residential status (and most visitors to the United States do not) you may find companies reluctant to employ you, even if you possess exceptionally good qualifications and experience. This could be because there are plenty of skilled people in the area and so there is no need to call on expertise from abroad. However, a more plausible reason is that the employer (like most American employers) has no experience of recruiting 'aliens' and is therefore unfamiliar with the procedures for obtaining a work visa.

To overcome this reluctance the onus is on you to explain the immigration rules: how the employer must apply to the US Department of Labor for labor certification and that when this comes through you will need to contact the Immigration and Naturalisation Service (INS). The American Council on International Personnel may also be able to advise. (For addresses, please see Appendix G.) While immigration attorneys can be used, they are not always necessary if the employer has good grounds for offering you the job.

Visits 'on spec' cost money, of course, and there is no guarantee that in the end you will find a job. You therefore need to make sure that you have adequate financial support to proceed with your job search, since you will not qualify for government handouts if you have never worked in America before.

Another consideration is that if you are recruited outside the United States, you will normally get extra perks, notably free travel to your post and back together with some help in moving your belongings. There is also a better chance that you will be dealing with people who know the ropes about work visas for aliens and are able to make all the necessary arrangements speedily.

A final point: make sure that you sign a contract, which sets out the terms and conditions of your employment in detail. Then, in the event of a dispute between your employer and yourself you have some form of legal protection.

YOU START AT THE TOP AND WORK YOUR WAY DOWN!

7
Working Conditions and Financial Obligations

One golden rule for a person planning to work overseas is: take nothing for granted. This applies just as much to the United States as it does to some country in the Third World; for while superficially things may look the same as they do back home, they seldom are.

This is certainly true with respect to the world of work. US employment laws and working practices may be different from those you are used to. Contracts, for instance, are less likely to be open-ended; in fact, many people are on short-term contracts and new agreements have to be negotiated every two or three years. Moreover, American employers are in a position to terminate a job at any time without justification.

In some respects employees in the United States receive less protection than workers in Europe. That is not to say that America has no labour laws; in fact, there is plenty of legislation both at the federal and state levels, some of it extremely detailed. It is designed to prevent unfair employment practices and discrimination, and to regulate the health and safety of employees.

Your best protection, however, is the contract that you sign. It should spell out the terms and conditions of your employment clearly, so that if your employer should renege on any parts of the agreement you can take him to court. As Americans are somewhat litigious by nature, legal disputes with employers are not uncommon.

YOUR CONTRACT

At the end of Chapter 4 you saw what conditions you should look for in a contract signed in the UK or Ireland.

What should I look for in a USA contract?
A contract signed in the United States should include:
- the name and address of your employer
- your job title and responsibilities

97

- the staff member you are answerable to
- the location of your employment
- your net salary and dates of payment
- the commencement date and duration of your employment
- the working hours.

Statutory benefits
In addition to pay there are three benefits that the employer is required to provide by law:

Social security payment
He has to make a contribution to your Social Security account (the equivalent to National Insurance in the UK) with the Federal Government.

Unemployment compensation
Your employer must pay into the Government insurance programme that pays unemployment benefit to employees who lose their jobs. The employee does not have to contribute to the scheme.

Workmen's compensation
The employer also has to bear the full cost of contributions to this scheme which provides benefits to employees injured or disabled at work.

Discretionary benefits
The other benefits are discretionary (*ie* employers are not required by law to provide them, though most of them offer at least some). When negotiating your contract you need to pay attention to these points.

Vacation
Vacation entitlements are modest by European standards: seldom more than two weeks per annum except for senior employees, while a new employee might only get one week off.

In addition there are various public holidays: New Year's Day, Memorial Day (last Monday in May), Independence Day (July 4), Labor Day (first Monday in September), Thanksgiving (fourth Thursday in November) and Christmas Day. Note that a lengthy break at Christmas is unusual.

Sick leave
Employees are allowed to take a specific number of days each year

for sickness or compassionate leave—typically six days in all. Note that visits to the dentist or doctor during the working day may be deducted from your sick leave entitlement.

Life insurance
Many employers offer low-cost or free life insurance, normally based on the employee's salary.

Medical insurance
Traditionally businesses have provided health care insurance for their staff, but as the cost of health care rockets some have started to cut back on benefits. When negotiating your contract you should make sure that the provision offered will be adequate for your needs. (See below.)

Pension plans
As in the UK there are company pension plans, some of them funded entirely by the employer, others requiring contributions from both employer and employee. If you are working on a short-term contract, you may be ineligible for such a scheme.

Other benefits
These would include profit sharing schemes (normally restricted to long-term employees), training allowances, social and sports facilities, counselling, low-cost loans. Company cars and luncheon vouchers are not very common.

MEDICAL MATTERS

In the United States there is no government funded health service catering for everybody on the lines of the National Health Service in the UK. The **Medicare** programme, which accounts for 15 per cent of Federal Government spending, is limited to the over-65s and long term disabled.

Medical costs in America are high and are rising fast. In 1990 health care spending came to $950 billion—13.7 per cent of GDP; the UK percentage is less than half that. Even a routine visit to the dentist can set you back a tidy sum. That is why you ought to make sure that you and any dependants you have in the United States have adequate medical insurance cover.

Fortunately, many employers have company medical plans for their staff, and around 90 per cent of employees with private health insurance are covered by such plans. However, a number of these plans cover only a proportion of the expenses incurred (normally between 70 and 90 per cent), and may exclude dental care. So you may need to explore the possibility of topping up your employer's scheme with an individual policy.

Sickness benefit is provided by:

- the Federal Government in the case of disabilities that are total and permanent
- certain states for short periods of illness or disability
- private insurance plans in other states. These are often funded by employers.

The Health Insurance Association of America publishes some useful consumer guides, including *The Consumer's Guide to Health Insurance*, *The Consumer's Guide to Medicare Supplement Insurance* and *The Consumer's Guide to Disability Insurance*.

WORKING PRACTICES

The working day is normally from 8am to 4.30pm in factories, 8.30am to 5pm for offices and the 40-hour week tends to be the norm. Americans tend to be sticklers for timekeeping, and you will be expected to arrive punctually and not slink off before the end of the working day. It is quite normal even for executives to clock in.

Employees are expected to pull their weight, and if you want to succeed in your job you must be prepared to work long hours; firms are quite ready to dismiss backsliders with no reasons given. There is no specific federal government regulation regarding termination of employment, but the normal practice is to give two weeks' notice or severance pay. If you are laid off you may be able to collect unemployment insurance, but not for an open-ended period.

By contrast, equal opportunity legislation tends to work in the employee's favour. The Equal Employment Opportunity Commission of the Federal Department of Labor prohibits discrimination on the basis of race, religion, colour, sex, national origin, handicap, age and virtually everything else. Americans are much more prone to taking employers to court than employees on this side of the Atlantic.

Many states have additional laws designed to counter discrimination in employment, sexual harassment and smoking in public places, and one needs to be aware of these. State laws can affect the way you apply for a job: in some states you should not enclose a photograph with your application. One clearly has to be circumspect in one's relationships towards subordinates of the opposite sex, while chain smokers are in danger of being ostracised.

Working practices often reflect the values of the society in which they operate. In the United States individualism, enterprise and financial success are highly regarded, especially in the urban areas. While British people share many of these attitudes, people from other cultures may find the American way of work perplexing because their societies have a different system of values.

If you come into this category, Geert Hofstede's *Cultures Consequences* is required reading. The Institute for Training in Intercultural Management in the Hague offers courses in understanding and working with other nationalities, as does its UK affiliate, Howell & Associates. Other organisations involved in preparing people for working in the United States are: the Centre for International Briefing, Employment Conditions Abroad and Going Places.

TAXATION

'In this world nothing can be said to be certain, except death and taxes', wrote Benjamin Franklin over 200 years ago. In the United States the tax system, like death, has the habit of catching up with you in the end, so you need to be aware of some of its features.

Federal Income Tax

If you take up employment in America, you are liable to be taxed unless you fall into one of the exempt categories, such as diplomats, students and exchange visitors.

Many Americans live in awe of the Internal Revenue Service (the US equivalent of the Inland Revenue) whose tentacles seem to be everywhere. Departing aliens, for instance, may not be permitted to leave the country unless they can produce a certificate of compliance (sometimes known as the sailing permit or departure permit) at the port of departure.

To obtain this certificate, if you have earnings in the United States you must first file Form 1040C to the IRS office in your district; if you have received no income from US sources you need to submit Form 2063. Mercifully, tourists, students and the staff of foreign governments and international organisations are exempt.

The ins and outs of US taxation are long and complex, and beyond the scope of this book. You can, though, get various guides free of charge from the Internal Revenue Service itself. The relevant ones are *US Tax Guide for Aliens* and *Your Federal Income Tax* (which is at least three times as long as this book!).

The first thing the IRS will want to establish is whether you are a non-resident alien or resident alien for tax purposes. Green card holders are automatically regarded as residents by the IRS, and people on non-immigrant visas who have been present in the United States for a substantial part of the year also fall into this category. The chart in Figure 11 will help you decide. Complications occur in the case of people who commute between the UK and America, and if you have been both a non-resident alien and a resident alien during the course of one tax year.

The US tax year coincides with the calendar year. If you are a non-resident alien in the eyes of the IRS, and engaged in a trade or business, you will need to apply for a **taxpayer identification number** at the local office of the Social Security Administration and file your income tax return on Form 1040NR. Resident aliens file Form 1040EZ, 1040A or 1040 and must apply for a taxpayer identification number too, as soon as they start earning income subject to US tax.

A US income tax form is a complex document, since there are several allowances you may be able to claim (including certain medical and dental expenses). Many Americans employ a certified public accountant (CPA) to complete their tax return for them—at a cost of a few hundred dollars—but if you work diligently through the tax guides mentioned above you should be able to do it yourself.

For employees a system similar to Pay As You Earn operates in the United States, though it is not obligatory. You must let your employer know whether you are a resident or non-resident alien and agree with him how much tax you expect to pay so that the correct amount of tax can be withheld. If you are a resident alien you need to let him have a **Certificate of Alien Claiming Residence in the United States** (Form 1078).

When you come to fill in your tax form at the end of the tax year, you may find you are due for a refund or additional payment if there is a discrepancy between what has been withheld and what you should have paid on your tax form. Note that there are deadlines for the submission.

State and local taxes

Most of the states also levy taxes on individuals (though until now Texas has been an exception). This takes the form of income tax, and the rates can vary considerably from state to state. To find out what proportion of your income you have to pay, you should contact the tax department of the state in which you intend to live and work.

(Addresses in Appendix G.) The table in Figure 14 will also give some indication.

You may also need to pay local taxes to the city or county in which you live, and these often take the form of a sales tax or a property tax. Residents of Metropolitan Atlanta, for instance, pay:

- federal tax
- state income tax
- property taxes (rates)
- a sales and use tax (currently 4 per cent).

Social Security

The federal government also deducts social security tax, which is similar to our National Insurance and goes towards your pension and Medicare. However, bear in mind that Medicare benefits are only available to certain groups. Because of reciprocal agreements between the United States and other countries, including the UK, as a non-resident alien you may well be able to pay UK National Insurance contributions instead. You may also have to contribute to a disability insurance scheme in certain states.

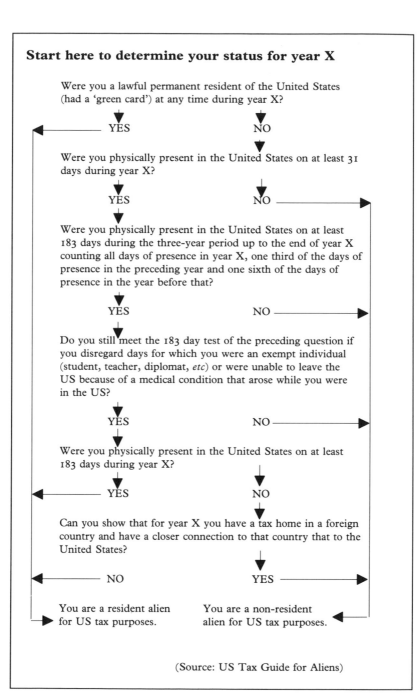

Start here to determine your status for year X

Were you a lawful permanent resident of the United States (had a 'green card') at any time during year X?

YES   NO

Were you physically present in the United States on at least 31 days during year X?

YES   NO

Were you physically present in the United States on at least 183 days during the three-year period up to the end of year X counting all days of presence in year X, one third of the days of presence in the preceding year and one sixth of the days of presence in the year before that?

YES   NO

Do you still meet the 183 day test of the preceding question if you disregard days for which you were an exempt individual (student, teacher, diplomat, *etc*) or were unable to leave the US because of a medical condition that arose while you were in the US?

YES   NO

Were you physically present in the United States on at least 183 days during year X?

YES   NO

Can you show that for year X you have a tax home in a foreign country and have a closer connection to that country that to the United States?

NO   YES

You are a resident alien for US tax purposes.   You are a non-resident alien for US tax purposes.

(Source: US Tax Guide for Aliens)

Fig. 11.   Determining your tax status.

104

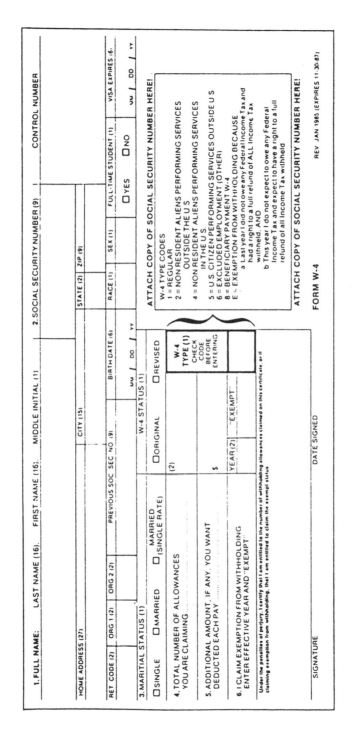

Fig. 12. Employer's tax deduction card.

EMPLOYEE'S PAY STATEMENT

C.G. NICKERSON SUPPLY CO.
4567 MELROSE
MIAMI, FL. 33199

HOURS		WAGES				DEDUCTIONS				
REGULAR	OVERTIME	REGULAR	OVERTIME	OTHER	GROSS PAY	FICA	WITHHOLDING TAX	HEALTH INSURANCE	CREDIT UNION	NET PAY

Fig. 13.   Example of an employee's pay statement showing basic and overtime pay, tax and other deductions.

US State and Local Taxes

[Preliminary. Data based on average family of four (two wage earners and two school age children) owning their own home and living in a city where taxes apply. Comprises State and local sales, income, auto, and real estate taxes.]

City	Total taxes paid, by gross family income level (dollars)				Total taxes paid as percent of income			
	$25,000	$50,000	$75,000	$100,000	$25,000	$50,000	$75,000	$100,000
Albuquerque, NM	1,478	3,434	5,943	8,461	5.9	6.9	7.9	8.5
Atlanta, GA	2,838	5,593	9,107	12,019	11.4	11.2	12.1	12.0
Baltimore, MD	4,068	8,246	12,791	16,659	16.3	16.5	17.1	16.7
Bridgeport, CT	4,519	9,416	16,270	21,185	18.1	18.8	21.7	21.2
Burlington, VT	1,909	4,132	7,197	10,134	7.6	8.3	9.6	10.1
Charleston, WV	1,691	3,542	6,373	8,836	6.8	7.1	8.5	8.8
Charlotte, NC	2,085	4,412	7,253	9,734	8.3	8.8	9.7	9.7
Chicago, IL	2,954	5,938	9,326	12,084	11.8	11.9	12.4	12.1
Columbus, OH	2,151	4,713	7,712	10,650	8.6	9.4	10.3	10.7
Columbia, SC	1,971	4,799	8,151	10,905	7.9	9.6	10.9	10.9
Des Moines, IA	1,844	4,120	6,770	9,109	7.4	8.2	9.0	9.1
Detroit, MI	4,723	9,680	14,773	19,290	18.9	19.4	19.7	91.3
Honolulu, HI	1,853	4,306	7,272	9,921	7.4	8.6	9.7	9.9
Indianapolis, IN	2,017	3,703	6,268	8,061	8.1	7.4	8.4	8.1
Jackson, MS	1,451	3,421	6,080	8,237	5.8	6.8	8.1	8.2
Kansas City, MO	1,965	4,358	7,024	9,224	7.9	8.7	9.4	9.2
Louisville, KY	2,439	5,100	8,099	10,777	9.8	10.2	10.8	10.8
Memphis, TN	1,718	2,896	4,506	5,702	6.9	5.8	6.0	5.7
Milwaukee, MI	3,274	7,288	11,425	15,071	13.1	14.6	15.2	15.1
Newark, NJ	5,853	11,445	17,696	23,420	23.4	22.9	23.6	23.4
Nw York City, NY	2,603	6,579	11,199	15,247	10.4	13.2	14.9	15.2
Omaha, NE	2,159	4,529	7,872	10,668	8.6	9.1	10.5	10.7
Philadelphia, PA	3,956	7,610	11,361	14,755	15.8	15.2	15.1	14.8
Portland, ME	2,132	5,144	9,361	12,759	8.5	10.3	12.5	12.8
Portland, OR	2,428	5,369	8,623	11,542	9.7	10.7	11.5	11.5
Providence, RI	4,271	8,393	13,542	17,945	17.1	16.8	18.1	17.9
Salt Lake City, UT	2,038	4,682	7,564	10,020	8.2	9.4	10.1	10.0
Sioux Falls, SD	1,837	3,180	5,312	6,701	7.3	6.4	7.1	6.7
Virginia Beach, VA	2,089	4,423	7,521	9,930	8.4	8.8	10.0	9.9
Washington, DC	2,278	5,041	8,416	11,556	9.1	10.1	11.2	11.6
Median[1]	1,970	4,306	7,253	9,921	7.9	8.6	9.7	9.9

[1] Median of all 51 cities.

Fig. 14. Estimated state and local taxes paid by a family of four in selected cities: 1992

(Source: Government of the District of Columbia, Department of Finance and Revenue, *Tax Rates and Tax Burdens in the District of Columbia: A Nationwide Comparison*, annual).

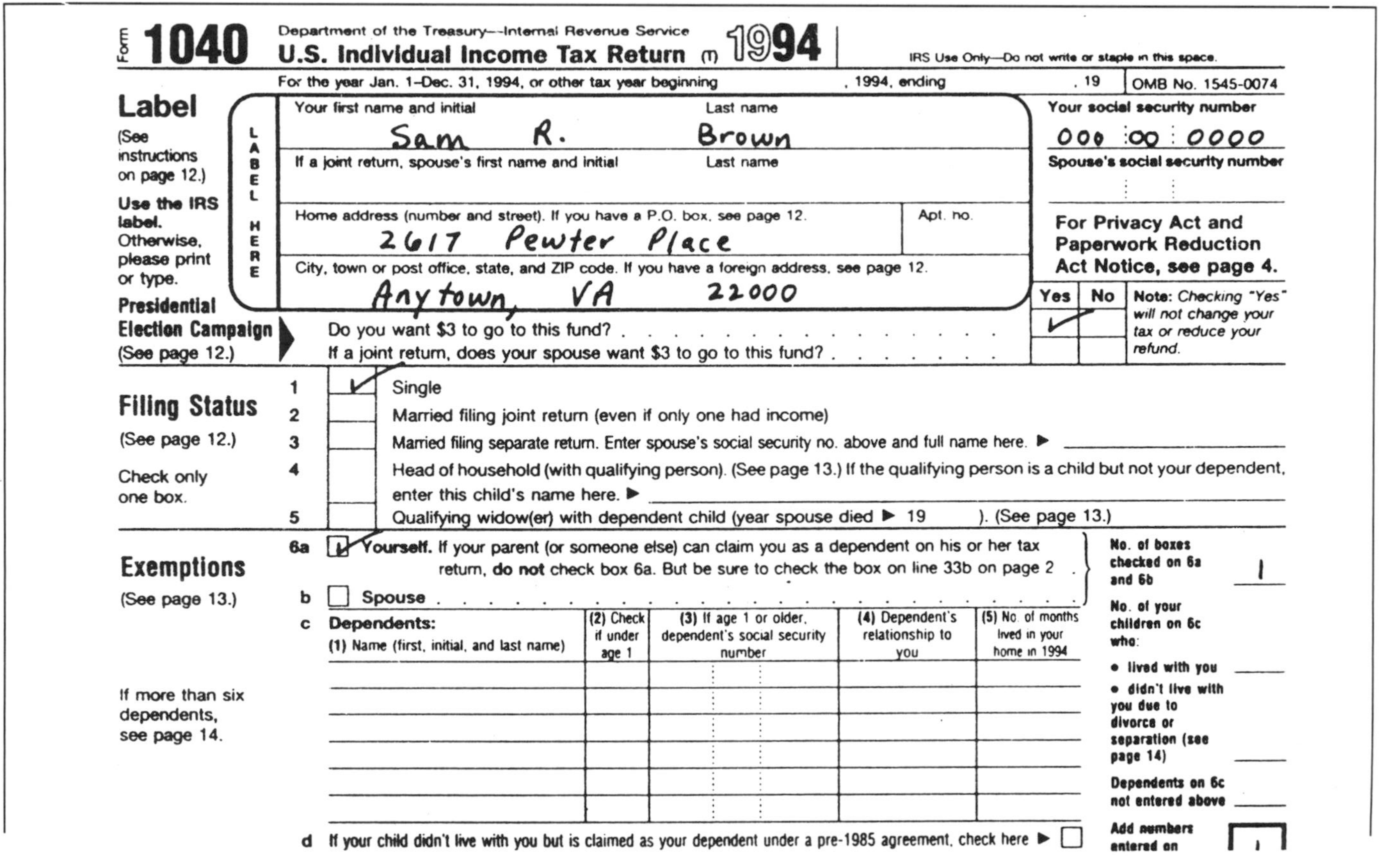

Fig. 15. USA income tax form: Dual Status Return.

● Total number of exemptions claimed

				lines above ▶	
Income	7	Wages, salaries, tips, etc. Attach Form(s) W-2	7	28,300	00
	8a	Taxable interest income (see page 15). Attach Schedule B if over $400	8a	395	00
Attach	b	Tax-exempt interest (see page 16). DON'T include on line 8a	8b		
Copy B of your Forms W-2, W-2G, and 1099-R here.	9	Dividend income. Attach Schedule B if over $400	9	120	00
	10	Taxable refunds, credits, or offsets of state and local income taxes (see page 16)	10		
	11	Alimony received	11		
If you did not get a W-2, see page 15.	12	Business income or (loss). Attach Schedule C or C-EZ	12		
	13	Capital gain or (loss). If required, attach Schedule D (see page 16)	13		
	14	Other gains or (losses). Attach Form 4797	14		
Enclose, but do not attach, any payment with your return.	15a	Total IRA distributions . 15a b Taxable amount (see page 17)	15b		
	16a	Total pensions and annuities 16a b Taxable amount (see page 17)	16b		
	17	Rental real estate, royalties, partnerships, S corporations, trusts, etc. Attach Schedule E	17		
	18	Farm income or (loss). Attach Schedule F	18		
	19	Unemployment compensation (see page 18)	19		
	20a	Social security benefits 20a b Taxable amount (see page 18)	20b		
	21	Other income. List type and amount—see page 18	21		
	22	Add the amounts in the far right column for lines 7 through 21. This is your **total income** ▶	22	28,815	00
Adjustments to Income	23a	Your IRA deduction (see page 19)	23a		
	b	Spouse's IRA deduction (see page 19)	23b		
Caution: See instructions ▶	24	Moving expenses. Attach Form 3903 or 3903-F	24	8,300 00	
	25	One-half of self-employment tax	25		
	26	Self-employed health insurance deduction (see page 21)	26		
	27	Keogh retirement plan and self-employed SEP deduction	27		
	28	Penalty on early withdrawal of savings	28		
	29	Alimony paid. Recipient's SSN ▶	29		
	30	Add lines 23a through 29. These are your **total adjustments** ▶	30	8,300	00
Adjusted Gross Income	31	Subtract line 30 from line 22. This is your **adjusted gross income**. If less than $25,296 and a child lived with you (less than $9,000 if a child didn't live with you), see "Earned Income Credit" on page 27 ▶	31	20,515	00

Cat. No. 11320B

Form **1040** (1994)

Tax Compu- tation

(See page 23.)

Tax from table — $2,594 34

Tax from Form 1040AB — $36

If you want the IRS to figure your tax, see page 24.

Credits

(See page 24.)

Other Taxes

32	Amount from line 31 (adjusted gross income)		20,515	00
33a	Check if: ☐ You were 65 or older, ☐ Blind; ☐ Spouse was 65 or older, ☐ Blind.	▸ 33a		
	Add the number of boxes checked above and enter the total here	▸ 33a		
b	If your parent (or someone else) can claim you as a dependent, check here	▸ 33b ☐		
c	If you are married filing separately and your spouse itemizes deductions or you are a dual-status alien, see page 23 and check here.	▸ 33c ☑		
34	Enter the larger of your: Itemized deductions from Schedule A, line 29, OR Standard deduction shown below for your filing status. **But if you checked any box on line 33a or b, go to page 23 to find your standard deduction.** If you checked box 33c, your standard deduction is zero. • Single—$3,800 • Head of household—$5,600 • Married filing jointly or Qualifying widow(er)—$6,350 • Married filing separately—$3,175		4,022	00
35	Subtract line 34 from line 32		19,493	00
36	If line 32 is $83,850 or less, multiply $2,450 by the total number of exemptions claimed on line 6e. If line 32 is over $83,850, see the worksheet on page 24 for the amount to enter		2,450	00
37	**Taxable income.** Subtract line 36 from line 35. If line 36 is more than line 35, enter -0-		17,043	00
38	Tax. Check if from a ☐ Tax Table, b ☐ Tax Rate Schedules, c ☐ Capital Gain Tax Worksheet, or d ☐ Form 8615 (see page 24). Amount from Form(s) 8814 ▸ •		2,590	00
39	Additional taxes. Check if from a ☐ Form 4970 b ☐ Form 4972			
40	Add lines 38 and 39	▲	2,590	00
41	Credit for child and dependent care expenses. Attach Form 2441	41		
42	Credit for the elderly or the disabled. Attach Schedule R	42		
43	Foreign tax credit. Attach Form 1116	43		
44	Other credits (see page 25). Check if from a ☐ Form 3800 b ☐ Form 8396 c ☐ Form 8801 d ☐ Form (specify)	44		
45	Add lines 41 through 44		-0-	
46	Subtract line 45 from line 40. If line 45 is more than line 40, enter -0-	▲	2,590	00
47	Self-employment tax. Attach Schedule SE			
48	Alternative minimum tax. Attach Form 6251			

Dual Status Return (*continued*).

49 Recapture taxes. Check if from a ☐ Form 4255 b ☐ Form 8611 c ☐ Form 8828	49	
50 Social security and Medicare tax on tip income not reported to employer. Attach Form 4137	50	
51 Tax on qualified retirement plans, including IRAs. If required, attach Form 5329	51	
52 Advance earned income credit payments from Form W-2	52	
53 Add lines 46 through 52. This is your **total tax** ▶	53	2,590 00

Payments

Attach Forms W-2, W-2G, and 1099-R on the front.

54 Federal income tax withheld. If any is from Form(s) 1099, check ▶ ☐	54	2,736 00
55 1994 estimated tax payments and amount applied from 1993 return	55	
56 Earned income credit. If required, attach Schedule EIC (see page 27). Nontaxable earned income: amount ▶ [ ] and type ▶ [ ]	56	
57 Amount paid with Form 4868 (extension request)	57	
58 Excess social security and RRTA tax withheld (see page 32)	58	
59 Other payments. Check if from a ☐ Form 2439 b ☐ Form 4136	59	
60 Add lines 54 through 59. These are your **total payments** ▶	60	2,736 00

Includes t36 from Form 10404R

Refund or Amount You Owe

61 If line 60 is more than line 53, subtract line 53 from line 60. This is the amount you **OVERPAID** ▶	61	176 00
62 Amount of line 61 you want **REFUNDED TO YOU** ▶	62	146 00
63 Amount of line 61 you want **APPLIED TO YOUR 1995 ESTIMATED TAX** ▶	63	
64 If line 53 is more than line 60, subtract line 60 from line 53. This is the **AMOUNT YOU OWE.** For details on how to pay, including what to write on your payment, see page 32	64	
65 Estimated tax penalty (see page 33). Also include on line 64	65	

Sign Here

Keep a copy of this return for your records.

Under penalties of perjury, I declare that I have examined this return and accompanying schedules and statements, and to the best of my knowledge and belief, they are true, correct, and complete. Declaration of preparer (other than taxpayer) is based on all information of which preparer has any knowledge.

Your signature ▶ *Aaron R. Brown* Date 3-16-95 Your occupation R+D Specialist

Spouse's signature. If a joint return, BOTH must sign. Date Spouse's occupation

Paid Preparer's Use Only

Preparer's signature ▶ Date Check if self-employed ☐ Preparer's social security no.

Firm's name (or yours if self-employed) and address ▶ E.I. No. ZIP code

SCHEDULES A&B
(Form 1040)

Department of the Treasury
Internal Revenue Service (T)

Schedule A—Itemized Deductions

(Schedule B is on back)

▶ Attach to Form 1040. ▶ See Instructions for Schedules A and B (Form 1040).

OMB No. 1545-0074

19**94**

Attachment
Sequence No. 07

Name(s) shown on Form 1040

Sam R. Brown

Your social security number

000 : 00 : 0000

Medical and Dental Expenses	**Caution:** *Do not include expenses reimbursed or paid by others.*				
	1	Medical and dental expenses (see page A-1) . . .	1		
	2	Enter amount from Form 1040, line 32.	2		
	3	Multiply line 2 above by 7.5% (.075) . . .	3		
	4	Subtract line 3 from line 1. If line 3 is more than line 1, enter -0-		4	
Taxes You Paid (See page A-1.)	5	State and local income taxes . . .	5	662 00	
	6	Real estate taxes (see page A-2) . . .	6		
	7	Personal property taxes . . .	7		
	8	Other taxes. List type and amount ▶	8		
	9	Add lines 5 through 8 . . .		9	662 00
Interest You Paid (See page A-2.) Note: Personal interest is not deductible.	10	Home mortgage interest and points reported to you on Form 1098	10		
	11	Home mortgage interest not reported to you on Form 1098. If paid to the person from whom you bought the home, see page A-3 and show that person's name, identifying no. and address ▶	11		
	12	Points not reported to you on Form 1098. See page A-3 for special rules . . .	12		
	13	Investment interest. If required, attach Form 4952. (See page A-3.)	13		
	14	Add lines 10 through 13 . . .		14	

Dual Status Return (*continued*).

Gifts to Charity	15	Gifts by cash or check. If any gift of $250 or more, see page A-3	15	360	00			
If you made a gift and got a benefit for it, see page A-3.	16	Other than by cash or check. If any gift of $250 or more, see page A-3. If over $500, you **MUST** attach Form 8283	16					
	17	Carryover from prior year	17					
	18	Add lines 15 through 17				18	360	00
Casualty and Theft Losses	19	Casualty or theft loss(es). Attach Form 4684. (See page A-4.)				19		
Job Expenses and Most Other Miscellaneous Deductions (See page A-5 for expenses to deduct here.)	20	Unreimbursed employee expenses—job travel, union dues, job education, etc. If required, you **MUST** attach Form 2106 or 2106-EZ. (See page A-5.) ▶	20					
	21	Tax preparation fees	21					
	22	Other expenses—investment, safe deposit box, etc. List type and amount ▶	22					
	23	Add lines 20 through 22	23					
	24	Enter amount from Form 1040, line 32.	24					
	25	Multiply line 24 above by 2% (.02)	25					
	26	Subtract line 25 from line 23. If line 25 is more than line 23, enter -0-				26		
Other Miscellaneous Deductions	27	Moving expenses incurred before 1994. Attach Form 3903 or 3903-F. (See page A-5.)				27		
	28	Other—from list on page A-5. List type and amount ▶				28		
Total Itemized Deductions	29	Is Form 1040, line 32, over $111,800 (over $55,900 if married filing separately)? **NO.** Your deduction is not limited. Add the amounts in the far right column for lines 4 through 28. Also, enter on Form 1040, line 34, the **larger** of this amount or your standard deduction. **YES.** Your deduction may be limited. See page A-5 for the amount to enter.			▶	29	4,022	00

For Paperwork Reduction Act Notice, see Form 1040 instructions.   Cat. No. 11330X   Schedule A (Form 1040) 1994

Form 1040NR

Department of the Treasury
Internal Revenue Service

U.S. Nonresident Alien Income Tax Return

For the year January 1–December 31, 1994, or other tax year
beginning _____ , 1994, and ending _____ , 19 ___

OMB No. 1545-0089

1994

Please print or type

Your first name and initial — Sam R.
Last name — Brown

Identifying or social security number — 000-00-0000

Present home address (number, street, and apt. no., or rural route). If a P.O. box, see page 5 of instructions.
2617 Pewter Place

Check if: ☑ Individual ☐ Estate or Trust

City, town or post office, state, and ZIP code. If a foreign address, see page 5 of instructions.
Anytown, VA 22000

For Paperwork Reduction Act Notice, see page 1 of instructions.

Country ▶ USA

Of what country were you a citizen or national during the tax year? ▶ United Kingdom

Give address in the country where you are a permanent resident. If same as above, write "Same." — Same

Give address outside the United States to which you want any refund check mailed. If same as above, write "Same." — N/A

Filing Status and Exemptions for Individuals (See page 5 of the instructions.)

Filing status. Check only one box.

1 ☐ Single resident of Canada or Mexico, or a single U.S. national
2 ☐ Other single nonresident alien
3 ☐ Married resident of Canada or Mexico, or a married U.S. national ⎱ If your spouse is filing a return, you
4 ☐ Married resident of Japan or the Republic of Korea ⎰ cannot take an exemption for him or her.
5 ☐ Other married nonresident alien
6 ☐ Qualifying widow(er) with dependent child (year spouse died ▶ 19 ___) (See page 5 of inst.)

Caution: *If your parent (or someone else) can claim you as a dependent on his or her tax return, do not check box 7a. But be sure to check the box below line 35 on page 2.*

	7a	7b
	Yourself	Spouse

No. of boxes checked on 7a and 7b ▲

7c Dependents:

(1) Name (first, initial, and last name)	(2) Check if under age 1	(3) If age 1 or older, dependent's social security number	(4) Dependent's relationship to you	(5) No. of months lived in your home in 1994

No. of your children on 7c who:

• lived with you ▲
•• didn't live with you due to divorce or separation ▲

↑ Copy B of your Forms W-2, W-2G, and 1099-R here

Dual Status Return (*continued*).

*Applies generally only to residents of Canada, Mexico, Japan, and the Republic of Korea and to U.S. nationals. (See page 6 of instructions.)

**Applies only to residents of Canada and Mexico and to U.S. nationals. (See page 6 of instructions.)

d If your child didn't live with you but is claimed as your dependent under a pre-1985 agreement, check here ▶ □

e Total number of exemptions claimed

**Dependents on 7c not entered above ▲

Add numbers entered on lines above ▲

Income Effectively Connected With U.S. Trade/Business		
8 Wages, salaries, tips, etc. Attach Form(s) W-2	8	6,500 00
9a Taxable interest income	9a	
b Tax-exempt interest (see page 7). DO NOT include on line 9a **9b**		
10 Dividend income	10	
11 Taxable refunds, credits, or offsets of state and local income taxes (see page 7)	11	
12 Scholarship and fellowship grants. Attach explanation (see page 7)	12	
13 Business income or (loss). Attach Schedule C or C-EZ (Form 1040)	13	
14 Capital gain or (loss). If required, attach Schedule D (Form 1040) (see page 7).	14	
15 Other gains or (losses). Attach Form 4797	15	
16a Total IRA distributions . **16a** 16b Taxable amount (see page 7)	16b	
17a Total pensions and annuities **17a** 17b Taxable amount (see page 8)	17b	
18 Rental real estate, royalties, partnerships, trusts, etc. Attach Schedule E (Form 1040)	18	
19 Farm income or (loss). Attach Schedule F (Form 1040).	19	
20 Unemployment compensation (see page 9)	20	
21 Other income. List type and amount—see page 9	21	
22 Total income exempt by a treaty from page 5, Item L **22**		
23 Add lines 8, 9a, 10–15, 16b, and 17b–21. This is your total effectively connected income ▶	23	6,500 00
Adjustments		
24 IRA deduction (see page 9) .	24	
25 Moving expenses. Attach Form 3903	25	
26 Self-employed health insurance deduction. **Caution:** See page 9	26	
27 Keogh retirement plan and self-employed SEP deduction	27	
28 Penalty on early withdrawal of savings	28	
29 Scholarship and fellowship grants excluded	29	
30 Add lines 24 through 29 (see instructions). These are your total adjustments ▶	30	0
31 Subtract line 30 from line 23. Enter here and on line 32. This is your adjusted gross income ▶	31	

Attach / Enclose, but do not attach, any payment with your return.

Cat No 11364D

Form **1040NR** (1994)

Tax Computation

32	Amount from line 31 (adjusted gross income)	32	
33	**Itemized deductions** from page 3, Schedule A, line 18	33	245 00
34	Subtract line 33 from line 32. If line 33 is more than line 32, enter -0-	34	
35	Exemptions (see page 10)	35	
	Caution: *If your parent (or someone else) can claim you as a dependent, check here* ▲ ☐		
36	**Taxable income.** Subtract line 35 from line 34. If line 35 is more than line 34, enter -0-	36	
37	Tax. Check if from ☐ Tax Table, ☐ Tax Rate Schedules, ☐ Capital Gain Tax Worksheet, or ☐ Form 8615 (see page 10). Amount from Form(s) 8814 ▲	37	
38	Additional taxes. Check if from ☐ Form 4970 ☐ Form 4972	38	
39	Add lines 37 and 38 ▲	39	

Credits

40	Credit for child and dependent care expenses. Attach Form 2441	40			
41	Foreign tax credit. Attach Form 1116	41			
42	Other credits (see page 11). Check if from ☐ Form 3800 ☐ Form 8801 ☐ Form (specify) _____	42			
43	Add lines 40 through 42			43	
44	Subtract line 43 from line 39. If line 43 is more than line 39, enter -0- ▲			44	

Other Taxes

45	Alternative minimum tax (see page 11). Attach Form 6251	45	
46	Recapture taxes (see page 12). Check if from ☐ Form 4255 ☐ Form 8611 ☐ Form 8828	46	
47	Tax on income not effectively connected with a U.S. trade or business from page 4, line 80	47	36 00
48	Social security and Medicare tax on tip income not reported to employer. Attach Form 4137	48	
49	Tax on qualified retirement plans, including IRAs. If required, attach Form 5329	49	
50	Transportation tax (see page 12)	50	
51	Add lines 44 through 50. This is your **total tax** ▲	51	

52	Federal income tax withheld. **If any is from Form(s) 1099, check** ▲ ☐	52	345 00
53	1994 estimated tax payments and amount applied from 1993 return	53	
54	**Earned income credit.** If required, attach Schedule EIC (Form 1040) (see page 13). Nontaxable earned income: amount ▲ _____ and type ▲ _____	54	

Dual Status Return (*continued*).

Payments

55	Amount paid with Form 4868 (extension request)	55
56	Excess social security and RRTA tax withheld (see page 13)	56
57	Other payments. Check if from ☐ Form 2439 ☐ Form 4136	57
58	Credit for amount paid with Form 1040-C	58
59	U.S. tax withheld at source:	
a	From page 4, line 77	59a
b	By partnerships under section 1446 (from Form(s) 8805 or 1042-S)	59b 3 6 00
60	U.S. tax withheld on dispositions of U.S. real property interests:	
a	From Form(s) 8288-A	60a
b	From Form(s) 1042-S	60b

61	Add lines 52 through 60b. These are your **total payments** ▲	61

Refund or Amount You Owe

62	If line 61 is more than line 51, subtract line 51 from line 61. This is the amount you **OVERPAID** ▲	62
63	Amount of line 62 you want **REFUNDED TO YOU.** ▲	63
64	Amount of line 62 you want **APPLIED TO YOUR 1995 ESTIMATED TAX** ▲	64
65	If line 51 is more than line 61, subtract line 61 from line 51. This is the **AMOUNT YOU OWE.** For details on how to pay, including what to write on your payment, see page 14 ▲	65 381 00
66	Estimated tax penalty (see page 14). Also, include on line 65	66

Sign Here

Under penalties of perjury, I declare that I have examined this return and accompanying schedules and statements, and to the best of my knowledge and belief, they are true, correct, and complete. Declaration of preparer (other than taxpayer) is based on all information of which preparer has any knowledge.

Keep a copy of this return for your records

Your signature ▲	Date	Your occupation in the United States

Paid Preparer's Use Only

Preparer's signature ▲	Date	Check if self-employed ☐	Preparer's social security no.
Firm's name (or yours if self-employed) and address ▲		E I No	
		ZIP code	

117

Schedule A—Itemized Deductions (See pages 14, 15, and 16.)

State and Local Income Taxes	1	State income taxes	1	245 00	
	2	Local income taxes	2		
	3	Add lines 1 and 2			3	245 00
Gifts to U.S. Charities		**Caution:** *If you made a gift and received a benefit in return, see page 14.*			
	4	Contributions by cash or check. If any gift of $250 or more, see page 15.	4		
	5	Other than cash or check. If any gift of $250 or more, see page 15. If over $500, you **MUST** attach Form 8283	5		
	6	Carryover from prior year	6		
	7	Add lines 4 through 6			7	
Casualty and Theft Losses	8	Casualty or theft loss(es). Attach Form 4684			8	
Job Expenses and Most Other Miscellaneous Deductions	9	Unreimbursed employee expenses—job travel, union dues, job education, etc. If required, you **MUST** attach Form 2106 or Form 2106-EZ. See page 16 ▶	9		
	10	Tax preparation fees	10		
	11	Other expenses. See page 16 for expenses to deduct here. List type and amount ▶			

07

Dual Status Return (*continued*).

12 Add lines 9 through 11	**12**
13 Enter the amount from Form 1040NR. line 32.	**13**
14 Multiply line 13 by 2% (.02)	**14**
15 Subtract line 14 from line 12. If line 14 is more than line 12, enter -0-.	**15**

Other Miscellaneous Deductions

16 Moving expenses incurred before 1994. Attach Form 3903. (See page 16.)	**16**
17 Other—certain expenses of disabled employees, estate tax on income of decedent, etc. List type and amount ▶	**17**

Total Itemized Deductions

18 Is Form 1040NR. line 32. over $111,800 (over $55,900 if you checked filing status box 3. 4. or 5 on page 1 of Form 1040NR)?

No. Your deduction is not limited. Add the amounts in the far right column for lines 3 through 17. Enter the total here and on Form 1040NR, line 33.

Yes. Your deduction may be limited. See page 16 for the amount to enter here and on Form 1040NR, line 33.

| **18** | 245 | 00 |

Tax on Income Not Effectively Con

Attach Forms 1042-S, SSA-1042

Nature of income		(a) U.S. tax withheld at source	
67 Dividends paid by:			
a U.S. corporations	67a	36	00
b Foreign corporations	67b		
68 Interest:			
a Mortgage	68a		
b Paid by foreign corporations	68b		
c Other	68c		
69 Industrial royalties (patents, trademarks, etc.)	69		
70 Motion picture or T.V. copyright royalties	70		
71 Other royalties (copyrights, recording, publishing, etc.)	71		
72 Real property income and natural resources royalties	72		
73 Pensions and annuities	73		
74 Social security benefits	74		
75 Gains (include capital gain from line 83 below)	75		
76 Other (specify) ▶	76		
77 **Total U.S. tax withheld at source.** Add column (a) of lines 67a through 76. Enter the total here and on Form 1040NR, line 59a ▶	77	36	00
78 Add lines 67a through 76 in columns (b)–(e)		78	

79 **Multiply line 78 by rate of tax at top of each column** | 79 |

80 **Tax on income not effectively connected with a U.S. trade or business.** Add 1040NR, line 47

Capital Gains and

Enter only the capital gains and losses from property sales or exchanges that are from sources within the United States and not effectively connected with a U.S. business. Do not include a gain or loss on disposing of a U.S. real property interest. Report these gains and losses on Schedule D (Form 1040).

Report property sales or exchanges that are effectively connected with a U.S. business on Schedule D (Form 1040), Form 4797, or both.

81(a) Kind of property and description (if necessary, attach statement of descriptive details not shown below)	(b) Date acquired (mo., day, yr.)

82 Add columns (f) and (g) of line 81

83 **Capital gain.** Combine columns (f) and (g) of line 82. Ent

Dual Status Return (*continued*).

nected With a U.S. Trade or Business

S. RRB-1042S. 1001 or similar form.

Enter amount of income under the **appropriate rate of tax** (see page 17)

(b) 10%	(c) 15%	(d) 30%	(e) Other (specify)	
			............%	............%
	240 00			
	240 00			
	36 00			

columns (b)–(e) of line 79. Enter the total here and on Form
. . . . ▶ | 80 | **36** | 00

Losses From Sales or Exchanges of Property

(c) Date sold (mo., day, yr)	(d) Sales price	(e) Cost or other basis	(f) LOSS If (e) is more than (d), subtract (d) from (e)	(g) GAIN If (d) is more than (e), subtract (e) from (d)
		82 (	)	

er the net gain here and on line 75 above (if a loss, enter -0-) ▶ | 83

Other Information (If an item does not apply to you, enter "N/A.")

A What country issued your passport? *United Kingdom*

B Were you ever a U.S. citizen? ☐ Yes ☑ No

C Give the purpose of your visit to the United States ▸

Temporary assignment

D Type of entry visa and visa number ▸ *H-1*
No. 654321 and type of current visa ▸ *Permanent*

E Did you give up your permanent residence as an immigrant in the United States this year? ☐ Yes ☐ No

F Dates you entered and left the United States during the year. Residents of Canada or Mexico entering and leaving the United States at frequent intervals, give name of country only ▸

Entered – March 18, 1994
Departed – May 25, 1994
Entered – September 10, 1994

K Have you excluded any gross income other than foreign source income not effectively connected with a U.S. trade or business?

☑ Yes ☐ No

If "Yes," show the amount, nature, and source of the excluded income. Also, give the reason it was excluded. (Do not include amounts shown in item L.) ▸

$93 U.S. bank interest not effectively connected with a U.S. trade or business

L If you claimed the benefits of a U.S. income tax treaty with a foreign country, please give the following information. Also, see page 17.

● Country ▸ *United Kingdom*

● Kind and amount of effectively connected income exempt from tax. Also, identify the applicable tax treaty article. Do not enter exempt income on lines 8–15, 16b, and 17b–21 of Form 1040NR. For 1994 (also, include this exempt income on line 22 of Form 1040NR) ▸

For 1993 ▸

● Kind and amount of income not effectively connected that is exempt from or subject to a reduced rate of tax. Also, identify the applicable tax treaty article. For 1994 ▸

Dual Status Return (*continued*).

Dividend income of $240 received 7-7-94 and 7-7-94 taxed at 15% under Article 10

G Give number of days (including vacation and nonwork days) you were in the United States during:
1992 **0** , 1993 **0** , and 1994 **182**

H If you are a resident of Canada, Mexico, Japan, or the Republic of Korea, or a U.S. national, did your spouse contribute to the support of any child claimed on Form 1040NR, line 7c? ☐ Yes ☐ No   N/A
If "Yes," state amount ▶ $ N/A

If you were a resident of Japan or the Republic of Korea for any part of the tax year, enter in the space below your total foreign source income not effectively connected with a U.S. trade or business. This information is needed so that the exemption for your spouse and dependents residing in the United States (if applicable) may be allowed in accordance with Article 4 of the income tax treaties between the United States and Japan or the United States and the Republic of Korea.

Total foreign source income not effectively connected with a U.S. trade or business ▶ $ N/A

I Did you file a U.S. income tax return for any year before 1994? ☐ Yes ☑ No
If "Yes," give the latest year and form number ▶ N/A and the Internal Revenue Service Center to which it was sent ▶

J To which Internal Revenue office did you pay any amounts claimed on Form 1040NR, lines 53, 55, and 58? N/A

For 1993 ▶ N/A

• Were you subject to tax in that country on any of the income you claim is entitled to the treaty benefits? ☑ Yes ☐ No

• Did you have a permanent establishment or fixed base (as defined by the tax treaty) in the United States at any time during 1994? ☐ Yes ☑ No

M If you file this return to report community income, give your spouse's name, address, and social security number. Also, show the address of the Internal Revenue Service Center where his or her return was filed ▶ N/A

N If you file this return for a trust, does the trust have a U.S. business? ☐ Yes ☐ No
If "Yes," give name and address ▶ N/A

8
Working for Yourself

So far in this book you have looked at ways of finding an employer in the United States. This chapter looks at another option worth consideration: working for yourself.

Self-employment is admittedly not an easy option, but for anyone who has experience of running his own business, setting up in the United States will not be so very different. Immigrants from all over the world have done this: and the many ethnic shops, restaurants and factories you find in the country prove that success often favours the bold.

If you plan to invest $1 million ($500,000 in certain designated areas) in the creation of a new business, the purchase of existing business or the infusion of capital into an existing business, you will probably qualify for full immigrant status. Investors with lesser amounts of capital will have to settle for a non-immigrant visa (see Chapter 2).

- L-1 Intra-company transfer visa: This applies where you are setting up a company as a branch, subsidiary or affiliate of a foreign operation. Once it has been established for a year you may qualify for a permanent visa. Some foreign nationals purchase a business and title the purchase in the name of the US subsidiary.

- E-1 Trade visa: This applies where you establish a company that trades between USA and your home country. Fifty-one per cent of trade must be between these two countries. There is no limit on the number of visa extensions.

- E-2 Treaty investor visa: This is the most common way for foreign investors to live and work in the US, and it is available to investors, managers, and employees with specialist knowledge.

The investment has to be substantial and depends on the nature of the business. The smaller the cost of establishing the business the higher the percentage of investment required.

WHAT'S MY FIRST STEP?

How does one set up on one's own account in the United States? There are basically four approaches you could consider:

- buy a business
- open a branch of your UK business in the United States
- set up a joint venture with an American company
- set up your own business from scratch.

Before you take the plunge it is vital to do some market research. To do this properly will involve one or more visits to the United States to find out the lie of the land.

If you are thinking of **acquiring a business** you need to ask around to see if the asking price is reasonable and the business has a bright future. This is not a time for throwing caution to the wind, and you should bear in mind that even some leading companies based in the UK have made disastrous acquisitions in America over the past decade.

A **branch office** is an excellent plan for anyone seeking to distribute or service his company's products in the United States. However, there is plenty of scope for the small businessman outside manufacturing; for example, as an international recruitment consultant, estate agent, relocation expert or business consultant servicing clients on both sides of the Atlantic.

A **joint venture** is also worth considering, not least because of the benefit in terms of market experience and local know-how an American partner can offer. However, you will need to proceed with caution and consider a number of possible partners before coming to any decision.

Starting from scratch is a risky activity, and you need to be confident of the viability of your project before embarking on it. New businesses wherever they are started tend to have a high casualty rate, with only a small proportion surviving until their fifth birthday.

UK sources of advice and assistance

Anyone planning to start a business in their own country requires advice and assistance. If you are planning to start a business—

however large or small—in a foreign country your need is even greater.

If you are a UK citizen there are a number of British organisations you can call on:

- Department of Trade and Industry, British Overseas Trade Board, Exports to North America Branch, which publishes the *UK Businessman's Guide to American Law, Business Practices and Taxation.*

- British Trade and Investment Office, British Consulate General, New York, which publishes a booklet entitled *Setting Up Your Own Business in the USA* and can provide a list of recommended lawyers.

- Other British missions in the United States—the Commercial Office of the Embassy in Washington and the various Consulates-General.

- The British-American Chamber of Commerce, in London, New York and California, and the British-Florida Chamber of Commerce.

US sources of advice and assistance

There are also plenty of organisations in the United States that may be able to provide you with advice. The larger you are, and the more likely you are to employ US residents and contribute to the US economy, the greater the range of financial incentives available to you.

The Department of Commerce

The International Trade Administration publishes *Investment in the USA*. The Industrial Development Section publishes the *Site Selection Handbook*, which has details of the financial assistance, tax incentives and special services for industrial development. The Bureau of Economic Analysis produces the *Survey of Current Business* and other publications. The Commercial Attaché at the US Embassy may be able to provide you with the information you need.

The state governments

Generally speaking, the individual states of the Union have a very positive attitude to foreigners wishing to set up in business, even if the business is relatively small. Different states compete with one another to attract newcomers, often offering tax and other incentives, and many produce detailed brochures on the advantages they offer to investors. Their economic development departments (listed in Appendix G) should be able to offer you advice. Many of them have offices in Europe and a few, notably California, Florida, New Jersey and New York, are represented in London.

Local chambers of commerce and trade or professional associations
City and state chambers of commerce are a useful source of local business intelligence, and should be able to suggest useful professional contacts. (Chambers of commerce are listed in Appendix G; a number of trade and professional associations appear in Appendix A.)

US Small Business Administration
Although created to assist US residents to set up their own businesses, the Administration produces a wide range of publications and videos of interest to any small scale entrepreneur, which cover all elements of business from financial management to marketing and crime prevention. In addition, Small Business Development Centers provide training, counselling and research; Small Business Institutes provide free management studies; SCORE (Service Corps of Retired Executives) provides free training and one-to-one counselling; and specialised financing is available. While you as a newcomer may not be eligible for all of these benefits, there is no harm in asking about them.

Other sources of advice
These include banks, lawyers, accountants and business consultants; in the larger centres you may find the affiliates of UK or Irish firms. There are also several excellent handbooks on starting businesses.

MATTERS FOR CONSIDERATION

American law can be baffling to a newcomer, and if you are setting up in business you will have to take care not to put a foot wrong. It is therefore advisable to engage the services of a reputable lawyer who can not only deal with the legal requirements of your business, but also ensure that you do not fall foul of the Immigration and Naturalisation Service.

As in the UK there are basically three types of business organisation:

- the sole proprietor
- the partnership
- the corporation.

It is up to you and your adviser to decide which of the three is most suitable for you. There are, incidentally, four other types of companies—the limited partnership, the statutory partnership association, the unincorporated association and the business trust, but these are rarely used these days.

All entities doing business in the United States are subject to laws enacted at three levels of government—federal, state and local. While there may be considerable similarity between the laws, there are also significant differences. If you are planning to employ people, you need to be conversant with the labour regulations of the state in which you operate.

The economic development office of the state may help to steer you through some of the red tape. Its officials can advise you about any licences you need to operate your business and of the regulations that apply to your activities. The relevant chamber of commerce or local branch of the Small Business Administration should also be able to help.

From the city, town or county in which you intend to operate you may well have to obtain a business licence and make sure that you are not contravening planning laws, building codes and other regulations. You will also have to register with the state tax office and the federal Internal Revenue Service, which can provide you with a *Going Into Business* Tax Kit.

If you start to employ people, the IRS will provide you with an employer's identification number, and you will need to contact the state labor department and various arms of the federal Department of Labor, notably:

- The Occupational Safety and Health Administration, which sets standards for health and safety at work

- Unemployment Insurance Service, which levies a contribution from employers to provide dole to the unemployed

- Employment Standards Administration, which regulates working hours, the employment of minors, minimum wages, *etc.*

WHAT BUSINESS?

The details mentioned above should indicate that people starting up on their own in the United States, as indeed anywhere, need to have their wits about them. Americans are not averse to driving hard bargains, and make no allowances for enterprises that are just finding their feet. All the more reason for doing a thorough investigation into the market in advance.

Many people prefer to make use of their professional skills, and this is very sensible. If you are qualified in some branch of the health care field, for instance, you could set up your own practice, though care needs to be taken to choose the right locality. Bear in mind that you will need to make sure your qualifications are recognised, and you may be required to take an examination.

Computer consultants and electronic systems designers should also be able to make a good living. There could also be scope for self-employed plumbers, electricians and gardeners, particularly in such states as Florida where there are large numbers of elderly people and a booming construction industry. However, you will need to make out a good case for yourself in order to get the necessary work visa.

You may find there is no real demand for the skills you deployed back home, in which case you will need to investigate alternatives. You could look into the possibility of buying a small business, such as a shop, a rest home or a restaurant. There is something of a vogue for British style pubs in California and Florida, and if you see yourself in the role of 'mine host' this could be an option for you.

Taking on a franchise is another possibility. A franchisor provides you with the knowhow (and sometimes equipment, marketing and supplies) in return for a fee and a percentage of the profits. However, not all franchises are as profitable and trouble-free as they may sound, and you should take appropriate advice (legal and financial) before you enter into any agreement. The International Franchise Association may be able to advise you of the standing of a particular franchisor.

You should however guard against jumping on a bandwagon, since such vehicles have a nasty habit of coming to an abrupt halt. Ideally, you need to be in a sector with good prospects for expansion. The final chapter will attempt to suggest which sectors these are.

9
Looking Ahead

Most of this book has concentrated on the here and now, but if you have long-term aspirations you have to look ahead. In the words of John Galsworthy: 'If you do not think about the future you cannot have one.'

This chapter looks into the future. It speculates about future job prospects in the United States, and in particular, the most promising job sectors and areas for employment. If, however, you are interested in exploring other options—returning home or perhaps moving on to some other country—these questions are also dealt with briefly.

WHAT ARE THE FUTURE JOB PROSPECTS?

At the time of going to press the United States is experiencing a recession, and this has a dampening effect on the jobs market. However, recessions do not affect every region equally, nor do they last forever. One of these days the US economy will experience an upturn, and this will mean more job opportunities.

This does not necessarily mean more of the same. Certain industries will require fewer staff, either because they are in decline or because of increases in productivity; the automobile and textile industries are cases in point. Others will require more staff, because they are expanding. The outstanding examples here are the health care and home care sectors.

Clearly it makes sense to look for jobs where there is going to be a growth in demand. Fortunately we have some useful forecasts to go by; every two years the Bureau of Labor Statistics of the US Department of Labor produces employment projections for each occupation. The latest projections to hand relate to the period 1994–2005.

Figure 16 shows the occupations that are expected to grow the fastest, with home health aides topping the bill and many other health care occupations in hot pursuit. Computer personnel and legal assistants are going to be much in demand, also human services workers (social workers), special education teachers and correction officers (prison officers)—a sign that crime is likely to increase as well.

Other occupations which are likely to undergo expansion by 40 per cent or more are: pre-school teachers, entertainment sector personnel, securities and financial sales workers, private detectives, gardeners and groundsmen. Prospects also look good for accountants, lawyers, opticians, cameramen and manicurists!

By contrast numerous manufacturing occupations are likely to decline, especially in the textile, electronics and plastics industries, as a result of automation. Fewer bookkeepers, accounting and auditing clerks will be needed in offices, and the number of typists is likely to fall as well. Telecommunications is also going to lose jobs. However, these are not sectors where much recruitment was done from abroad anyway.

To return to the expanding occupational sectors, while many of the extra jobs mentioned will be taken up by Americans, not all of them will be. Reviewing data showing the mathematical proficiency of pupils in the twelfth grade, an American labour expert notes that 'a very small pool of young people today appear educationally prepared for many of the occupations projected to grow most rapidly in the 1990–2005 period'.[1]

However, predictions need to be taken with a pinch of salt as they may be based on inaccurate data. In the 1980s the National Science Foundation predicted a shortfall of trained engineers and scientists by 2005, yet at present there is a glut of PhD graduates in engineering (electrical, civil and chemical), maths, bioscience and economics.

THE MOST PROMISING AREAS

Americans are much more mobile than Europeans, and far more prepared to move to where the action is. Consequently during the seventies and eighties there was a migration from the north and east of the country to the booming Sunbelt region stretching from southern California to Virginia. The Rocky Mountain states also experienced growth during this period, while the Great Plains experienced decline.

These areas continue to look promising. The value of exports from Arizona, Utah, Idaho, Colorado and Oregon doubled between 1990

[1]Ronald Kutscher in his article *New BLS Projections: Findings and Implications* (Monthly Labor Review, November 1991).

Occupation	EMPLOYMENT (1,000)				PERCENT CHANGE 1994–2005		
	1994	Low	2005 Moderate	High	Low	Moderate	High
Personal and home care aides	179	382	391	397	114.0	118.7	122.3
Home health aides	420	832	848	863	98.3	102.0	105.7
Systems analysts	483	893	928	972	84.9	92.1	101.3
Computer engineers	195	355	372	394	81.8	90.4	101.9
Physical and corrective therapy assistants and aides	78	141	142	143	82.3	83.1	84.5
Electronic pagination system workers	18	32	33	34	77.2	82.8	88.2
Occupational therapy assistants and aides	16	28	29	29	80.0	82.1	86.5
Physical therapists	102	182	183	185	78.9	80.0	81.9
Residential counselors	165	284	290	295	72.7	76.5	79.5
Human services workers	168	284	293	303	68.8	74.5	80.0
Occupational therapists	54	91	93	95	68.7	72.2	77.3
Manicurists	38	63	64	64	68.7	69.5	69.9
Medical assistants	206	329	327	324	59.9	59.0	57.9
Paralegals	110	170	175	179	54.3	58.3	62.4
Medical records technicians	81	125	126	130	53.5	55.8	59.8
Teachers, special education	388	545	593	648	40.6	53.0	67.2
Amusement and recreation attendants	267	398	406	414	49.2	52.0	55.2
Correction officers	310	430	468	513	38.5	50.9	65.2
Operations research analysts	44	65	67	69	45.5	50.0	55.8
Guards	867	1248	1282	1322	44.0	47.9	52.5
Speech-language pathologists and audiologists	85	120	125	130	40.3	46.0	52.8
Detectives, except public	55	77	79	80	41.7	44.3	47.2
Surgical technologists	46	64	65	68	39.3	42.5	48.6
Dental hygienists	127	182	180	178	43.3	42.1	40.1
Dental assistants	190	271	269	266	43.1	41.9	40.0
Adjustment clerks	373	505	521	540	35.1	39.6	44.6
Teacher aides and educational assistants	932	1211	1296	1393	29.9	39.0	49.5
Data processing equipment repairers	75	100	104	108	33.3	38.2	44.1
Nursery and greenhouse managers	19	26	26	26	38.3	37.5	37.3
Securities and financial services sales workers	246	328	335	343	33.6	36.6	39.5
Bill and account collectors	250	334	342	351	33.3	36.5	40.1
Respiratory therapists	73	96	99	104	32.3	36.4	43.8
Pest controllers and assistants	56	75	76	78	33.2	35.6	38.6
Emergency medical technicians	138	178	187	197	29.0	35.6	42.6

Fig. 16. Fastest growing occupations: 1994 to 2005
(US Bureau of Labor Statistics)

Occupation	EMPLOYMENT (1,000)				PERCENT CHANGE 1994–2005		
	1994	Low	2005 Moderate	High	Low	Moderate	High
Letterpress operators	14	4	4	4	-72.2	-71.3	-70.5
Typesetting and composing machine operators	20	6	6	6	-72.0	-71.1	-70.2
Directory assistance operators	33	10	10	10	-71.5	-70.4	-69.4
Station installers and repairers, telephone	37	10	11	11	-71.5	-70.4	-69.4
Central office operators	48	14	14	15	-71.4	-70.3	-69.2
Billing, posting, and calculating machine operators	96	32	32	33	-67.2	-66.7	-66.1
Data entry keyers, composing	19	6	6	7	-67.7	-66.6	-65.5
Shoe sewing machine operators and tenders	14	4	5	7	-70.9	-63.6	-53.8
Roustabouts	28	13	13	16	-54.2	-55.0	-43.5
Peripheral EDP equipment operators	30	13	13	14	-56.9	-54.8	-52.3
Cooks, private household	9	5	5	4	-48.1	-49.2	-50.5
Motion picture projectionists	8	4	4	4	-46.4	-47.3	-48.0
Rail yard engineers, dinkey operators, and hostlers	6	3	4	4	-44.3	-40.4	-36.5
Central office and PBX installers and repairers	84	50	51	53	-41.0	-39.1	-37.1
Computer operators, except peripheral equipment	259	157	162	168	-39.6	-37.7	-35.3
Statement clerks	25	15	16	16	-39.8	-37.7	-35.5
Housekeepers and butlers	20	13	12	12	-36.1	-37.5	-39.1
Drilling/boring machine tool setters and set-up operators	45	28	30	32	-38.1	-34.9	-29.6
Fitters, structural metal, precision	14	9	9	10	-38.3	-34.6	-29.4
Mining, quarrying, and tunneling occupations	18	11	12	13	-39.5	-33.9	-27.8
Typists and word processors	646	418	434	452	-35.2	-32.8	-30.0
Photoengraving and lithographic machine operators	5	3	3	3	-33.7	-32.1	-30.5
Boiler operators and tenders, low pressure	18	12	12	13	-34.5	-31.9	-29.1
Railroad brake, signal, and switch operators	19	12	13	14	-35.8	-30.8	-26.1
Lathe and turning machine tool setters and set-up operators	71	47	50	54	-34.2	-30.6	-24.9
Cement and gluing machine operators and tenders	36	24	25	27	-34.0	-30.1	-25.3
EKG technicians	16	11	11	12	-31.5	-29.7	-26.6
Machine tool cutting operators and tenders, metal and plastic	119	80	85	92	-32.8	-28.9	-22.8
Paste-up workers	22	16	16	17	-30.1	-27.8	-25.7
Shoe and leather workers and repairers, precision	24	16	17	19	-33.8	-27.6	-19.4
Bank tellers	559	391	407	423	-30.1	-27.3	-24.4

Fig. 17.   Fastest declining occupations: 1994 to 2005
(BLS).

and 1995 thanks to proximity to fast growing markets in Asia and Latin America, and a 1996 DRI/McGraw Hill survey estimated that two thirds of the job growth of the next five years will come in the south and west (which includes Alaska and New Mexico). States in the south east such as Maryland, Delaware, Kentucky, West Virginia, Oklahoma and the District of Columbia will see ten per cent job growth.

As far as one can predict, the need for oil is going to continue, so 'the oil patch', as it is sometimes known, will continue to prosper, apart from a few blips now and then. One would expect the high-tech industries that have sprung up in the region to have a bright future. Defence related industries, however, look less secure.

Prospects in the MidWest look less good, with the possible exception of Nebraska which currently boasts the lowest unemployment rate in the US and is keen to attract skilled employees. The North East offers the worst prospects for employment and growth because of its high costs and downsizing in financial services, utilities and defence. However, New York City has always been the leading centre for finance, publishing, fashion and entertainment, and is likely to remain so into the distant future.

RETURNING HOME TO AN ESTABLISHED POSITION

If you are on the permanent staff of a company you can expect a transfer home sooner or later. This can be a relief to some; but more often than not it will be a wrench, particularly if you have come to enjoy the American life style.

'Re-entry', as the return home is sometimes described, is not always a smooth process, and you will need to call on your capacity for adaptation once more. The International Committee of the Institute of Personnel and Development offers sound advice:

- Take time to wind down properly.
- Assess and review the change in yourself and those at home.
- Gradually re-establish relations with friends, relatives and professional contacts.
- Plan long- and short-term goals along with strategies for achieving them.
- Accept that you will probably suffer some reverse culture shock, particularly of an organisational, financial and psychological nature.

MOVING ON

If you are on a contract, you may have the option of renewing it; but on the other hand you may well feel it is time to get up and go. Americans believe that if you want to get on you move on rather than stay with the same company for years on end.

There are five main options to consider:

Get another job in the United States

You are well placed to find yourself a better position with another employer. This is easy if you are a resident alien with a 'green card'; but if you are on a temporary visa your new employer will have to be informed and told about the business of obtaining labour certification. This can of course take time, so you need to plan ahead.

Start your own business in the United States

It is relatively easy to buy a small business or to set up your own, but if you are not a permanent resident you will need to obtain the appropriate visa. See also Chapter 8.

Find a job back home

If you are on an exchange visitor visa you will be expected to return home, as your stay in America has been in the nature of an educational visit designed to develop your career in your own country rather than in the United States.

People who have been overseas for a number of years often need time to readjust, and would be wise to take note of the IPD advice to permanent employees given above. It is also advisable to set about the process of finding yourself a job in the UK well before your departure. Keep your eye on the job columns in UK publications and send off speculative applications.

Seek an overseas posting elsewhere

It is a good idea to approach contacts who know you first of all. Your present employer, for instance, may have operations overseas, and if you have been recruited through an agency, they may have other overseas postings that might be suitable.

The United States is a good place for overseas job hunting, particularly for South America and the Pacific Rim. American companies often recruit non-Americans for overseas assignments, partly because they are more adaptable but also because there are usually fewer visa problems. There are a number of manuals that will set you off in the right direction. For instance, *How to Get a Job Abroad* or

How to Teach Abroad (if you are a teacher). (See Appendix H.)

Sign up for a study course

The international jobs market is a very competitive place, and if you want to stay in it you need to keep abreast of modern developments in your field. If you do not, you will soon cease to be an attractive proposition to employers. No company is going to employ a has-been —especially a foreign has-been—when they can pick someone more recently qualified who may well be cheaper to employ.

You may be lucky enough to be with an employer who offers training facilities, though if you are employed on contract terms the chances are that you will not benefit from them. Otherwise, why not look into the possibility of home study courses, part-time tuition at night school, or consider taking a sabbatical?

If you plan to stay in the United States, take a look at handbooks such as the *NHSC Directory of Home Study Schools*, the *Handbook of Trade and Technical Careers and Training* or one of the guides to higher education mentioned in the Educational Arrangements section in Chapter 5.

GETTING ADVICE

At some stage in your career you may decide that you need advice, particularly if you are contemplating changing direction.

Where can I find advice in the USA?

In the United States you will find a range of facilities at your disposal.

College career services
Most colleges, universities and community colleges have career counselling centres offering workshops, individual counselling and other programmes, and you should be able to use these services even if you are not following a course at the institution. Several can be contacted on the Internet via career.com.

Libraries
Many public libraries have career information centres which bring together a wide range of materials relating to careers and job finding. Some of them also provide courses or lectures on career choice.

Adult education centres
Some of these provide career guidance in the form of courses, seminars or individual counselling sessions.

Voluntary organisations
A number of voluntary organisations exist to help job seekers, often those from minority groups. One of these—Catalyst—is devoted to women's career development and produces a range of useful pamphlets and books, including *When Can You Start?* and *What to Do with the Rest of Your Life?*

Employers
A number of the larger firms now have career development officers, usually within the personnel and training departments, who can help you plan ahead. They also bring in outplacement agencies to counsel staff who are made redundant.

Private careers counsellors
The International Association of Counseling Services produces a *Directory of Counseling Services*, and Richard N Bolles's *What Color is your Parachute?* also lists selected job counsellors. Catalyst also produces a guide: *The Catalyst National Network of Career Resource Centers*. You might also contact the National Employment Counselors Association.

If you return to the UK and require some form of counselling, the British Association of Counselling can suggest qualified people you can turn to or you might approach the careers service of a local education authority. *How to Manage Your Career*, Roger Jones, also offers some useful pointers.

THE KEY TO SUCCESS

Hopefully by this stage no reader has any illusions that finding a job in America is an easy task, especially for a non-American. No job is going to come looking for you; instead you need to put in considerable effort to search out suitable opportunities, more so than if you are seeking a job in your own country.

Persistence, however, is not sufficient; you also need to be well informed. An expatriate jobs magazine boasts, 'The *Nexus* commitment is research, research and more research,' and this is precisely the attitude you need to adopt if you are serious about working in the United States.

The remainder of this book is devoted to helping you with your research into job opportunities. Follow up the various leads, offer a good account of yourself, and one day you may well surmount the odds and attain your objective: a worthwhile and interesting job in the USA. Good luck!

Appendix A
Job Sectors

Accountancy

One plan is to join a large international accountancy firm such as Arthur Andersen and see if it is possible to transfer to the US or join a British company with important interests in the US. Opportunities arise from time to time for recently qualified ACAs in mainstream auditing.

Certified public accountants (CPAs) need a licence and are regulated by the accountancy board of the state in which they practise. This could entail taking a four-part exam prepared by the American Institute of Certified Public Accountants. Registered public accountants are being phased out. The National Association of Management Accountants offers a certificate in management accounting and the Institute of Internal Auditors also offers a certificate.

To find out more about the requirements you should contact either your own professional institute in the UK, the accountancy board of the state where you wish to work, or one of the American professional associations.

Useful addresses
American Institute of Certified Public Accountants, 1211 Avenue of the Americas, New York, NY 10036-8775.
National Association of Management Accountants, 10 Paragon Drive, Montvale, NJ 07645.
National Society of Public Accountants, 1010 N Fairfax Street, Alexandria, VA 22314.
Institute of Internal Auditors, 249 Maitland Ave, Altamonte Springs, FL 32701-4201.

Recruitment consultants
Beament Leslie Thomas, Harrison Willis, Davis Kidd, Financial Recruitment Int'l.

Advertising, public relations, marketing and retailing

A very competitive but expanding business, and you might do best to try one of the British firms operating in this area.

Useful addresses and publications

Public Relations Society of America Inc, 33 Irving Place, 15/16th Street, New York, NY 10003-2376.

American Association of Advertising Agencies, 666 Third Ave, New York, NY 10017.

American Advertising Federation, 1400 K Street, Suite 1000, Washington DC 20005.

American Marketing Association, 250 S Wacker Drive, Chicago, IL 60606. (Publishes *The Green Book, Directory of Market Research Companies.*)

Market Research Association, 2189 Silas Deane Hwy, Suite 5, Rocky Hill, CT06067.

National Retail Federation, 100 W 31st St, NewYork, NY 10001.

Public Relations News, 27 E 80th St, New York, NY 10021-0333.

Public Relations Career Directory, R. W. Fry (ed) (Career Press Inc).

PR Reporter, PO Box 600, Exeter, NJ 03833.

Handbook of Advertising & Marketing Services, Executive Communications Inc, 919 Third Ave, 9th Floor, New York, NY 10022-3903.

Bradford's Directory of Market Research & Management Consultants, PO Box 276, Fairfax, VA 22030-0276.

Standard Directory of Advertising Agencies, National Register Publishing, 11500 W Olympic Blvd, Suite 355, Los Angeles, CA 90064-1527.

Career Opportunities in Advertising and PR, Shelly Field (Facts on File).

Major employers

Among the leading companies in this field are:

Interpublic Group of Companies, 1271 Avenue of the Americas, New York, NY 10020.

The Owl Group, 466 Lexington Ave, New York, NY 10017.

A C Nielson & Co, Nielson Plaza, Northbrook, IL 60062.

Ogilvy Group, 309 W 39th St, New York, NY10019.

Recruitment consultants

DGH, DM, Knight Chapman.

Aerospace

There is a growing demand for aerospace engineers, and several job advertisements have appeared in UK newspapers recently. The main manufacturing areas are California, Texas and Washington State.

Useful addresses
American Institute of Aeronautics and Astronautics, The Aerospace Center, 370 L'Enfant Promenade SW, Washington, DC 20024.

Major employers
Boeing Company Inc, PO Box 3707, Seattle, WA 98124.
General Dynamics Corp, Pierre LaClede Center, St Louis, MO 63105.
General Electric Company, 3135 Easton Turnpike, Fairfield, CT 06431.
Lockheed Corp, 4500 Park Granada Blvd, Calabas, CA 91399.
McDonnell Douglas, PO Box 516, St Louis, MO 63166.
Northrop Corp, 1840 Century Park East, Los Angeles, CA 90067.
Rockwell International Corp, 600 Grant Street, Pittsburg, PA 15219.
United Technologies Group, United Technologies Building, Hartford, CT 06101.

Recruitment consultants
Moxon Dolphin Kerby, Butler, FHELP.

Agriculture
Generally speaking there are few opportunities in this field, unless you fancy becoming a cowboy and the low pay that comes with it. Pay is better if you perform as a rodeo cowboy, but the profession is competitive and the work exhausting. If you have cash to spare, you could consider buying a ranch or farm, but prospects in this sector are none too bright. Prospects for agricultural scientists are better.

Useful addresses
National Cattlemen's Association, PO Box 3469, Englewood, CO 80155.
Dude Ranchers' Association, Box 471, Laporte, CO 80535.
Professional Rodeo Cowboys' Association, 101 Prorodeo Drive, Colorado Springs, CO 80901.
American Farm Bureau Federation, 225 Touhy Ave, Park Ridge, IL 60008.
American Society for Agricultural Science, 701 North Saint Asaph St, Alexandria, VA 22314.

Architecture
To practise architecture in the US you need to be registered with the National Architectural Accrediting Board in most states or work under a registered architect. Landscape architects tend to be concentrated in the sunbelt states.

Useful addresses
American Institute of Architects, 1735 New York Avenue NW, Washington, DC 20006.

American Society of Landscape Architects, 4401 Connecticut Avenue, Washington, DC 20008.

Banking and finance

Opportunities when they occur would tend to be for experienced people in very specialist fields, *eg* Eurobonds. There are a number of British financial institutions with branches in the US, and you could always apply for a transfer.

Useful addresses and publications
American Bankers' Association, 1120 Connecticut Ave, NW, Washington, DC 20036.
American Financial Services Association, 919 19th Street NW, Washington, DC 20006.
American Financial Directory and *American Bank Directory*, McFadden Business Publications, 6195 Crooked Creek Road, Norcross, GA 30092-3105.
US Savings and Loans Directory (Rand McNally).
Insurance and Financial Services Careers, Wallace Witners, PO Box 40169, 1509 Madison Ave, Memphis, TN 38174.

Recruitment consultants
NPA, Financial Recruitment Int'l.

Construction

Nine out of ten construction managers work in the contract construction industry and the same applies to most of the other specialists in this sphere. Perhaps the best plan is to subscribe to one of the American construction magazines to find out where the main areas of activity are. In the past decade the sunbelt states, especially Florida, have seen a great deal of construction activity. Prospects look particularly promising for infrastructure projects. If you have worked on contract for an American construction firm in the past—in the Middle East, for instance—you could ask for suggestions.

Useful addresses
American Society of Civil Engineers, 345 E 47th St, New York, NY 10017.
Associated General Contractors of America, 1957 E St, NW, Washington, DC 20006.
Associated Builders & Contractors, 729 15th Street NW, Washington, DC 20005.
American Society of Cost Engineers, PO Box 1557, Morgantown, WV 26505-1557.
American Society of Professional Estimators, 6911 Richmond Highway, Suite 230, Alexandria, VA 22306.

Construction Management Association of America, Suite 180, 1893 Preston White Drive, Reston, VA 22091.
United Brotherhood of Carpenters and Joiners of America, 101 Constitution Avenue NW, Washington, DC 20001.

Recruitment consultants
Morson, Sherwood, Alasdair Graham, Rosta.

Creative

The jobs outlook for artists and designers is good, and a few people go to the US to operate on a freelance basis. This is, however, a competitive field and there could be visa problems.

Useful addresses and publications
American Society of Interior Designers, 608 Massachusetts Ave NE, Washington, DC 20002.
American Institute of Graphic Artists, 1059 Third Avenue, New York, NY 10021.
Graphic Artists Guild, 11 W 20th St, 8th Floor, New York, NY 10003.
Industrial Designers Society of America, 1142 E Walker Road, Great Falls, VA 22066.
Professional Photographers of America Inc, 57 Forsythe St, Suite 1600, Atlanta, GA 30303.
Career Opportunities in the Music Industry, Shelly Field (Facts on File).

Electronics

This is a field which employs a large number of foreign engineers, usually on contract, and jobs advertisements appear from time to time in the British press. A number of these jobs are in defence-related industries, so there has been a decline in opportunities in this sector.

For further information:
Institute of Electrical and Electronics Engineers, 345 E 47th St, New York, NY 10017.

Major employers
Advanced Micro Devices Inc, 901 Thompson Place, Sunnyvale, CA 94086.
Amp Inc, 470 Friendship Road, Harrisburg, PA 17105.
CTS Corp, 905 North W Boulevard, Elkhart, IN 46514.
E G & G Inc, 45 William Street, Wellesley, MA 02181.
Emerson Electric Co, 8000 W Florissant Avenue, St Louis, MO 63136.
Motorola, 1313 E Algonquin Road, Roselle, IL 60196.
Perkin-Elmer Corp, 761 Main Avenue, Norwalk, CT 06859-0001.
RCA Corp, 30 Rockefeller Plaza, New York, NY 10020.
Square D, 1415 S Roselle Rd, Palatine, IL 60067.

Tektronix, PO Box 500, Beaverton, OR 97077.
Westinghouse Corp, Westinghouse Building, Gateway Centre, Pittsburgh, PA 15222.

Recruitment consultants
Anders Glaser Wills, Beechwood, Morson, Moxon Dolphin Kerby, Randall Massey.

Engineering

In recent years there has been a decline in the number of graduates in engineering in the US, and to make good this shortfall there should be good opportunities for foreign engineers. If your work affects life, health or property you will need to register with the state in which you operate. Salaries in industry start at around $30,000 and can reach $90,000 at senior management level.

Useful addresses and publications
National Society for Professional Engineers, 1420 King Street, Alexandria, VA 22314.
Society of Women Engineers, 120 Wall St, 11th Floor, New York, NY 10005.
American Institute of Chemical Engineers, 345 E 47th St, New York, NY 10017.
American Society of Civil Engineers, 1015 15th St NW, Suite 600, Washington, DC 20005.
American Society of Mechanical Engineers, 345 E 47th St, New York, NY 10017.
Peterson's Engineering, Science and Computer Jobs, 202 Carnegie Center, Box 2123, Princeton, NJ 08543.
JETS Guidance, 1420 King Street, Alexandria, VA 22314. (Central distribution point for information on engineering careers in the US.)
Peterson's Engineering, Science and Computer Jobs, 202 Carnegie Center, Box 2123, Princeton, NJ 08543.
Institute of Industrial Engineers, 25 Technology Park, Atlanta, GA 30092-2988.

Recruitment consultants
Anders Glaser Wills, Beechwood, Morson, Moxon Dolphin Kerby, Randall Massey, Wrightson Wood, Fircroft, Sherwood, Butler, Alasdair Graham, FHELP, Rosta.

Entertainment and performing arts

As in the UK this is an overcrowded profession, with the overwhelming majority of its practitioners 'resting' at a given moment. While Robert Redford may get a fabulous salary, most people live very modestly and have to supplement their earnings. Also, unless you happen to be very distinguished yourself or a member of a very distinguished company, you may well find difficulty in obtaining the necessary work visa.

Many of the dance companies are centred on New York. If you want to be a film extra you will have to register with Central Casting . . . and unless you have some very unusual features there is a long waiting list.

Useful contacts and publications
Associated Actors and Artistes of America, 165 W 46th Street, New York, NY 10036.
American Federation of Musicians, 150 Broadway, Suite 600, New York, NY 10036.
American Dance Guild, 33 W 21st Street, 3rd Floor, New York, NY 10010. (Publishes *Jobs Express Registry*.)
American Guild of Musical Artists, 1727 Broadway, New York, NY 10019.
Art Search—National Employment Service Bulletin for the Performing Arts, Theatre Communications Group Inc, 355 Lexington Ave, New York, NY 10017.
Theatre Careers—A Comprehensive Guide to Non-Acting Careers, J. W. Greenburg (Holt Rinehart Winston).
Career Opporunities in Theater and the Performing Arts, Shelly Field (Facts on File).

Environment, forestry and nature conservation
Since the majority of jobs are with the federal or state governments, these are the organisations you need to approach. This is a particularly good sector for vacation employment.

Useful addresses and publications
American Forestry Association, PO Box 2000, Washington, DC 20013.
Society of American Foresters, 5400 Grosvenor Lane, Bethesda, MD 20814.
US Department of Agriculture, Forest Service, 14th St and Independence Avenue SW, Washington, DC 20250.
US Department of Agriculture, Soil Conservation Service, PO Box 2890, Washington, DC 20013.
US Fish and Wildlife Service, Department of the Interior, Washington, DC 20250.
Bureau of Land Management, Department of the Interior, Washington, DC 20240.
Society for Range Management, 1839 York Street, Denver, CO 80206.
Environmental Opportunities, PO Box 670, Walpole, NH 03608.
A Complete Guide to Environmental Careers, CEIP, 68 Harrison Ave, Boston, MA 02111.

Conservation Directory, US National Wildlife Federation, 1412 16th Street NW, Washington, DC 20036.
Outdoor Careers, Ellen Shenk (Stackpole).

Health care
(See also under **Medical** and **Nursing**)

An ageing population and advances in medical technology mean that this sector is likely to grow rapidly, especially the home health care sector. However, it is not sure whether the US will produce enough qualified people to cope with the demand, in which case there will be plenty of opportunities for foreigners.

It is worth bearing in mind that in order to practise your profession, whether on a self-employed basis or in a hospital, you will normally have to be licensed by the state in which you are active. This may involve taking an exam and having approved qualifications. Osteopathy, incidentally, is particularly widespread in the sunbelt states.

A number of British and Irish employment consultants recruit for the United States and are acquainted with the rules and regulations. Otherwise you should contact the appropriate body in the US for further details. Physiotherapists and nurses currently benefit from Schedule A exemption from labor certification.

Useful addresses

American Chiropractors' Association, 1701 Clarendon Boulevard, Arlington, VA 22209.

American College of Healthcare Executives, 840 North Lake Shore Drive, Chicago, IL 60611.

American Dental Association, 211 E Chicago Ave, Chicago, IL 60611.

American Dental Hygienists' Association, 444 N Michigan Ave, Suite 3400, Chicago, IL 60611.

American Medical Technologists, 710 Higgins Rd, Park Ridge, IL 60068.

American Occupational Therapy Association, 1383 Piccard Drive, Rockville, MD 20849-1725.

American Optometric Association, 243 North Lindberg Boulevard, St Louis, MO 63141.

American Osteopathic Association, 142 E Ontario Street, Chicago, IL 60611.

American Podiatric (footcare) Medical Association, 9312 Old Georgetown Road, Bethesda, MD 20814-1621.

American Psychological Association, 750 1st Street NE, Washington, DC 20002-42420.

American Physical Therapy Association, 1111 N Fairfax Street, Alexandria, VA 22314.

Opticians' Association of America, 10341 Democracy Lane, PO Box 10110, Fairfax, VA 22030.

National Health Council, Health Careers Program, 1730 M Street NW, Suite 500, Washington, DC 20036.

International Chiropractors' Association, 1110 N Glebe Rd, Suite 1000, Arlington, VA 22201.

Private Care Association, 801 Princeton Ave SW, Suite 426, Birmingham, AL 35211. (Placement service for carers for the elderly.)

Major employers

American Medical International, 414 N Camden Drive, Beverly Hills, CA 90201.

Charter Medical Corporation, 577 Mulberry Street, PO Box 209, Macon, GA 31298.

Hospital Corporation of America, 1 Park Plaza, Nashville, TN 37203.

Humana Inc, PO Box 1438, Louisville, KY 40201.

Manor Care Inc, 10750 Columbia Pike, Silver Springs, MD 20901.

National Medical Enterprises, 11620 Wilshire Boulevard, Los Angeles, CA 90025.

Job listings

Jobmart, Association of Homes for the Ageing, 1129 20th Street NW, Suite 200, Washington, DC 20036.

Employment in National Institutes of Health, Clinical Center, National Institute of Health, Bethesda, MD 20892.

Recruitment consultants

Angel, Grafton, Medic, Nurse America, USA Careers, FHELP.

Hotels and catering

The industry is a useful source of vacation jobs, particularly in the main holiday areas where jobs as waiters and barmen are fairly easy to come by, especially if you arrive early in the season. If you are a student, see the BUNAC entry in Chapter 3. This is a sector which is easy to get into and employs a large number of foreigners, some of them illegal immigrants.

More senior posts are difficult to come by because of visa restrictions, unless you happen to be a senior executive with a British owned international hotel chain. However, there are no such restrictions on jobs on US based luxury cruises which are handled by VIP Luxury Cruise Management Division.

This is also a sector which is ideal for the entrepreneur with cash to invest or a friendly backer.

Useful addresses and publications

American Hotel and Motel Association, 1201 New York Avenue NW, Washington, DC 20005-3931.

National Restaurant Association, 1200 17th St NW, Washington, DC 20036.

Official Guide to Food Service and Hospitality Management Careers, International Publishing Co of America, 665 La Villa Drive, Miami Springs, FL 33166.

Career Opportunities in the Food and Beverage Industry, Barbara Sims-Bell (Facts on File).

Major employers

Brock Hotels Corp, 4441 West Airport Freeway, Irving, TX 75062.

Holiday Inns Inc, 3742 Lamar Avenue, Memphis, TN 38195.

Marriott Corp, 1 Marriott Drive, Washington, DC 20058.

Recruitment consultants

Profile, VIP.

Information technology

Another fruitful area for jobs which offers very good prospects. Computer positions in the US are advertised regularly in computer journals and there are a number of recruitment consultants handling these jobs in the UK.

Useful addresses and publications

Association for Systems Management, 1433 Bagley Road W, Cleveland, OH 44138-0370.

Peterson's Engineering, Science and Computer Jobs, 202 Carnegie Center, Box 2123, Princeton, NJ 08543.

Major employers

Automatic Data Processing, 1 ADP Boulevard, Roseland, NJ 07068.

Burroughs Corp, Burroughs Place, Detroit, MI 48232.

Computer Sciences Corporation, 2100 E Grand Ave, El Segundo, CA 90245.

Control Data Corp, 8100 34th Avenue S, Bloomington, MN 55440.

Data General Corp, 4400 Computer Drive, Westboro, MA 01580.

Electronic Data Systems Corp, 7171 Forest Lane, Dallas, TX 75230.

Hewlett Packard Co, 3000 Hanover Street, Palo Alto, CA 94304.

Honeywell Inc, Honeywell Plaza, Minneapolis, MN 55408.

IBM, Old Orchard Road, Armonk, NY 10504.

Intel Corp, 3535 Garrett Drive, Santa Clara, CA 95051.

Wang Laboratories Inc, 1 Industrial Avenue, Lowell, MA 01851.

Recruitment consultants

Beechwood, Computer People, DGH, Hunterskil, James Baker, MDA, Randall Massey, Track International, Prescot, Forsyth, TRC, Computing Resource Centre, Sector, Computech, Butler, HB.

Insurance

The headquarters of the main American insurance companies are based in Boston, Chicago, Hartford, New York and Philadelphia. However, several British insurance companies operate in the US and it might be easier to try for a transfer.

Useful addresses and publications
Alliance of American Insurers, 20 N Wacker Drive, Chicago, IL 60606.
Insurance Information Institute, 110 William St, New York, NY 10038.
Society of Actuaries, 475 N Martindale Road, Schaumburg, IL 60173-2226.
Society of Chartered Property and Casualty Underwriters, Kahler Hall, CB/9, 720 Providence Road, Malvern, PA 19355.
Insurance and Financial Services Careers (Wallace Witners), PO Box 40169, 1509 Madison Ave, Memphis, TN 38174.

Major employers
Aetna Life & Casualty Co, 151 Farmington Avenue, Hartford, CT 06156.
American International Group, 70 Pine Street, New York, NY 10270.
Cigna Corp, 1 Logan Square, Philadelphia, PA 19103.
Marsh & McLennan (insurance broking), 1166 Avenue of the Americas, New York, NY 10036.

Recruitment consultant
Insurance Personnel Selection.

Law

This is a sector which is likely to experience expansion in coming years, and this is particularly true for legal assistants (paralegals). American law is similar to British Common Law, so there should be few problems; however the Americans make no distinction between barristers and solicitors. To practise as a lawyer you may need to take the Multistate Bar Examination (MBE) and perhaps a written ethics examination as well. To obtain information about the requirements you should contact the Clerk to the Supreme Court of the state in which you will be practising or the State Board of Bar Examiners. The Law Society in London can also advise.

Useful addresses
American Bar Association, 750 North Lake Short Drive, Chicago, IL 60611.
    (Publishes *Regulation of Foreign Lawyers* which deals with the jurisdictions in a number of states.)
National Association of Legal Assistants Inc, 1516 S Boston, Suite 200, Tulsa, OK 74119.
National Federation of Paralegal Associations, PO Box 33108, Kansas City,

MO 64114-0108. (Publishes information on job prospects in particular areas.)

National Employment Listing Service for the Criminal Justice System and Social Services, Criminal Justice Center, Sam Houston State University, Huntsville, TX 77341.

FBI, US Dept of Justice, Washington, DC 20535.

Recruitment consultants
Quarry Dougall, Harrison Willis.

Librarianship and information science
Opportunities tend to be few and far between, unless you have specialist skills that are in demand.

Useful addresses
American Library Association, 50 E Huron St, Chicago, IL 60611.
American Society for Information Science, 8720 Georgia Ave, Suite 501, Silver Spring, MD 20910-3602.

Management
The best idea would probably be to ask your organisation for a transfer to the US. However, management and management consultancy posts are advertised from time to time in the British press. Prospects for management analysts, of whom 50 per cent are self-employed, look particularly good.

Useful addresses and publications
Administrative Management Society, 4622 Street Road, Trevose, PA 19147.
American Management Association, 135 W 50th St, New York, NY 10019.
Society for Human Resource Management, 606 N Washington St, Alexandria, VA 22314.
Association of Management Consultants, 521 5th Ave, 35th Floor, New York, NY 10175.
National Management Association, 2210 Ann Arbor Boulevard, Dayton, OH 45439.
Peterson's Business and Management Jobs, 202 Carnegie Center, Box 2123, Princeton, NJ 08543.
VGM's Handbook of Business and Management Careers, C.T. Norback, ed (VGM Career Books).

Recruitment consultants
Beament Leslie Thomas, DM Merton.

Medicine

At one time doctors and surgeons encountered few barriers to entering and practising in the US, but since 1977 they have needed to apply for labour certification (unless they are eminent in their field) and pass a visa qualifying examination or the National Board of Medical Examiners exam (Parts I and II). It is possible to do non-clinical work on a B2 visa provided it is non-remunerative, and on a J-1 visa provided it is related to your training programme.

Physicians intending to become permanently resident must first work for three years on H-1B visa status.

The North East has the highest doctor-patient ratio, so your chances will be increased if you head for areas where the ratio is lower, *eg* the southern states. The Dept of Health and Human Resources can provide a list of areas where medical practitioners are in short supply.

Working as a doctor in the US can be extremely remunerative. However, medical insurance companies are now seeking to keep costs down by shifting to managed health care programmes that rely to a greater extent on medical assistants. The era of fat fees for consultations could be drawing to a close.

Useful addresses
American Medical Association, 515 N State St, Chicago, IL 60610.

Mining

There are a few signs of expansion in this sector. (See also **Petroleum Engineering**.)

Useful addresses
Society for Mining, Metallurgy and Exploration, PO Box 625002, Littleton, CO 80127-5002.
Minerals, Metals & Materials Society, 420 Commonwealth Drive, Warrendale, PA 15086.
Geological Society of America, PO Box 9140, 3300 Penrose Place, Boulder, CO 80301.
American Institute of Mining, Metallurgical and Petroleum Engineers, 345 E 47th St, 14th Floor, New York, NY 10017.

Recruitment consultant
British Mining Consultants.

Miscellaneous trades

There could be opportunities as a self-employed person provided you can get a visa. A number of trades are heavily unionised and you may have to join a union in order to get a good job.

Useful addresses
United Auto Workers, 8000 E Jefferson, Detroit, MI 48214.
International Brotherhood of Electrical Workers, 1125 15th St, NW, Suite 1201, Washington, DC 20005.
National Association of Plumbing, Heating and Cooling Contractors, PO Box 6808, Falls Church, VA 22046.
National Association of Television and Electronic Services of America, 5930 S Pulaski St, Chicago, IL 60629.
The American Welding Society, 550 NW LeJeune Rd, Miami, FL 33135.

Nursing
(See also **Health Care**)
There are excellent opportunities for nurses in the USA since health care is an expanding sector. However, before you can practise in the US, in nearly every state except Arkansas you need to pass a licensing examination. This can either be a state board exam or the CGFNS examination which is held three times a year at various locations around the world, including London. Several agencies in the UK recruit nursing staff and some US hospital companies have offices in London. The Royal College of Nursing has information packs on nursing in the US.

There are four nursing grades:

- Licensed Practical Nurse. An LPN works under the supervision of doctor or registered nurse in hospitals, private homes, surgeries and clinics.
- Registered Nurse. The next step up the ladder. Two-thirds of RNs work in hospitals, and the rest work in nursing homes, community clinics, private clinics and industry.
- Certified Nurse-Midwife. A CNM is a registered nurse with additional training.
- Nurse Practitioner. The highest grade of all. This is a registered nurse with additional training who is licensed to perform routine medical procedures.

Useful addresses
American College of Nurse-Midwives, 1012 14th St NW, Washington, DC 20005.
American Nurses' Association, 600 Maryland Ave SW, Suite 100W, Washington, DC 20024-2571.

Federation of Nurses and Healthcare Professionals, 555 New Jersey Avenue NW, Washington, DC 20006.
National League for Nursing, 350 Hudson Street, New York, NY 10014.

American Hospital Association, Division of Nursing, 840 North Lake Shore Drive, Chicago, IL 60611.
Commission on Graduates of Foreign Nursing Schools (CGFNS), 3624 Market Street, Philadelphia, PA 19104.
National Association for Healthcare Recruitment, Box 5769, Akron OH 44372.

Recruitment consultants
Angel, Grafton, Medic Intl, Nurse America.

Personnel and training
There are good prospects in this area, particularly in the employment agency sector, but a foreigner would need to become fully versed in US employment legislation in order to obtain a management post. There are advantages in becoming a certified personnel consultant.

Useful addresses
National Association of Personnel Consultants, 3133 Mount Vernon Avenue, Alexandria, VA 22305.
American Society for Training and Development, 1640 King Street, PO Box 1443, Alexandria, VA 22313.
International Personnel Management Association, 1617 Duke Street, Alexandria, VA 22314.

Petroleum (oil and gas) engineering
There are a number of foreigners working in this sector, and job advertisements appear from time to time in the British press. Texas, Oklahoma, Louisiana, California and Alaska are the main areas for this industry. (See also **Mining**.)

Useful address
Society of Petroleum Engineers, PO Box 833836, Richardson, TX 75083-3836.

Major employers
Atlantic Richfield, 515 South Flower Street, Los Angeles, CA 90071.
Chevron, 225 Bush Street, San Francisco, CA 94104.
Exxon Corp, 225 East John W Carpenter Freeway, Irving, TX 75062-2298.
Halliburton Co, 500 N Akard St, Dallas, TX 75201.
Occidental Petroleum Corp, 10889 Wilshire Boulevard, Los Angeles, CA 90024.

Phillips Petroleum Co, Adams Building, Bartlesville, OK 74004.
Texaco, 2000 Westchester Avenue, White Plains, NY 10650.
Unocal, 1201 W 5th St, Los Angeles, CA 90017.

Recruitment consultant
Anders Glaser Wills, Morson, ABB Lutech, Sherwood, Rosta, Alasdair
Graham.

Pharmacy/Pharmaceuticals

If you wish to practise as a pharmacist all states require that you be
licensed. For this you will need a qualification from an accredited
pharmacy college (some states accept foreign study programmes), to
pass a state board exam, to demonstrate good character and serve an
internship under the supervision of a licensed pharmacist.

Useful addresses
American Pharmaceutical Association, 2215 Constitution Ave, NW,
Washington, Dc 20037.
National Association of Boards of Pharmacy, 700 Busse Highway, Park Ridge,
IL 60068.
American Society of Hospital Pharmacists, 7272 Wisconsin Ave, Bethesda,
MD 20814.

Major employers
Abbott Laboratories, Abbott Park, North Chicago, IL 60064.
American Home Products Corp, 685 Third Avenue, New York, NY 10017.
Dupont de Nemours & Co, 1007 Market Street, Wilmington, DE 19898.
Bristol-Myers Co, 345 Park Avenue, New York, NY 10154.
Lilly & Co, 307 East McCarty Street, Indianapolis, IN 46285.
Merck & Co, PO Box 2000, Rahway, NJ 07065.
Sterling Drug Inc, 90 Park Avenue, New York, NY 10016.
Upjohn Co, 7000 Portage Road, Kalamazoo, MI 49001.
Warner Lambert Co, 201 Tabor Road, Morris Plains, NJ 07950.

Recruitment consultants
Knight Chapman, Butler.

Printing

There would appear to be few opportunities in this sector for
foreigners, except in a self-employed capacity.

Useful address
Printing Industries of America Inc, 100 Daingerfield Rd, Alexandria, VA
22314.

Property

Estate agents (called real estate agents in the US) are required to pass a state licensing exam. Land surveyors also need to be licensed. There could be opportunities serving the needs of the growing British communities in California and Florida.

Useful addresses

Building Owners and Managers Association, 1201 New York Ave NW, Suite 300, Washington, DC 20005.

International Association of Corporate Real Estate Executives, Suite 10, 440 Columbia Drive, West Palm Beach, FL 33409.

National Association of Realtors, 430 N Michigan Ave, Chicago, IL 60611-4087.

National Property Management Association, 380 Main St, Suite 290, Dunedin, FL 34698.

American Congress on Surveying and Mapping, 5410 Grosvenor Lane, Bethesda, MD 20814-2122.

Public sector jobs

(See also **Teaching, Social services**.) The widest range of jobs is found in the public sector at the federal, state or local level, though some of these jobs will be open only to US citizens. The US Office of Personnel Management has a network of Federal Job Centers involved in recruitment in cities throughout the country and the states have a similar system. If you are in the US, this should be the first place to head for.

Alternatively, you could write to the department of the Federal Government, state, county or municipality which is likely to be interested in your qualifications.

Useful addresses and publications

Federal Job Information Center, US Office of Personnel Management, 1900 East Street NW, Washington, DC 20415. Tel: 202 606 2700.

National Employment Listing Service for the Criminal Justice System and Social Services, Criminal Justice Center, Sam Houston State University, Huntsville, TX 77341.

National Association of the Counties, 440 First Street NW, Washington, DC 20001.

International City Management Association, 777 North Capitol Street NE, Washington, DC 20002. (Publish *The Municipal Yearbook*.)

International Association of Fire Fighters, 1750 New York Ave, NW, Washington, DC 20006.

National Federation of Federal Employees, 1016 16th Street NW, Washington, DC 20036.

American Federation of Government Employees, 80 F Street NW, Washington, DC 20001.

Fraternal Order of Police, 2100 Gardiner Lane, Louisville, KY 40205-2900.

Federal Employment Bulletin, PO Box 11715, Washington, DC 20008. (Fortnightly bulletin.)

How to Get a Federal Job—A Guide to Finding and Applying for a Job with the US Government Anywhere in the US, K. Kraus (Facts on File).

Federal Career Opportunities, Federal Research Services, Inc, 370 Maple Ave W, PO Box 1059, Vienna, VA 22180.

National Directory of State Agencies (Cambridge Information Group).

Book of the States, Council of State Governments, Iron Works Pike, Lexington, KY 40578.

Publishing and the media

This is a competitive field, but opportunities are expected to grow as more local newspapers are established. A number of British publishing companies, such as Elsevier Reed, are active in the US, and if you are on the staff of one of these you could look into the possibility of a transfer. The US has a vast number of local radio stations and you could try your luck there.

Useful addresses and publications

Magazine Publishers of America, 575 Lexington Ave, New York, NY 10022.

National Association of Broadcasters, 1771 N St, NW, Washington, DC 20036.

Newspaper Guild, 8611 Second Street NW, Silver Springs, MD 20910.

National Newspaper Publishers Association, 3200 13th Street NW, Washington, DC 20010.

Editor and Publisher Market Guide and *Editor and Publisher International Yearbook*, 11 W 19th St, New York, NY 10011- 4202.

National Directory of Magazines, Oxbridge Communications, 150 Fifth Ave, Suite 301, New York, NY 10011-4311.

Ulrich's International Periodicals Directory, R. R. Bowker.

Literary Market Place, R. R. Bowker.

Career Opportunities in TV, Cable and Video, MK & RM Reed (Facts on File).

Major employers

Capital Cities/ABC Inc, 77 W 66th St, New York, NY 10023.

Dun & Bradstreet Corp, 299 Park Avenue, New York, NY 10171.

Gannett Co, 100 Wilson Blvd, Arlington, VA 22209.

Grolier Inc, Sherman Turnpike, Danbury, CT 06816.

Harte-Hanks Communications, 40 NE Loop 410, San Antonio, TX 78216.

Knight Ridder Newspapers Inc, 1 Herald Plaza, Miami, FL 33101.

New York Times, 229 W 43rd Street, New York, NY 10036.

Taft Broadcasting Co, 1718 Young Street, Cincinnati, OH 45210.

Time Warner Inc, Time & Life Building, Rockefeller Cntr, New York, NY
10020.

Religion
Ministers of religion come into a special visa category, which could
mean it is easier for them to enter the US than a layman. Most of
the American religious denominations have their counterparts in the
British Isles, and if you are interested in working in the US it is likely
that you will make arrangements through your own religious organisation. The Roman Catholic Church is currently experiencing a
shortage of priests and is particularly anxious to increase its numbers
and there is a shortage of rabbis away from the main urban areas.

As religion is not taught in public sector schools, the only openings
for teachers of religious instruction are in church and private schools
and colleges.

Reference
Yearbook of American and Canadian Churches, Abingdon Press.

Scientific work
The United States possesses excellent facilities for scientific research
in industry, in academic institutions and the public sector, and these
have attracted scientists from all over the world.

Useful addresses and publications
American Chemical Society, 1155 16th St, NW, Washington, DC 20036.
American Institute of Physics, 335 E 45th St, New York, NY 10017.
American Mathematical Society, PO Box 6248, Providence, RI 02940.
American Institute of Biological Sciences, 730 11th Street NW, Washington,
   DC 20001-4521.
American Society of Biological Chemists, 9650 Rockville Pike, Bethesda, MD
   20014.
American Statistical Association, 1429 Duke Street, Alexandria, VA 22314.
Jobs Bulletin, Association for Women in Science, 1522 K St, NW Suite 820,
   Washington, DC 20005.
VGM's Handbook of Scientific and Technical Careers: C. T. Norback (ed)
   (VGM Career Books).

Secretarial work
There is always a need for good secretaries, though there could be
problems in gaining labor certification unless the prospective employer is able to make out a good case. If you have residential status
there are plenty of employment agencies offering both temporary or
permanent employment.

Useful addresses
Professional Secretaries International, 10502 NW Ambassador Drive, PO
Box 10502, Kansas City, MO 64195-0404.
National Association of Legal Secretaries, 2250 E 73rd St, Tulsa, OK 74136.
Office and Professional Employees International Union, 265 W 14th Street,
New York, NY 10011.

Social services and voluntary organisations

(See also **Public sector jobs.**) Two-fifths of social workers work in
the public sector, often at the municipal or county levels. Most of the
rest are employed in voluntary agencies (also called 'non-profits').
Many states have licensing or registration requirements for social
workers. This is an expanding profession, partly as a result of the
ageing population.

Useful organisations and publications
National Association for Social Workers, 750 1st St NE, Suite 700, Washing-
ton, DC 20002. (Offers voluntary certification ACSW or ACBSW.)
Intercristo, PO Box 33487, 19303 Freemont Ave N, Seattle, WA 98133. (A
Christian organisation which offers a job placement and job information
service. It publishes a quarterly newsletter *On the Job* and operates
Prospectus, a database of 40,000 openings in non-profit Christian organisa-
tions. However it is not in a position to arrange jobs for people living
outside the US.)
Community Jobs, 1520 16th Street NW, Washington, DC 20036.
Employment Listings for the Social Services, 10 Angelica Drive, Framingham,
MA 01701.
National Employment Listing Service for the Criminal Justice System and
Social Services, Criminal Justice Center, Sam Houston State University,
Huntsville, TX 77341.
Careers in the Non-Profit Sectors, T. Mc Adam (ed), Taft Group, 5130
MacArthur Blvd NW, Washington DC 20016.
Profitable Careers in Non-Profits, W. Lewis and C. Milano (John Wiley)
Taft Directory of Non-Profit Organisations S. E. Elnick (ed) (Taft Group).
Jobs and Careers with Non-profit Organisations, Ron Krannich (Garrett Park).
*Doing Well by Doing Good: The Complete Guide to Jobs in the Non-Profit
Sector*, Terry W. McAdam (Fund Raising).

Sport and recreation

Around half of leisure workers are employed in the public sector. The
rest work in commercial and voluntary organisations, some of them
quite small affairs. There is plenty of seasonal vacation work available,
much of it carried out by students (see Chapter 3). There is also an
increasing need for experienced groundsmen.

Useful addresses and publications
National Recreation and Park Association, 2775 S Quincy St, Suite 300, Arlington, VA 22206-2204. (Publishes a twice-monthly bulletin of job openings.)
American Camping Association, Bradford Woods, 5000 State Road 67 N, Martinsville, IN 46151.
Professional Golfers Association, 100 Ave of Champions, Palm Beach Gardens, FL 33418.
US Professional Tennis Association, 3535 Briar Park Drive, Houston, TX 77042.
Athletics Employment Weekly, Box 86, Warsaw, IL 62379.
Career Opportunities in the Sports Industry, Shelly Field (Facts on File).

Major employers
Bally Manufacturing Corp, 8700 W Bryn Mawr Avenue, Chicago, IL 60631. (Amusement parks.)
Walt Disney Productions, 500 South Buena Vista, Burbank, CA 91521. (Disneyworld.)
YMCA National Office, 101 N Wacker Street, Chicago, IL 60606.

Teaching and lecturing

(See also **Religion**.) If your principal objective is to gain teaching experience for up to one year in the USA, your best plan would be to go to the US on an exchange programme. Among the organisations that organise teacher/lecturer exchanges are the Central Bureau and the Fulbright Commission. Chapter 3 deals with exchanges in more detail.

For longer periods your employer will normally need to apply for labor certification, unless you are pre-eminent in your field. School teachers wishing to teach in the public sector need to have their credentials accepted by the teaching certification department of the state in which they wish to teach, and this applies to US teachers as much as to foreign ones. The addresses are given in Appendix G. In some states, you need to be a US citizen in order to become a teacher in a state school, notably the District of Columbia, Florida, Idaho, Indiana, Maryland, Mississippi, Nevada, New Jersey, North Dakota, Pennsylvania, Nebraska, South Dakota, Texas, Washington, South Carolina and West Virginia.

Lists of schools and school districts are obtainable from the relevant state department of education (which is listed in Appendix G). Some state education departments maintain a placement bureau that you can contact, but more often than not recruitment is the responsibility of the school district or individual school. There are also teacher placement agencies which may charge a fee.

Teachers seeking posts in private schools do not usually need to meet the same certification requirements as those seeking posts in public sector schools. Applications should normally be directed to the principal of the school in question.

Academic vacancies are listed on the Internet: http://volvo.gslis. utexas.edu/~acadres/geographic.html.

Useful addresses and publications

The National Association of State Directors of Teacher Education Certification (NASDTEC), PO Box 2431, Sacramento, CA 95814. (Publishes the *Manual on Certification and Preparation of Educational Personnel in the US*.)

Association of School College and University Staffing (ASCUS), Box 4411, Madison, WI 53711. (Publishes the *Directory of Public Schools Systems in the US* and *A Job Search Handbook for Educators*.)

National Association of Teachers' Agencies, PO Box 223, Georgetown, MA 01833. (Can provide a list of teacher placement agencies.)

The Handbook of Private Schools, Porter Sargent Publishers, Inc, 11 Beacon Street, Boston, MA 02108.

Independent Educational Services, 20 Nassau St, Princeton, NJ 08542. (Teacher recruitment agency.)

American Federation of Teachers, 555 New Jersey Ave NW, Washington, DC 20001.

Foreign and Domestic Teachers Bureau, PO Box 1063, Vancouver, WA 98666. (Teacher recruitment agency.)

National Education Selection, 189 Clifford St, Newark, NJ 07105. (Publishes a teachers' vacancy list nine times a year.)

Modern Language Association, 10 Astor Place, 5th Floor, New York, NY 10003. (Publishes job information lists, which include teaching posts.)

American Association of University Professors, 1012 14th Street, Washington, DC 20005.

The US-UK Educational Commission, 62 Doughty Street, London WC1N 2LS. Tel: (0171) 404 6994. (Has a small library and can provide further information on the US educational system.)

Telecommunications

(See also **Electronics**.) Job opportunities in this sector look set to decline as a result of improved technology.

Useful addresses

United States Independent Telephone Association, 1801 K St NW, Suite 1201, Washington, DC 20006.

Major employers

AT & T Technologies, 550 Madison Avenue, New York, NY 10022.

GTE Corporation, 1 Stamford Forum, Stamford, CT 06904.
United Telecommunications Inc, 2330 Shawnee Mission Parkway, Shawnee
Mission, KS 66205.

Recruitment consultants
Moxon Dolphin Kerby, Butler.

Transport
Not many openings in this sector for non-Americans.

Useful addresses and publications
Future Aviation Professionals of America, 4959 Massachusetts Blvd, Atlanta,
GA 30337.
Air Line Pilots Association, 1625 Massachusetts Avenue NW, Washington,
DC 20036.
American Trucking Associations Inc, 2200 Mill Rd, Alexandria, VA 22314.
Official Guide to Airline Careers, (S&S Trade).
Career Opportunities in Travel & Tourism, John K. Hanks (Facts on File).

United Nations
The headquarters of the UN and a number of its agencies are based
in the United States, and if you land a job here your visa problems
will be solved. Some of the posts will involve foreign travel and
possibly postings outside the US. There are two kinds of posts:

- Professional posts: specialists in economics, science, data processing, *etc*; translators, interpreters, précis writers, *etc*.

- General service posts: secretarial, administrative, information,
  clerical, accounting, *etc*.

Useful addresses
Professional Recruitment Service, Room 2465, UN Secretariat, New York,
NY 10017.
United Nations Children's Fund (UNICEF), 866 UN Plaza, 6th Floor, New
York, NY 10017.
United Nations Institute for Training and Research, 801 UN Plaza, New
York, NY 10017.
International Monetary Fund, 700 19th Street NW, Washington, DC 20006.
World Bank, including International Bank for Reconstruction and Develop-
ment, International Development Association, International Finance
Corporation, 1818 H Street NW, Washington DC 20433.

Veterinary medicine

There are good prospects for vets. However you will need a licence to practise; this is gained through taking a two day state board proficiency examination.

Useful address
American Veterinary Medical Association, Suite 100, 1931 N Meacham Road, Schaumburg, IL 60173-4360.

Writing
(See also **Publishing and the Media.**)
Society for Technical Communication, 815 15th Street NW, Suite 516, Washington, DC 20005. (Technical writers' association.)
National Writers Union, 873 Broadway, New York, NY 10003.
Writers Guild of America, 8955 Beverly Blvd, West Hollywood, CA 90048. Also 555 W 57th St, New York, NY 10019. (TV, cinema, radio writers.)
Career Opportunities for Writers, R. Guiley (Facts on File).
Writers Market (annual), Writer's Digest Books, 1 Dana Ave, Cincinnati, OH 45207. Distributor: Freelance Market News, 4 Dale Street, Manchester M1 1JB. Tel: (0161) 228 2362.

Further information

A more comprehensive list of professional and trade associations is provided in:

Encyclopedia of Associations (Gale Research).
Career Guide to Professional Associations—A Directory of Organizations by Occupational Field, (Sulzberger & Graham).
Professional and Trade Association Job Finder—A Directory of Employment Resources offered by Associations and other Organisations: S. N. Feingold and A. Nicholson (Garrett Park Press).

Appendix B
UK Recruitment Organisations

Anders Glaser Wills

Capital House, 10th Floor, Hounslow Place, East Street, Southampton SO1
0BU. Tel: (01703) 223511. Fax: (01703) 227911.

Job sectors: Automotive, aerospace, IT, petrochemical, power generation,
marine engineering.

Type of employer: Multinational engineering and construction firms.

Method of recruitment: Advertising, candidate register.

Advertising media used: National newspapers and specialist publications.

Qualifications and experience required: Minimum qualification HND, but
most of the jobs are for graduates. Five years' experience desirable.

Additional information: Part of the CDI Corporation, the largest supplier of
temporary technical staff in the US with around 250 offices. Also recruits
for Africa, Europe, Middle East and Far East. (FRES)

Angel International Recruitment

50 Fleet Street, London EC4Y 1BE. Tel: (0171) 583 1661. Fax: (0171) 940
2018.

Job sectors: Nursing.

Type of employer: Hospitals and private clinics.

Method of recruitment: Advertising, candidate register, recommendation.

Advertising media used: Nursing Times, national newspapers.

Qualifications and experience required: Trained nurses only who have passed
CGFNS; at least two years' post-qualification experience.

Additional information: Places between 50–100 annually in US; also recruits
for other countries. (FRES)

Beechwood Recruitment Ltd

221 High Street, London W3 9BY. Tel: (0181) 992 8647. Fax (0181) 992
5658. E-mail: 100623.1514@compuserve.com

Job sectors: Engineering, scientific, technology, sales and marketing, software
and computing.

Type of employer: Most, particularly multinationals, manufacturers and
defence industry.

Method of recruitment: Advertising, candidate register, recommendation.

Advertising media used: National press, trade press, local papers.
Qualifications and experience required: Minimum HNC level; 22–45 age range.
Additional information: Salaries range from £15,000 to £40,000. Also recruits for other countries worldwide. (FRES)

Butler International

Kings Mill, Kings Mill Lane, South Nutfield, Redhill, Surrey RH1 5NE. Tel: (01737) 822000. Fax: (01737) 823031.
Job sectors: Engineering and information technology.
Type of employer: Multinational industrial and manufacturing firms. Main sectors: aerospace, automotive, telecommunications, chemicals, pharmaceuticals, information technology, general manufacturing.
Method of recruitment: Advertising, executive search, candidate register, referrals.
Advertising media used: Daily Telegraph, specialist magazines and journals.
Qualifications and experience: Engineers and IT specialists with HNC or BSc and a minimum of 3 years' experience. Salary range: £18,000–£80,000. Contract rates: £12–£35+ per hour.
Additional information: One of the largest specialist technical recruitment companies in the USA with 50 offices there. Over 6,000 contractors employed at any one time.

Computech International Resources

34 Francis Grove, Wimbledon, London SW19 4DY. Tel: (0181) 288 4880. Fax: (0181) 288 4882. E-mail: computech@dial.piper.com; also www:computec-intl.com.
Job sectors: IT.
Type of employer: Fortune 500 companies.
Methods of recruitment: Advertising, database, referrals, executive search.
Advertising media used: Computing, Computer Weekly, Internet.
Qualifications and experience: IT skills such as SAP, Oracle Financials, GSM, Hogan, Adabas Natural, Smalltalk, Baan/Triton.
Additional information: Also recruits for Canada, Australia and New Zealand.

Computer People

Victory House, 7 Selsdon Way, London E14 9GL. Tel: (0171) 510 2000. Fax: (0171) 510 2291.
Job sectors: Information technology.
Type of employer: Large commercial organisations.
Method of recruitment: Advertising, candidate register, executive search, recommendation.
Advertising media used: Computing, Computer Weekly.
Qualifications and experience required: Various levels of skill required, particularly with experience of Unix, IBM and CASE technology.
Additional information: Handles 150 placements on average per year; network of 12 offices in USA; salary range $30,000 to $100,000. (FRES)

Computing Resource Centre Ltd
West Lodge, 407 Uxbridge Road, London W3 9SH. Tel: (0181) 896 3110.
    Fax: (0181) 896 2912. E-mail: recruitment@crcdirect.co.uk.
Job sectors: Computing (SAP)
Type of employer: Multinationals, management consultancies.
Method of recruitment: Recommendation, executive search, advertisement.
Advertising media used: The Times, Computing.
Qualifications and experience required: Hands-on SAP experience (either
    computer implementation or business experience).
Additional information: US office open since end of 1995; also recruits for
    Europe. (FRES).

DGH Management and Recruitment Consultants
Broomebourne Farm, Further Quarter, High Halden, Kent TN26 3HL. Tel:
    (01233) 850104. Fax: (01233) 850105.
Job sectors: Sales and marketing.
Type of employer: Multinationals.
Method of recruitment: Executive search.
Qualifications and experience required: Degree in Science or Business pre-
    ferred; age 30–40; at least 5 years' experience in IT, data communications
    or telecommunications sales.
Additional information: Also recruits for Europe and the Far East.

The Forsyth Group
Claridge House, 29 Barnes High Street, London SW13 9LW. Tel: (0181)
    878 9189. Fax: (0181) 878 8586. E-mail: forsyth@ibm.net.
Job sector: Information technology.
Type of employer: From large vendors of hardware and software to small
    niche oriented organisations.
Method of recruitment: Executive search, advertisement, candidate database.
Qualifications and experience: Candidates with a highly technical background
    and with Internet programming skills are of particular interest for the
    US.
Additional information: Associate company based in Boston, MA. Also
    recruits for Europe.

Grafton International
94 High Street, Belfast BT1 2BG. Tel: (01232) 242824. Fax: (01232) 246429.
Job sectors: Healthcare (nurses).
Type of employer: Private and university hospitals.
Method of recruitment: Advertising and candidate register.
Advertising media used: Nursing Times, OSJ, Telegraph.
Qualifications and experience required: RGN plus 2 years' postgraduate
    experience and CGFNS.
Additional information: Recruits more than 100 annually. Age range 21-60.
    Salary range: £20,000–£50,000. (FRES)

Harrison Willis
Cardinal House, 39/40 Albermarle Street, London W1X 3FD. Tel: (0171)
629 4463. Fax: (0171) 491 4705.
Job sectors: Accountancy (normally main-stream audit).
Type of employer: Accountancy practices.
Method of recruitment: Advertising, candidate register, executive search,
recommendation.
Advertising media used: Accountancy.
Qualifications and experience required: Full ACA qualification, majority of
posts are for people in their twenties with up to three years' post
qualification experience.
Additional information: Also recruits for positions worldwide. (FRES)

Harrison Willis (Legal)
17 Red Lion Square, London WC1R 4QH. Tel: (0171) 404 4646. Fax: (0171)
831 7969.
Job sector: Law.
Type of employer: Practices, firms.
Method of recruitment: Advertising, recommendation.
Advertising media used: The Times, The Lawyer, Law Society Gazette.
Qualifications and experience required: Qualified solicitor or barrister.
Additional information: Also recruits for positions world wide. (FRES)

James Baker Associates
46 Queens Road, Reading RG1 4BD. Tel: (0118) 950 5022. Fax: (0118) 950
5056.
Job sectors: IT, high technology.
Type of employer: Multinationals, large national companies and consultancy
organisations.
Method of recruitment: Advertising, selection, database.
Advertising media used: Computer Weekly, Computing, national newspapers.
Qualifications and experience required: Technical graduates aged up to 30 with
a minimum of three years' experience; normally highly specialist computer
skills are required.
Additional information: Also recruits for Europe, the Middle East, *etc.*

Medic International Ltd
4 Thameside Centre, Kew Bridge Road, Brentford, Middlesex TW8 0HB.
Tel: (0181) 568 1993. Fax: (0181) 568 1961.
Job sectors: Medical (occupational therapists and physiotherapists).
Type of employer: Various.
Method of recruitment: Advertising, recommendation, candidate register.
Advertising media used: Professional journals.
Qualifications and experience required: British qualifications normally ac-
ceptable but need to be assessed by US Registration Board.

Additional information: Three-week orientation programme provided; also recruits for countries worldwide. (FRES)

Morson International

Stableford Hall, Monton, Eccles, Manchester M30 8AP. Tel: (0161) 707 1516. Fax: (0161) 788 8372.

Job sectors: Engineering, especially oil and gas construction, petrochemicals, aerospace.

Type of employer: Multinational.

Method of recruitment: Advertising, candidate register.

Advertising media used: National press.

Qualifications and experience required: At least a degree or HND in engineering. Multidisciplinary experience (*eg* electrical, mechanical, piping, instrumentation).

Additional information: Places around 100 engineers a year in US at salaries in £25,000–£50,000 range. Office in the US: 5353 West Alabama, Suite 525, Houston, TX 77056. Also recruits for Europe. (FRES)

Moxon Dolphin Kerby Ltd

178–202 Great Portland Street, London W1N 6JJ. Tel: (0171) 631 4411. Fax: (0171) 636 5592.

Job sectors: Hi-tech: electronics, aerospace, semiconductors, telecommunications.

Type of employer: Multinationals, major corporations, R & D facilities.

Method of recruitment: Advertising; executive search; register.

Advertising media used: Daily Telegraph, Sunday Times, Electronics Weekly, New Scientist.

Qualifications and experience required: At least a first degree plus three to four years' experience in relevant disciplines.

Additional information: Places between 50 and 100 people annually; also recruits for Canada, Europe and the Middle East; four offices in the United States. (ASSC)

Quarry Dougall

37–41 Bedford Row, London WC1R 4JH. Tel: (071) 405 6062. Fax: (071) 831 6394.

Job sectors: Law (lawyers and paralegals).

Type of employer: Partnerships, national and multinational companies, institutions.

Method of recruitment: Advertising, candidate register, recommendation.

Advertising media used: Times, The Lawyer, Law Society Gazette.

Qualifications and experience required: Legal qualification and ideally also admitted in the US; specialist experience in an area of the law with similar application in the US.

Additional information: Operates in association with Mestel & Co, Inc; also recruits for other countries worldwide. (FRES)

Randall Massey Consultants

Ambrose House, 30–33 Milton Road, Swindon SN1 5JA. Tel: (01793) 614700. Fax: (01793) 619243.

Job sectors: Electronics, IT.

Type of employer: High-tech vendors and users.

Method of recruitment: Advertising, executive search.

Advertising media used: Sunday Times; Daily Telegraph.

Qualifications and experience required: Degree in electronics or computer science; 25-35 years old; unique skill set (*eg* in mobile communications or semi-conductors).

Additional information: Also recruits for Europe and Hong Kong.

Sector Personnel

12 Well Court, London EC4M 9DN. Tel: (0171) 489 0165. Fax: (0171) 236 2824. E-mail: sector@cix.compulink.co.uk.

Job sector: Information technology.

Type of employer: Mainly private sector.

Methods of recruitment: All.

Advertising media used: Computer Weekly, Computing, Fax Me (Jobscrvc.com).

Qualifications and experience: Candidates must meet current visa require-ments: degree plus 4 years IT experience, HND plus 6 years IT experience, or 12 years experience.

Additional information: Associate offices in USA.

Sherwood Engineering Recruitment

Sherwood House, Aldwarne Road, Parkgate, Rotherham S62 6BU. Tel: (01709) 710800. Fax: (01709) 710880. E-mail: 100443. 2644@compuserve.com.

Job sectors: Construction and process industry.

Type of employer: Multinational.

Method of recruitment: All.

Advertising media used: E-mail, newspapers in various areas.

Qualifications and experience required: Construction and process related technical staff with overseas experience from foreman supervisor to project director level.

Additional information: Recruits for positions worldwide.

Track International

PO Box 1, Perranporth, Cornwall TR6 0YG. Tel: (01872) 573937. Fax: (01872) 571282. E-mail: trackint.com; Compuserve: 100020,1156.

Job sectors: IT.

Type of employer: Various.

Method of recruitment: Advertising.

Advertising media used: Teletext, Computer Weekly.

Qualifications and experience required: Graduates in the appropriate discipline aged up to 35.

Additional information: Also recruits for Europe and South Africa.

TRC Ltd

Suite 510, Walmar House, 296 Regent Street, London W1R 5HD. Tel: (0171) 436 4424.

Job sector: IT.

Type of employer: Blue chip multinationals.

Method of recruitment: Executive search, advertisement, candidate register.

Advertising media used: Job Search, Job Mart and the specialist press.

Qualifications and experience required: Graduate specialists in the SAP integrated software package.

Additional information: Also recruits for the Middle East, Far East and Africa.

VIP International

17 Charing Cross Road, London WC2H 0EP. Tel: (0171) 930 0541. Fax: (0171) 930 2860. E-mail: vip.intl@dial.pipex.com.

Job sectors: Hotel and catering management.

Type of employer: Public sector and multinational companies.

Method of recruitment: Advertising, candidate register, executive search, recommendation.

Advertising media used: Hotel Management, Caterer, Evening Standard, etc.

Qualifications and experience required: Aged 23 + with appropriate qualifications and ideally junior management experience in first class establishments.

Additional information: Few management positions in the US itself, but hundreds of opportunities on board US-based luxury cruises handled by VIP Luxury Cruise Management and Recruitment Division. (FRES).

Organisations which occasionally recruit for the US

ABB Lutech Resources Ltd, South Point, Sutton Court Road, Sutton, Surrey SM1 4TZ. Tel: (0181) 288 0920. Fax: (0181) 288 0921. Recruits for a few positions in process engineering in multinational firms through advertisements in *Daily Telegraph*. Candidates need to be graduates with a minimum of 5 years experience in petrochemical or oil/gas industry. Design engineering experience essential. Parent company has offices in New Jersey and Houston, USA. Also recruits for Europe, Middle East and Nigeria.

Barnett Consulting Group, Providence House, River Street, Windsor, Berks SL4 1QT. Tel: (01753) 856723. Recruits senior and middle management for a variety of sectors.

Beament Leslie Thomas, 107–111 Fleet Street, London EC4A 2AB. Tel: (0171) 353 5606. Places taxation specialists and management consultants with firms of accountants and consultants. Professional qualifications and relevant experience are required. Age range: mid 20s to early 30s. (FRES)

British Mining Consultants, PO Box 18, Mill Lane, Huthwaite, Sutton in Ashfield, Notts NG17 2NS. Tel: (01623) 441444. Fax: (01623) 440330. Recruits geologists, mining engineers and mine managers in association with a US subsidiary.

Davies Kidd, Hamilton House, 1 Temple Avenue, London EC4Y 0HA. Tel: (0171) 353 4212. Recruits young recently qualified ACAs who have trained with medium to large accountancy firms for audit work. Also recruits for Europe, the Middle East and the Pacific Rim.

DM Management Consultants Ltd, 19 Clarges Street, London W1Y 7PG. Tel: (0171) 499 8030. E-mail: pmt.dmma.dial.pipex.com. A specialist in strategic marketing and direct marketing mail order appointments. The normal requirement is for graduate senior and general managers in their mid-20s, 30s and 40s.

FHELP Marketing, Henrietta Villa, Common Mead Avenue, Gillingham, Dorset SP8 4NB. Tel: (01747) 822651. Fax: (01747) 825845. Recruits engineering, aeronautical, medical and teaching professionals and civilians for equipment maintenance in military and air force bases. Advertises posts in *Daily* and *Sunday Telegraph* and maintains candidate database. Also recruits for positions worldwide and has office in USA.

Financial Recruitment International, Southmead, Long Hey Road, Caldy, Wirral L48 1LY. Tel: (0151) 625 0565. Fax: (0151) 625 0058. Recruits accountants with ACA or equivalent qualification as audit seniors for banking, insurance, fund management and public practice. Also recruits for the Caribbean, Europe, Middle East and Far East.

Fircroft Group, Trinity House, 114 Northenden Road, Sale, Cheshire M33 3HD. Tel: (0161) 905 2020. Fax: (0161) 969 1743. Recruits a small number of graduate engineers (all disciplines) with at least five years' experience for multinationals. Has a network of offices in the US. Also recruits for the Far East and (to a lesser extent) the Middle East. (FRES)

Alasdair Graham Associates Ltd, 97 Ayr Road, Newton Mearns, Glasgow G77 6RA. Tel: (0141) 639 3345. Fax: (0141) 639 2918. Recruits professional engineers aged 30–55 to work in multinational oil, gas, water, power and construction companies for salaries in excess of US$50,000. Has associate office in Houston and also recruits for Australia, Middle East, SE Asia, Europe and North Africa. (FRES).

HB Associates, 101 High Street, Evesham, Worcs WR11 4DN. Tel: (01386) 49856. Fax: (01386) 41925. E-mail: hbgroup.co.uk. Recruits graduate software engineers aged 25–35 for multinational computer/IT corporations. Advertises in *IS Opportunities*, maintains a candidate register, and undertakes executive search. Associate office in Boston, USA. Also recruits for France and Germany.

Hunterskil, Project House, 110–113 Tottenham Court Road, London W1P 9HG. Tel: (0171) 383 3888. Fax: (0171) 387 2048. Recruits IT professionals with a minimum of three years' commercial experience. Advertises in *Computer Weekly* and *Freelance Informer*. (FRES)

Insurance Personnel Selection, Lloyd's Avenue House, 6 Lloyd's Avenue, London EC3N 3ES. Tel: (0171) 481 8111. Fax: (0171) 481 0994. Places skilled insurance and reinsurance staff qualified to ACII standard with multinational insurance brokers and companies. The majority of candidates come through recommendation. (FRES)

MDA Computer Group (Dart Resourcing Group), Sceptre House, 169/173 Regent Street, London W1R 7FB. Tel: (0171) 439 1776. Fax: (0171) 439 7871. Recruits experienced and qualified IT specialists through advertising, candidate register and executive search. Branches in Birmingham, Bristol, Manchester and Slough. (Member of Computing Services Association.)

Merton Associates, Merton House, 70 Grafton Way, London W1P 5LE. Tel: (0171) 388 2051. Recruits around ten senior managers a year for the United States using executive search methods. Salaries are normally in excess of $75,000.

NPA Management Services Ltd, 12 Well Court, London EC4M 4DN. Tel: (0171) 248 3812. Fax: (0171) 221 4538. Recruits high level international banking specialists in the 25–50 age range for foreign exchange and treasury operations and corporate finance. Normally requires degree in relevant discipline (*eg* law, accountancy) plus experience. (ASSC).

Prescot Computer Recruitment, 33A Lauderdale Drive, Richmond, Surrey TW10 7BS. Tel: (0181) 948 0729. Fax: (0181) 332 6055. Recruits computer professionals with at least three years' experience.

Profile Management & Specialist Recruitment Ltd, 201 Haverstock Hill, Belsize Park, London NW3 4QG. Tel: (0171) 431 1616. Fax: (0171) 794 4229. E-mail: chad@pres.rec.demon.co.uk. Recruits senior management for hotels and restaurants. Positions are not advertised. (FRES)

Rosta Engineering Ltd, 87A Castle Street, Edgeley, Stockport SK3 9AR. Tel: (0161) 477 2111. Fax: (0161) 480 4599. Recruits technical and engineering personnel for the automotive, petrochemical and construction industries. All types of design personnel, administrators, managers, as well as construction supervisors, inspectors and managers. Advertises in Daily Telegraph and maintains candidate database. Also recruits for Pakistan, Korea, Australia, Nigeria and Middle East. (FRES).

Wrightson Wood Ltd, 11 Grosvenor Place, London SW1X 7HH. Tel: (0171) 245 9371. Executive search agency specialising in industrial manufacturing and engineering. A member of International Executive Search Associates (INESA), a consortium which includes Gilbert Tweed Associates in the US.

Notes
FRES: Member of the Federation of Recruitment and Employment Services, 36–38 Mortimer Street, London W1N 7RB. Tel: (0171) 323 4300.
ASSC: Member of Association of Search and Selection Consultants, 24 St James's Square, London SW1Y 4HZ. Tel: (0171) 839 7788.

The information in this chapter is based on the replies to a questionnaire circulated to international recruitment agencies whose recruitment requirements may change. The list does not claim to be comprehensive and inclusion in this section does not imply recommendation by the author or publisher.

Appendix C
US Recruitment Organisations

Executive recruitment
This is a select list of executive recruitment consultancies with offices in the British Isles and the United States—and often other countries too. It is important to realise that the British or Irish office listed will not necessarily recruit for jobs in the United States, nor will US branches be equipped to deal with applications from abroad. Please refer to the relevant sections in Chapters 4 and 6. The Executive Grapevine produces an international directory of executive recruitment consultants.

Abbott Smith Associates, PO Box 318, Millbrook, NY 12545; 55 Clarence Gate Gdns, Glentworth St, London NW1 6RS. Tel: (0171) 258 1457. Personnel and training professionals. Also Chicago.

Boyden International Inc., 260 Madison Ave, New York, NY 10022-3574; 24 Queen Anne's Gate, London SW1H 9AA. Tel: (0171) 222 9033. Also Atlanta, Boston, Cleveland, Dallas, Fort Lauderdale, Houston, Los Angeles, Minneapolis, Morristown, Pittsburg, San Francisco, Stamford, Washington.

DPSC, 24 Wyckoff Avenue, Waldwick, NJ 07463; PO Box 38, Tadworth, Surrey, KT20 7UR. Tel: (01737) 814116. Also Wellesley (MA).

Robert Half International, 565 5th Ave, New York, NY 10036-7660; Walter House, Strand, London WC2R 0PT. Tel: (0171) 836 3545. One hundred and forty offices throughout US.

Heidrick & Struggles, 245 Park Ave, New York, NY 10147-0152; 100 Piccadilly, London W1V 9FN. Tel: (0171) 491 3124. Also Atlanta, Boston, Chicago, Cleveland, Dallas, Greenwich (CT), Jacksonville (FL), Menlo Park, Minneapolis, San Francisco, Washington.

AT Kearney Inc, 222 S Riverside Plaza, Chicago, IL 60606-5904; Stockley House, 130 Wilton Road, London SW1V 1LQ. Tel: (0171) 834 6886.

Also Alexandria (VA), Atlanta, Chicago, Dallas, Denver, Los Angeles, Miami, New York, Scottsdale (AZ).

Korn Ferry Carré Orban International, 237 Park Ave, New York, NY 10017-3142; 252 Regent Street, London W1R 5DA. Tel: (0171) 312 3100. Also Atlanta, Boston, Chicago, Denver, Houston, Los Angeles, Minneapolis, Palo Alto, San Francisco, Seattle, Stamford, Washington.

KPMG Executive Recruiters, 345 Park Ave, New York, NY 10154-0111; 1–2 Dorset Rise, London EC4Y 8AE. Tel: (0171) 236 8000. Branches throughout US.

Marlar International, 410 Severn Ave, Suite 403, Annapolis, MD 21403-2524; 16 Berkeley Street, London W1X 5AG. Tel: (0171) 495 1772. Also Los Angeles.

Norman Broadbent International, 200 Park Ave, 18th Floor, New York, NY 10166; 65 Curzon St, London W1Y 7PE. Tel: (0171) 629 9626.

Russell Reynolds Associates, 200 Park Avenue, 23rd Floor, New York, NY 10166-0105; 24 St James's Square, London SW1Y 4HZ. Tel: (0171) 839 7788. Also Atlanta, Boston, Chicago, Cleveland, Dallas, Los Angeles, Minneapolis, San Francisco, Stamford, Washington.

Spencer Stuart & Associates, 52 E 52nd St, New York, NY 10055-0001; 16 Connaught Place, London W2 2ED. Tel: (0171) 493 1238. Also Atlanta, Chicago, Dallas, Houston, Los Angeles, Philadelphia, San Francisco, Stamford.

TASA, 875 3rd Ave, Suite 1501, New York, NY 10022; 15 Carteret Street, London SW1H 9DJ. Tel: (0171) 233 1234. Also Palo Alto.

Egon Zehnder International Inc, 55 E 59th St, 14th Floor, New York, NY 10022-1112; Devonshire House, Mayfair Place, London W1X 5FH. Tel: (0171) 493 3882. Also Atlanta, Chicago, Los Angeles.

Ward Howell International (Whitehead Mann), 99 Park Avenue, New York, NY 10016; also 44 Welbeck Street, London W1M 7HF. Tel: (0171) 737 8736. Also Barrington (IL), Chicago, Dallas, Encino (CA), Houston, Los Angeles, San Francisco, Stamford.

Whitney Group, 12 E 49th St, Tower 49, New York, NY 10017; 17 Buckingham Gate, London SW1E 6LB. Tel: (0171) 630 9255. Financial sector.

Temporary help services and other employment agencies

To list all such agencies and their branches would require a book several times the size of this one. Normally, you would apply to such an agency once you have arrived in the United States, and the best policy is to thumb through the Employment Agency section of the local *Yellow Pages*. Some telephone directories list agencies according to their specialisation.

The agencies listed below are just a sample of what is available. Most of them have several branches.

Careers Unlimited, 1401 E Lansing Drive, E Lansing, MI 48823.
CDI Temporary Services, 10 Penn Center, Philadelphia, PA 19103.
Kelly Services, 999 W Big Beaver Road, Troy, MI 48084.
Lloyd Personnel Consultants, 10 Cutter Mill Road, Great Neck, NY 10021.
Manpower Inc, PO Box 2053, Milwaukee, WI 53201.
Manus Services Corp, Manus Building, PO Box 440406, Seattle, WA 98114.
Norrell Temporary Services, 3535 Piedmont Rd NE, Atlanta, GA 30305.
Olsten Corporation, 1 Merrick Ave, Westbury, NY 11590.
Personnel Recruiters Inc, 150 Morris Ave, Springfield, NJ 07081.
Scientific Placement Inc, PO Box 19949, Houston, TX 77224.
Temporaries Inc, 1015 18th Street, Suite 504, Washington, DC 20036.
Uniforce Temporary Services, 1335 Jericho Turnpike, PO Box 5055, New Hyde Park, NY 11040.
Western Temporary Services, 301 Lennon Lane, Walnut Creek, CA 94598.
Wordforce Inc, 902 Broadway, New York, NY 10010.

Trade associations

There are a number of trade associations to which many of these organisations belong. They include:

● National Association of Temporary Services
● Association of Executive Recruiting Consultants
● National Association of Personnel Consultants

Directories

Among the directories that list recruitment agencies are:

Executive Employment Guide, The American Management Association Inc, 135 W 50th Street, New York, NY 10020.
Directory of Executive Recruiters, J. H. Kennedy Publications.
Directory of Personnel Consultants by Specialisation, National Association of Personnel Consultants.

Appendix D
Newspaper and Specialist Journals

Key
W: weekly; F: fortnightly; M: monthly; B: bi-monthly; Q: quarterly; A: annual.

UK expatriate newspapers and magazines

Overseas Jobs Express, F, Premier House, Shoreham Airport, Sussex BN43 5FF. Tel: (01273) 440220. Fax: (01273) 440229. Internet: http://www.overseasjobs.com.

Nexus, M, Expat Network, PO Box 380, Croydon CR9 2ZQ. Tel: (0181) 760 5100. Fax: (0181) 760 0469. E-mail: expatnetwork@cityscape.co.uk.

Job Finder, F, Overseas Consultants, PO Box 152, Douglas, Isle of Man.

Home & Away, M, Expats International, 29 Lacon Road, London SE22 9HE. Tel: (0181) 299 4986.

The Expatriate, M, FMI Publishers Ltd, 175 Vauxhall Bridge Road, London SW1V 1ER. Tel: (0171) 233 8595. Fax: (0171) 233 8718.

Going USA, M., Outbound Newspapers, 1 Commercial Road, Eastbourne BN21 3XQ. Tel: (01323) 412001.

Expatriate Today, Q, Directory Profiles, 148 Upper Richmond Road West, London SW14 8DP. Tel: (0181) 392 2838).

Network, Q, 6 Fold Court, Chaddesley Corbett, Worcs DY19 4SA. Tel: (01562) 777124. Fax: (01562) 777125.

The Weekly Telegraph, W, PO Box 14, Harold Hill, Romford, Essex RM3 8EQ. Tel: (01708) 381000.

The International and *Resident Abroad*, M, Financial Times Magazines, Greystoke Place, Fetter Lane, London EC4A 1ND. Tel: (0171) 405 6969.

The Guardian Weekly, 164 Deansgate, Manchester M60 2RR. Tel: (0161) 832 7200.

*Includes job vacancies.

US newspapers

Virtually all US newspapers are regional papers. The few exceptions are:

Christian Science Monitor, 1 Norway Street, Boston, MA 02115; Eggington

House, 25–28 Buckingham Gate, London SW1E 6LD. Tel: (0171) 630 8666.

USA Today, 1000 Wilson Boulevard, Arlington, VA 22209.

Wall Street Journal, 200 Liberty Street, New York, NY 10281. Has four regional editions.

Leading local and regional newspapers which carry job advertisements are listed in Appendix G under the states in which they circulate.

Specialist US journals

(For a more comprehensive selection of journals see *Benn's International Media Guide* or *Ulrich's International Periodicals Directory*.)

Advertising Age, W, Crain Communications, 20–22 Bedford Row, London WC1R 4EB.

America's Textiles, M, Robert G Horsfield, Daisy Bank, Chinley, Stockport SK12 6DA. Tel: (01663) 50242.

American Banker, D, One State Street, Plaza, New York, NY 10004.

American Printer, M, Intertec Publishing, 29 N Wacker Street, Chicago, IL 60606.

Architectural Record, M, McGraw-Hill.

Automotive Engineering, M, 400 Commonwealth Drive, Warrendale, PA 15096. (UK rep: (0171) 834 7676.)

Aviation Daily, D, McGraw-Hill.

Broadcasting and Cable, W, Cahners.

Building Design and Construction, M, Cahners.

Business Week, W, McGraw Hill.

CPI Purchasing, M, Cahners. Purchasing for the chemical process industries.

Chemical and Engineering News, W, Technomedia. (UK rep: (01734) 343302.)

Chemical Week (Chemical Wk Assoc.). (UK rep: (0171) 430 2900.).

Civil Engineering, M, E 47th Street, New York, NY 10017-2.

Coal Week, McGraw Hill. Includes metallurgy, mining and petroleum.

Computerworld Newspaper, W, CW Communications, Box 880, 375 Cochituate Road, Framingham, MA 01701. (UK rep: (0171) 978 1440).

Construction Equipment, M, Cahners.

Construction Products, M, Cahners.

Consulting-Specifying Engineer, M, Cahners. Mechanical/electrical/ electronic system design engineers for construction industry.

Contractor, M, Cahners. Airconditioning, heating and plumbing.

Control Engineering, M, Cahners.

Daily Variety, D, Cahners. Entertainment.

Data Communications, M, McGraw-Hill.

Datamation, F, Cahners. Information processing.

Design News, F, Cahners. Design engineers in the original equipment market.

Digital Review, W, Cahners. DEC computing.

Editor and Publisher, W, 11 W 19th St, New York, NY 10011.

Electric Utility Week, W, McGraw-Hill.

Electric Construction and Maintenance, M, Intertech Publishing, 29 N Wacker Street, Chicago, IL 60606.

Electrical World, M, McGraw-Hill.

Electronic Packaging and Production, M, Cahners. Design and production of electronic circuits, products and equipment.

Emergency Medicine, F, Cahners.

Engineering News-Record, W, McGraw-Hill.

Furniture Today, W, Cahners.

Graphic Arts Monthly, Cahners. Printing, typesetting, binding, etc.

Hospital Medicine, M, Cahners.

Hotels, M, Cahners.

Industrial Distribution, M, Cahners.

Industry Week, W, Penton.

Interior Design, M, Cahners.

Library Journal, F, Cahners.

Modern Materials Handling, M, Cahners.

Modern Plastics, McGraw-Hill.

Nursingworld Journal, M, 470 Boston Post Road, Weston, MA 02193.

Packaging, M, Cahners.

Plant Engineering, F, Cahners.

Plastics News, W, Crain Communications.

Power, M, McGraw-Hill.

Printing News/East, W, Cahners. Printing and allied industries in Greater New York.

Publishers Weekly, Cahners.

Purchasing Magazine, F, Cahners.

Restaurants and Institutions, F, Cahners.

Security, M, Cahners. Security and loss prevention operations.

Security Distributing and Marketing, M, Cahners.

Semiconductor International, M, Cahners.

Textile World, M, UK Rep: John Maycock Associates. Tel (0114) 266 7050.

Traffic Management, M, Cahners.

Variety, F, Cahners. Entertainment.

Publishers

Cahners Publishing Company is a division of Elsevier Reed Publishing and has an office in the UK: 27 Paul Street, London EC2A 4JU. Tel: (0171) 628 7030. Its HQ in the USA is 275 Washington Street, Newton, MA 02158. Tel: 617 964 3030.

McGraw Hill, Wimbledon Bridge House, 1 Hartfield Road, London SW19 3RU. Tel: (0181) 543 1234.

Penton Publishing, 1100 Superior Avenue, Cleveland OH 44114. Publish a wide range of industrial titles. UK Rep: (01295) 271003.

Ziff-Davis Publishing, One Park Ave, New York, NY 10016 publish a number of aerospace and computing titles. (Seymour Press, 334 Brixton Road, London SW9 7AG. Tel: (0171) 733 4444.)

Romaine Pierson Publishers, 80 Shore Road, Port Washington, NY 11050 publish a range of journals of interest to the medical profession.

US job lists

Academic Journal, M, Brookfield Publishing Co, PO Box 221, Brookfield Center, CT 06805.

California Connections, F, California Connections Publications, Box 90396, Long Beach, CA 90809. Directory of private and public sector employment opportunities.

Career Opportunities News, B, Garrett Park Press, PO Box 1901, Garrett Park, MD 20896.

Career Resource Guide and Digest, National College Placement Association, PO Box 5112, Mill Valley, CA 94942.

Community Jobs, M, Community Career Resource Center, 1516 P Street NW, Washington, DC 20005.

Employment Listings for the Social Services, 10 Angelica Drive, Framingham, MA 01701.

Environmental Opportunities, PO Box 670, Walpole, NH 03608.

Federal Career Opportunities, Federal Research Services, 370 Maple Avenue W, Box 1059, Vienna, VA 22180.

Federal Employment Bulletin, PO Box 11715, Washington, DC 20008.

Insurance and Financial Services Careers, A, Wallace Witmer Co, PO Box 40169, 1509 Madison Avenue, Memphis, TN 34174.

Job Bulletin, M, Association for Women in Science, 1522 K St NW, Washington, DC 20005.

Job Openings, US Government Printing Office, Washington, DC 20402.

Job Openings for Economists, American Economics Association, 2014 Broadway, Nashville, TN 37203-2418.

ML Job Information Lists, Modern Language Association, 10 Astor Place, 5th Floor, New York, NY 10003.

National Business Employment Weekly, 420 Lexington Avenue, New York, NY 10170.

National Employment Listing Service for the Criminal Justice System and Social Services, Criminal Justice Center, Sam Houston State University, Huntsville, TX 77341.

NRPA Job Bulletin, National Recreation and Park Association, 2775 S Quincy St, Arlington, VA 22206-2204.

Occupations in Demand at Job Service Offices, Consumer Information Center, Pueblo, CO 81009.

Teacher Vacancy List, M, National Education Selection, 189 Clifford Street, Newark, NJ 07105.

For a more comprehensive list of journals that carry employment advertising, please refer to *900,000 Plus Jobs Annually—Published Sources of Employment Listings*, S. N. Feingold and G. A. Hansard-Winkler (Garrett Park Press).

Miscellaneous

Occupational Outlook Quarterly, Bureau of Labor Statistics, US Dept of Labor. Articles on jobs and job prospects.

Career World, Curriculum Innovations Inc, 3500 Western Ave, Highland Park, IL 60035. Career guides.

Careers Magazine, 1001 Avenue of the Americas, New York, NY 10018. Quarterly magazine aimed at schools.

US Employment Opportunities–Career News Service. Washington Research Associates, 2103 N Lincoln St, Arlington, VA 22207. Annual with quarterly updates.

Career Opportunities News (bi-monthly), Garrett Park Press.

Appendix E
Job Applications

You may have discovered the ideal job opportunity, but that is only the first step on the road to landing the job. Along the way you have to convince the employer of your suitability for the post, which means presenting yourself in a positive light from the very first contact.

In a competitive jobs market modesty and reticence have to be abandoned if you are to propel yourself to the interview stage. Americans on the whole tend to be good at selling themselves, and you need to take a leaf out of their book.

Get off on the right foot with documentation that looks good and reads well. Use good quality notepaper of A4 size, and either type or word-process your correspondence unless your handwriting is exceptionally neat and legible.

An increasing number of people now understand what it takes to make an effective application. For those who are unsure of the process this section offers a few pointers.

Answering an advertisement

The agency or employer will often request a CV, or 'résumé' in American parlance. You should include a covering letter with it as a matter of course since this gives you an opportunity to draw attention to your strong points.

The letter should set out:

- WHY you want the job
- WHAT qualifications and experience you have
- HOW you measure up to the job description.

CV or résumé?

In the United States you do not submit a CV (personal history) but

Tel: 011 44 71 111 9999

20 Balmoral Avenue
London W19 1ZZ
United Kingdom

February 29, 199X

Caroline North
Vice-President, Human Resources
Iowa Investment Bank, Inc.
5432 Maine Street,
Shenandoah, IA 50300
USA

Dear Ms North,

I wish to apply for the post of international business manager of your organisation as advertised in the *Red Oak Daily Tribune*. I believe this is a challenging post which will offer me scope to make full use of my extensive financial skills.

Since graduating in Economics from the London School of Economics I have worked for a prestigious merchant bank in the City of London and have been promoted twice. I have gained experience in share dealing, investment management and international financing, and have made several successful foreign business trips on behalf of the bank, particularly to Brussels, Frankfurt and Paris.

With my sound knowledge of the European banking scene I believe I am well placed to assist you in your plans to increase your international profile. I am, incidentally, familiar with United States banking practice having done a three month placement with the New York firm of Goldschmidt and Silber three years back.

I very much look forward to meeting you in order to discuss your requirements in depth.

Sincerely yours,

James E Stuart

Fig. 18. Sample application letter.

181

a résumé, which is almost the same thing, but not quite. Generally speaking, a British style CV offers more information than an American style résumé, because federal and state laws designed to combat discrimination in the workplace restrict the type of information that should be divulged to an employer (*eg* age, sex, race, religion).

American employers appreciate the much fuller British style CVs, and if you are applying to an address on this side of the Atlantic you should not hesitate to submit a full-blown CV. If you are applying within the US you should proceed with caution; to include details of your age, date of birth, sex and family status, or to enclose a photograph, might contravene state laws on equal employment rights and render your application invalid.

Your CV/résumé should be concise, typed and, if possible, tailored to the job you are after. Ideally, it should cover no more than one sheet of A4 paper. If your career has been rich and varied, you may have to compromise by providing a one-page summary of your career followed by a more extended version.

There are broadly speaking two types of résumé:

- The chronological CV/résumé which details the positions you have held in chronological (or reverse chronological) order and is by far the commoner of the two;

- The functional CV/résumé which presents your work experience in terms of skills and responsibilities.

A typical chronological CV/résumé should contain the following information.

- Your name, address for correspondence and contact telephone number(s). A fax number or E-mail address is also useful.

- Your job objective. This is often included in American résumés as a matter of course, and might be quite a good idea for a speculative application.

- Your career: positions held, employers, dates. It is quite common in the UK to begin with your present job and work backward.

- Your education and qualifications. Make sure that the latter are comprehensible to an American who may not have a clue what MIMM, FCIS, AIBA or different classes of degree stand for. People near the beginning of their careers may prefer to put details of their education and qualifications before the career section.

- Other details: membership of professional associations, public offices held, hobbies (within reason), additional skills.

Regard your résumé as your personal sales brochure and be prepared to blow your own trumpet. You need to present a positive image to potential employers.

The interview

Before the interview make sure you are fully clued up about the organisation you are going to visit. If details are hard to come by, ring up the public relations officer and ask for a brochure or a copy of the annual report.

There are certain golden rules to observe during the interview:

- be on time
- dress smartly
- be natural
- look at the interviewer
- be polite
- stay calm
- draw attention to your strengths.

Remember that you need to convince your prospective employer that:

- you have a positive attitude to the job and organisation
- you will be both punctual and regular in attendance
- you enjoy good health
- you have relevant experience
- you are a person who can be relied on
- you can adapt to the requirements of the organisation and job.

Follow up letter

Courtesy can pay dividends in the long run. After the interview it is a good idea to send a letter to the interviewer, thanking him for seeing you and confirming that you are still interested in the job. In order to speed up delivery you might consider sending your message by fax.

Owen Gwynedd

Address: 20 Caernarfon Street, Llangarth, Wales LH1 1BB
Telephone: (0123) 987654 (evenings and weekends); (0123) 456789
               (daytime)
Date of Birth: 31 November 1962
Birthplace: Pwllheli, North Wales
Family Status: Married with one child
Nationality: British

Education and Qualifications:
1973–80   Llywelyn Fawr School, Cardiff
               5 O Levels; A Levels in Welsh, Physics
1980–82   Bleddyn ap Cynfyn Technical College, Bala
               Higher National Diploma in Mechanical Engineering
1982–83   Institute of Petroleum Studies, Aberdeen
               Certificate in Drilling Rig Maintenance

Employment Record:
1983–87   Welsh Petroleum Co, Harlech, Wales
               Maintenance Engineer on an offshore drilling rig
               operating off the Lleyn Peninsula
1987–90   Antrim Exploration Ltd, Ballymena, N Ireland
               Chief Driller with the Abu Dhabi project
1990–now   Instructor in oil rig maintenance

Interests:
Rugby Football
Choral Singing
Collecting antiques

Other Information:
Excellent health
Willingness to relocate
Clean PSV driving licence
Member of Professional Society of Oil Rig Operatives
Languages: Welsh, Arabic
Overseas experience: Spain, Abu Dhabi, Oman

Fig. 19. Sample British style CV.

Résumé of
Elisabeth Mary Tudor

14 Leicester Terrace
Raleigh
Essex ES1 2YY
United Kingdom
Tel: 011 44 911 98765

JOB OBJECTIVE: Features Editor

EMPLOYMENT

1989–present   Assistant Editor, *Historic Britain* magazine
Leicester Publishing, Windsor, Berks, UK.
Edited articles; liaised with printers and designers;
dealt with enquiries; assisted with promotions

1988–89   Editorial Assistant,
Boleyn Books, Sydney, Australia.
Assisted with copy editing, general office duties, as
well as promotional work.

ADDITIONAL EXPERIENCE

Reporter for college newspaper.
Vacation employment as assistant manager of a
fashion boutique in Raleigh.
Vacation employment as a market research
interviewer.

EDUCATION

1987–88   Greenwich Polytechnic, London, UK
Diploma in Publishing.

1983–1987   University of St Albans, UK
BA in History

1976–1983   Shakespeare High School, Southwark, London, UK
General Certificate of Education A Levels
(equiv. post-high school diploma) in History,
Latin, Mathematics and Zoology

ADDITIONAL INFORMATION

Fluent in French and Italian
Typing speed: 50 words a minute
Driving licence
Member of Guild of Publishing Assistants

Fig. 20. Sample chronological résumé

Richard Gloucester

HOME ADDRESS	CURRENT ADDRESS
26 Clarence Drive	9872 York Blvd
Buckingham, BX90 9XX	Bosworth
Great Britain	OK 98765
Tel: 011 44 111 22222	Tel: 888 999 7777

JOB OBJECTIVE:
>Senior position in either the sales or training division of a progressive telecommunication company.

MANAGEMENT EXPERIENCE
>Managed Middle East sales team of Stanley Telecommunications, and increased our exports to the area by 50 per cent in three years. Supervised the installation of telephone exchanges in Yemen and Qatar.

SALES EXPERIENCE
>Planned several sales campaigns within the UK for Brakenbury Industrial which led to a considerable increase in profits.
>Streamlined customer after-sales service for Brakenbury which led to a significant increase in repeat orders.
>Sold telecommunications equipment to seven countries in the Middle East, more than doubling company turnover in this area.

TRAINING EXPERIENCE
>Instructed apprentices at Stanley Communications in basic electrical skills, gaining a national training award for the firm.
>Lectured part-time in telecommunications engineering at Ratcliff Technical College. Several of my students went on to higher education.
>Devised and directed training programme for export sales department of Brakenbury Industrial.

EDUCATION
>Higher National Diploma in Telecommunications (post high school diploma) from Rivers College, Richmond, Yorkshire, UK.
>City and Guilds Certificate in Supervisory Management (by correspondence).

OTHER DETAILS
>Member of British Institute of Management
>Treasurer of Oxford branch of the Lions Club
>Hobbies: Football, gliding and rallying

Fig. 21. Sample functional résumé.

Tel: (555) 666 7777   3605 Sunset Strip
                                              Aquitaine
                                              WV 54321

                                              July 4, 199X

Mr R D Franklin
Adams Lincoln Inc
519 Hayes Blvd
Arcadia
FL 00999

Dear Mr Franklin,

I am a robotics design engineer and keen to make full use of my skills and experience. As I know that Adams Lincoln is a world leader in this field, I wonder if you expect to have any vacancies in the near future.

Let me tell you a little about myself. After graduating in computer science from Oxford University, England, I studied for a Master's degree in Robotics at York University, England. I then took a position as a development officer at the National Robotics Research Institute in Much Hadham, and was involved in pioneering the use of robots in mountain bike manufacture. One of my inventions was a runner up in the European Robotics Awards earlier this year.

I am now keen to apply my knowledge within a commercial organisation and to learn more about the state of robotics technology in the United States. I intend to visit Florida during the coming month and would like to take the opportunity to call on you—with no obligation on either side.

I will telephone you when I arrive in the States to arrange an appointment.

Sincerely yours,

Henry Plantagenet

Enc. Résumé

Fig. 22. Sample speculative letter.

Tel: 011 44 987 6543

91 Battlefield Close
Hastings HS9 7JJ, UK
December 16, 199X

Mr T Jefferson
President
Colorado Computing Services
1490 Island Road
Miles City, MT 59600

Dear Mr Jefferson,

Thank you for seeing me yesterday during your visit to London. I enjoyed learning about your organisation and the new developments you are planning, and confirm that I am still keen to join your staff.

I hope that your trip proved worthwhile and you had a pleasant flight back to the US. Please let me know if you require any further information from me.

Yours sincerely,

William Norman

Tel: (123) 456 7890

156 Marlborough Heights
Halle, IL 77755
7/24/9X

Mr W Wilson
Director of Human Resources
Alabama Associates
Fort Carolina, TX 12345

Dear Mr Wilson,

Thank you for your letter of July 20 regarding my application for a position.

I enjoyed my visit to your firm which is clearly poised for an exciting future, and would like to thank all those who met me.

I am naturally sorry that you saw fit to appoint another person. Nevertheless, I hope you will keep my details on file in case another vacancy occurs in the future for which I would be better suited.

Sincerely yours,
George Hanover

Fig. 21. Sample follow-up letters.

If you know by this time that you have not been selected, mention that you would be glad to be considered for any future vacancies that may occur.

Appendix F
Useful Addresses: United Kingdom

Aaronson & Co, 308 Earls Court Road, London SW5 9BA. Tel: (0171) 373 9516. Fax: (0171) 835 1014. (Immigration lawyers.)

American Chamber of Commerce, 75 Brook Street, London W1Y 2EB. Tel: (0171) 493 0381. (Has small reference library, but appointments to use it have to be made in advance.)

Amertrans, Bushey Mill Lane, Watford, WD2 4JG. Tel: (01923) 54444. Fax: (01923) 2233555. (International removers.)

Animal Aunts, 45 Fairview Road, Headley Down, Hants GU35 3HQ. Tel: (01428) 712611 (Offers pet and house-minding service.)

Association of Temporary and Interim Executive Services, 36–38 Mortimer Street, London W1N 7RB. Tel (0171) 323 4300.

BBC World Service, PO Box 76, Bush House, Strand, London WC2B 4PH. Tel: (0171) 240 7790 (Publishes *London Calling*, a monthly bulletin of radio and TV programmes transmitted throughout the world and the magazine *BBC Worldwide*.)

BCL Immigration Services, 40 South Audley Street, Mayfair, London W1Y 5DH. Tel: (0171) 495 3999. Fax: (0171) 495 3991. E-mail: sanwar@bclimser.demon.co.uk. (Immigration consultant.)

British American Chamber for Commerce, 10 Lower John Street, London W1R 3PE. Tel: (0171) 287 2676.

British Association for Counselling, 1 Regent Place, Rugby CV21 2PJ. Tel: (01788) 578328.

British Association of Executive Search Consultants, 24 St James's Square, London SW1Y 4HZ. Tel (0171) 839 7788.

British Association of Removers, 3 Churchill Court, Station Road, North Harrow HA2 7SA. Tel: (0181) 861 3331. Fax: (0181) 861 3332.

British Overseas Trade Board (BOTB), Department of Trade and Industry, 1 Victoria Street, London SW1H 0ET. Tel: (0171) 215 5000.

Brown Shipley Lomond Ltd, 84 Coombe Road, New Malden, Surrey. Tel: (0181) 949 8811. (Financial advisers.)

BUPA Expacare, Russell Mews, Brighton BN1 2NR. Tel: (01273) 208181. (Health insurance.)

California State Office, 27 Dover Street, London W1X 3PA. Tel: (0171) 629 8211. Fax: (0171) 629 8223.

Career Development Centre for Women, 97 Mallard Place, Twickenham, Middlesex TW1 4SW. Tel: (0181) 892 3806.

CBI Employee Relocation Council, Centre Point, 103 New Oxford Street, London WC1A 1DV. Tel: (0171) 379 7400. Fax: (0171) 240 1578. (Advises companies moving staff; publishes *Relocation News*.)

Centre for International Briefing, Farnham Castle, Surrey GU9 0AG. Tel: (01252) 721194. Fax: (01252) 711283.

Christians Abroad, 1 Stockwell Green, London SW9 9HP. Tel: (0171) 737 7811. (Advice and contacts for people moving abroad.)

Company Pension Information Centre, 7 Old Park Lane, London W1Y 3LJ.

Council for the Accreditation of Correspondence Colleges, 27 Marylebone Road, London NW1 5JS. Tel: (0171) 935 5391.

Davies Turner, 334 Queenstown Road, London SW8 4HG. Tel: (0171) 622 9361. Fax: (0171) 622 6688. (International removers.)

Dean Associates, 51 High Street, Emsworth, Hants PO10 7AN. Tel: (01243) 378022. (Educational information on day schooling for the children of families living abroad temporarily.)

Department of Health Leaflets Unit, PO Box 21, Honeypot Lane, Stanmore, Middx HA7 1AY. Tel (0800) 555777.

Department of Social Security, Overseas Branch, Benton Park Road, Newcastle upon Tyne, NE98 1YX. Tel: (0191) 213 5000.

Department of Trade and Industry, Exports to North America Branch, Kingsgate House, 66–74 Victoria Street, London SW1E 6SW. Tel: (0171) 215 4601.

ECIS (European Council for International Schools), 21 Lavant Street, Petersfield, Hants GU32 3EW. Tel: (01230) 68244. Fax: (01730) 67914. (Publishes a directory of international schools.)

Economist Subscription Fulfilment Service, PO Box 14, Harold Hill, Romford RM3 8EQ. Tel: (014023) 81555. Fax: (014023) 81211.

Employment Conditions Abroad, Anchor House, 15 Britten Street, London SW3 3TY. Tel: (0171) 351 7151. (Briefings and country reports.)

Europea IMG, Fivash House, 9 Denne Parade, Horsham RH12 1JD. Tel: (01403) 63860. (Medical insurance.)

Exeter Friendly Society, Beech Hill House, Walnut Gardens, Exeter EX4 4DG. Tel: (01392) 498063. (Medical insurance.)

Expatriate Advisory Services, 14 Gordon Road, West Bridgeford, Nottingham NG2 5LN. Tel: (0115) 9816572. Fax: (0115) 9455076. (Financial advisers.)

Expat Network, 500 Purley Way, Croydon CR0 4NZ. Tel: (0181) 760 5100. Fax: (0181) 760 0469. (Expatriate service organisation.)

Expats International, 29 Lacon Road, London SE22 9HE. Tel: (0181) 299 4986. (Expatriate service organisation.)

Federation of Recruitment and Employment Services, 36–38 Mortimer Street, London W1N 7RB. Tel: (0171) 323 4300.

Gary M. Ferman, 19/20 Grosvenor Street, London W1X 9FD. Tel: (0171) 499 5702. Fax: (0171) 236 2533. (Immgration lawyer.)

Florida Government Office, 18–24 Westbourne Grove, London W2 5RH. Tel: (0171) 727 8388. Fax: (0171) 792 8633.

Wilfred T Fry Ltd, Crescent House, Crescent Road, Worthing BN11 1RN. Tel: (01903) 23145. Fax: (01903) 200868. (Financial advisers.)

Gabbitas Educational Consultants, Carrington House, 126–130 Regent Street, London W1R 6EE. Tel: (0171) 439 2071. Fax: (0171) 437 1764.

Global International Fowarding Ltd, 16 Perivale Industrial Park, Greenford UB6 7RW. Tel: (0181) 997 4321. (International removers.)

Going Places, 80 Coombe Road, New Malden, Surrey KT3 4QS. Tel: (0181) 949 8811. (Briefings.)

Golden Arrow Shippers, Horsford Kennels, Lydbury North, Shropshire SY7 8AY. Tel: (015888) 240. (Pet transportation experts.)

Richard S. Goldstein, 20 Stratton Street, Mayfair, London W1X 5FL. Tel: (0171) 491 6675. Fax: (0171) 629 7900. (Immigration lawyer. Also New York.)

Gudeon & Farrell, 181 Kensington High Street, London W8 6SH. Tel: (0171) 937 1542. Fax: (0171) 493 7915. (Immigration lawyers.)

Hall-Godwins (Overseas) Consulting Co., Briarcliff House, Kingsmead, Farnborough, Hants GU14 7TE. Tel: (01252) 5217071. (Financial advisers.)

Healthsearch Ltd, 9 Newland Street, Rugby CV22 7BL. Tel: (01788) 541855. (Advice on healthcare plans.)

Diane B. Hinch, 24 Grosvenor Street, London W1X 9FB. Tel: (0171) 917 9680. Fax: (0171) 917 6002. (Immigration lawyer. Also California.)

Homesitters Ltd, The Old Bakery, Western Road, Tring, Herts HP23 4BB. Tel: (01442) 891188. (Caretaking service.)

Hylton Potts, 7 Cheval Place, Knightsbridge, London SW7 1EW. Tel: (0171) 225 1881. Fax: (0171) 584 3751. (Immigration lawyer.)

Inland Revenue Claims Branch, Foreign Division, Merton Road, Bootle L69 9BL.

ISIS (Independent Schools Information Service), 56 Buckingham Gate, London SW1E 6AG. Tel: (0171) 630 8793.

Institute of Freight Forwarders, Redfern House, Browells Lane, Feltham, Middlesex. Tel: (0181) 844 2266.

LaVigne & Lane PA, 150 Minories, London EC3N 1LS. Tel: (0171) 264 2110. Fax: (0171) 264 2107. (Immigration lawyer. Also in Orlando, Florida.)

Leeson's Employment and Accommodation Data Services (LEADS), 4 Cranley Road, Ilford, Essex IG2 6AG. Tel: (0181) 554 0232. (Employment services for migrants.)

Manor Car Storage, PO Box 28, Clavering, Saffron Walden, Essex CB11 4RA. Tel: (01799) 550021.

Mercers College, Ware, Herts SG12 9BU. Tel: (01920) 465926. (Correspondence courses for children.)

New York State Government Office, 25 Haymarket, London SW1Y 1PY. Tel: (0171) 839 5079. Fax: (0171) 839 5401.

Nexus Business Publications, Warwick House, Swanley, Kent BR8 8HY. Tel: (01322) 660070. (Publishers of *Independent and Boarding Schools World Handbook*.)

Overseas Resettlement Secretary, Board for Social Responsibility, Church House, Dean's Yard, London SW1P 3NZ. Tel: (0171) 222 9011. (Can arrange contacts at destination.)

Par Air Services, Warren Lane, Colchester, Essex CO3 5LN. Tel: (01206) 330332. (Pet shipping agents.)

PPP, Crescent Road, Tunbridge Wells TN1 2PL. Tel: (01892) 40111. Fax: (01892) 510102. (Health insurance.)

Joel Z. Robinson, 4 Helmet Row, London EC1V 3QV. Tel: (0171) 253 2404. Fax: (0171) 253 0760. (Immigration lawyer. Also New York.)

Walter F. Rudeloff, 4 King's Walk, London EC4Y 7DL. Tel: (0171) 267 1297. Fax: (0171) 267 1297. (Immigration lawyer.)

SFIA (School Fees Insurance Agency) Educational Trust Ltd, SFIA House, 15 Forlease Road, Maidenhead, Berks SL6 1JA. Tel: (01628) 34291. (Publishers of *The Parent's Guide to Independent Schools.*)

Society of Pensions Consultants, Ludgate House, Ludgate Circus, London EC4A 2AB. Tel: (0171) 353 1688.

Stan Steinger, Macmillan House, 95 Kensington High Street, London W8 4SG. Tel: (0171) 937 7733. Fax: (0171) 937 8185. (Immigration lawyer. Also California and Iowa.)

TraQs Consulting, Riding Court Road, Datchet, Berks SL3 9LE. Tel: (01753) 582020. (Tax planning software.)

David Turner, 12 Queen Anne Street, London W1M 0AU. Tel: (0171) 437 3806. Fax: (0171) 310 1644. E-mail: dtplus@dircon.co.uk. (Immigration lawyer.)

TSW Tax Consultants, 66 New Bond Street, London W1Y 9DF. Tel: (0171) 491 2535.

UK Expatriates Professional Advisory Services Ltd, 84 Grange Road, Middlesborough TS1 2LS. Tel: (01642) 221211 (Tax advisers.)

United States Embassy, 42 Elgin Street, Ballsbridge, Dublin. Tel: (Dublin) 688777.

United States Embassy, 24 Grosvenor Square, London W1A 2JB. Tel: (0171) 499 9000.

Visa Branch, 5 Upper Grosvenor Street, London W1A 2JB. Tel: (0171) 499 7010. General information line: 0891 200290.

US Information Service, 55/56 Upper Brook Street, London W1A 2LH. Tel: (0171) 408 8060.

United States Consulate-General, Queen's House, Queen Street, Belfast BT1 6EQ. Tel: (01232) 328239. (Has Visa Office.)

United States Consulate-General, 3 Regent Terrace, Edinburgh EH7 5BW. Tel: (0131) 556 8315. Fax: (0131) 557 6023.

Visit USA Association: Tel: 0891 600530. (Travel information.)

US-UK Educational Commission, 62 Doughty Street, London WC1N 2LS. Tel: (0171) 404 6994.

US Visa Consultants, 27 York Street, London W1H 1PY. Tel: (0171) 224 3629. Fax: (0171) 224 3859.

Walker & Walker Emigration, 24 Church Street, Kirkby in Ashfield, Nottingham NG17 8LE. Tel: (0115) 9753240.

Women's Corona Society, c/o Commonwealth Institute, Kensington High
   Street, London W8 6NQ. Tel: (0171) 610 4407.
WES Home School, St George's House, 14–17 Wells Street, London W1P
   3FP. Tel: (0171) 637 2644.

For a futher list of immigration lawyers and consultants please consult
Obtaining Visas and Work Permits (How To Books).

Appendix G
Useful Addresses: United States

National

American Automobile Association, 1000 AAA Drive, Heathrow, FL 32746.

American Council on International Personnel, 515 Madison Avenue, 15th Floor, New York, NY 10022. (Advice on the employment of aliens.)

Association of Executive Search Consultants, 230 Park Ave, Suite 1549, New York, NY 10169.

British American Chamber of Commerce, 52 Vanderbolt Avenue, New York, NY 10017. Similar organisations in California and Florida.

British Embassy, 3100 Massachusetts Ave NW, Washington, DC 20009. British Consulates in California (Los Angeles, San Francisco), Florida (Miami), Georgia (Atlanta), Illinois (Chicago), Massachusetts (Boston), New York, Texas (Dallas, Houston), Washington State (Seattle).

Catalyst, 250 Park Ave S, 5th Floor, New York, NY 10003-1459.

Department of Commerce, 14th St and Constitution Ave, Washington, DC 20230.

Department of Health and Human Services, 200 Independence Avenue SW, Washington, DC 20201.

Department of Labor, 200 Constitution Ave, Washington, DC 20210.

Equal Employment Opportunity Commission, 1801 L Street, NW, Washington, DC 20507.

Health Insurance Association of America, Suite 8802, 555 13th Street, NW, Washington, DC 20570. Publications are available from HIAA Fulfillment, PO Box 41455, Washington, DC 20018.

Intercristo, Christian Placement Network, 19303 Fremont Avenue N, Seattle, WA 98133. (Job placement service.)

Internal Revenue Service, PO Box 25866, Richmond, VA 23289; Rancho Cordova, CA 95743-0001; PO Box 9903, Bloomington, IL 61799. People living outside the US can contact IRS at the nearest US Embassy or the Assistant Commissioner International, IRS, 950 L'Enfant Plaza South SW, Washington, DC 20024.

International Association of Counseling Services, 101 South Whiting Street, Suite 211, Alexandria VA 22304.

Irish Embassy, 2234 Massachusetts Avenue NW, Washington, DC 20008. Tel: 202 462 3939.

National Association of Corporate and Professional Recruiters, 4000 Woodstone Way, Louisville, KY 40241.

National Association of Executive Recruiters, 222 S Westmonte Drive, Suite 101, Altamonte Springs, FL 32714.

National Association of Personnel Services, 3133 Mt Vernon Ave, Alexandria, VA 22305.

National Association of Temporary Services, 119 South Saint Asaph St, Alexandria, VA 22314.

National Employment Counselors Association, 5999 Stevenson Avenue, Alexandria, VA 22304.

National Labor Relations Board, 1717 Pennsylvania Avenue NW, Washington, DC 20570.

National Park Service, Room 1013, US Department of the Interior, 18th and C Street NW, Washington, DC 20240.

US Customs Service, PO Box 7118, Washington, DC 20044. Also at US Embassy, London.

US Forest Service, US Department of Agriculture, PO Box 69090, 14th and Independence Avenue, Washington, DC 20250.

US Small Business Administration, PO Box 1000, Fort Worth, TX 76119; 409 3rd Street, SW, Washington, DC 20416. Website: www.sbaonline.sba.gov.

40 Plus Clubs, 1718 P Street NW, Washington, DC 20036.

By state

Alabama

Birmingham News, 2200 4th Av N, Birmingham, AL 35202-25533.

Huntsville Times, Box 1007, Huntsville, AL 35807-5501.

Montgomery Advertiser, Box 1000, Montgomery, AL 36101-1000.

Department of Economic and Community Affairs, 3465 Norman Bridge Road, Montgomery, AL 36105.

Department of Education, State Office Bldg, Montgomery, AL 36130.

Employment Services Division, Department of Industrial Relations, 649 Monroe St, Montgomery, AL 36130.

Department of Labor, 64 N Union St, Montgomery, AL 36130.

Department of Revenue, Gordon Persons Bldg, Montgomery, AL 36130.

Birmingham Chamber of Commerce, PO Box 10127, Birmingham, AL 35202.

Montgomery Area Chamber of Commerce, PO Box 79, 41 Commerce St, Montgomery, AL 36101.

Alaska

Anchorage Daily News, Box 149001, Anchorage, AK 99514-9001.

INS District Office, Room 401, 632 West 6th Ave, Anchorage, AK 99501.

Alaska Industrial Development Authority, 1577 C St, Suite 304, Anchorage, AK 99501.

Department of Education, PO Box F, Juneau, AK 99811.

Division of Employment Services, Department of Labor, PO Box 3-7000, Juneau, AK 99802.

Department of Labor, PO Box 1149, Juneau, AK 99802.

Department of Revenue, PO Box S, Juneau, AK 99811.

Anchorage Chamber of Commerce, 415 F Street, Anchorage, AK 99501-2254.

Juneau Chamber of Commerce, 1107 W 8th St, Juneau, AK 99802.

Arizona

Arizona Republic, Box 1950, 120 E Van Buren St, Phoenix, AZ 85034.

Arizona Daily Star, 4850 S Park Ave, Tucson, AZ 85726.

INS District Office, Federal Building, 230 North First Ave, Phoenix, AZ 85025.

Department of Commerce, 1700 W Washington, 4th Floor, W Wing, State Capitol, Phoenix, AZ 85007.

Department of Education, 1535 W Jefferson, Phoenix, AZ 85007.

Employment Services Division, Department of Economic Security, 1300 W Washington, Phoenix, AZ 85005.

Industrial Commission, 800 W Washington, Phoenix, AZ 85005.

Department of Revenue, 1600 W Monroe, 9th Fl, Phoenix, AZ 85007.

Phoenix Metropolitan Chamber of Commerce, 34 W Monroe St, Phoenix, AZ 85003.

Arkansas

Arkansas Democrat, Box 2221, Capitol Ave, Little Rock, AR 72203.

Department of Education, Capitol Mall, Little Rock, AR 72201.

Employment Security Division, Department of Labor, Capitol Mall, Little Rock, AR 72201.

Department of Labor, 10421 W Markham #100, Little Rock, AR 72205.

Industrial Development Comm, 1 Capitol Mall, Little Rock, AR 72201.

Revenue Division, Ledbetter Bldg, Seventh and Wolf Street, Little Rock, AR 72201.

Greater Little Rock Chamber of Commerce, 1 Spring St, Little Rock, AR 72201.

California

Bakersfield Californian, Box 440, Bakersfield, CA 93302.

British Weekly, 1626 North Wilcox Ave, #337, Hollywood, CA 90028. UK Rep: Gibbs House, Kennel Ride, Ascot, Berks SL5 7NT.

Fresno Bee, 1626 E St, Fresno, CA 93786.

Press Telegraph, 604 Pine Ave, Long Beach, CA 90844.

Los Angeles Times, Times-Mirror Square, Los Angeles, CA 90053.

Tribune, 409 13th St, Oakland, CA 94612.

Sacramento Union, 301 Capitol Mall, Sacramento, CA 95812.

San Diego Union, Box 191, San Diego, CA 92112.

San Francisco Chronicle, 925 Mission St, San Francisco, CA 94103.
San Francisco Examiner, 925 Mission St, San Francisco, CA 94103.
San Jose Mercury News, 750 Ridder Park Drive, San Jose, CA 95190.
Orange County Register, 625 N Grand Ave, Santa Ana, CA 92711.
Union Jack Newspaper, PO Box 1823, La Mes, CA 91944-1823.
Wall Street Journal, 6500 Wilshire Blvd, Suite 1400, Los Angeles, CA 90048.
British Consulates: Suite 312, 3701 Wilshire Boulevard, Los Angeles, CA
    90010. Tel: 213 385 7381; 1 Sansome Street, Suite 850, San Francisco,
    CA 94101. Tel: 415 981 3030.
British American Chamber of Commerce, c/o Barclay's Bank, 3150 California
    Street, San Francisco, CA 94115.
INS Regional Office, Terminal Island, San Pedro, CA 90731.
INS Western Service Center, 2400 Avila Rd, 2nd Floor, Laguna Nigual, CA
    92677. Tel: 714 643 4880.
INS District Offices: 300 N Los Angeles St, Los Angeles, CA 90012; 880
    Front Street, San Diego, CA 92188; Appraisers Building, 630 Sansome
    St, San Francisco, CA 94111.
Department of Commerce, 1121 L Street, Suite 600, Sacramento, CA 95814.
    London Office: 27 Dover Street, London W1X 3PA. Tel: (0171) 629
    8211.
Department of Education, 721 Capitol Mall, Sacramento, CA 95814.
Employment Development Department, 800 Capitol Mall, Sacramento, CA
    95814.
US Dept of Labor, 71 Stevenson Street, San Francisco, CA 94119.
Department of Industrial Relations, 455 Golden Gate Ave, San Francisco,
    CA 94102; 1121 L St, Sacramento, CA 95814.
Department of Revenue, PO Box 1468, Sacramento, CA 95807.
Hollywood Chamber of Commerce, 6255 Sunset Blvd, PO Box 2068,
    Hollywood, CA 90028.
Los Angeles Area Chamber of Commerce, 404 South Bixel St, Los Angeles,
    CA 90017.
Metropolitan Sacramento Chamber of Commerce, 917 Seventh St, Sacra-
    mento, CA 95814.
Greater San Diego Chamber of Commerce, 110 West St, Suite 1600, San
    Diego, CA 92101.
San Francisco Chamber of Commerce, 465 California St, San Francisco, CA
    94104.
South Pasadena Chamber of Commerce, 1005 Fair Oaks Ave, South Pasa-
    dena, CA 91030.

Colorado
Denver Post, 1560 Broadway, Denver, CO 80201.
Rocky Mountain News, 400 W Colfax Ave, Denver, CO 80204.
INS, 12027 Federal Office Building, Denver, CO 80202.
Office of Economic Development, 136 State Capitol, Denver, CO 80203.
Department of Education, 201 E Colfax, Denver, CO 80203.
US Dept of Labor, 1961 Stout Street, 16th Floor, Denver, CO 80294.

Department of Labor and Employment, 600 Grant St, Suite 900, Denver, CO 80203. Employment services.

Division of Labor, 1313 Sherman St, Denver, CO 80203.

Department of Revenue, 1375 Sherman St, Denver, CO 80203.

Greater Denver Chamber of Commerce, 1600 Sherman St, Denver, CO 80203-1620.

Connecticut

Hartford Courant, 285 Broad St, Hartford, CT 06115.

New Haven Register, 40 Sargent Drive, New Haven, CT 06511.

INS District Office, 900 Asylum Ave, Hartford, CT 96105.

Department of Economic Development, 865 Brook St, Rocky Hill, CT 06067.

Department of Education, 165 Capitol Ave, Hartford, CT 06106.

Department of Labor, 200 Folly Brook Blvd, Wethersfield, CT 06109.

Department of Revenue Services, 92 Farmington Ave, Hartford, CT 06106.

Greater Hartford Chamber of Commerce, 250 Constitution Plaza, Hartford, CT 06103.

Delaware

News Journal, PO Box 1111, Wilmington, DE 19899.

Development Office, 99 Kings Hwy, Dover, DE 19901.

Department of Public Instruction, Townsend Bldg, Dover, DE 19901.

Office of Personnel, Townsend Bldg, Dover, DE 19903.

Department of Labor, 820 N French Street, Wilmington, DE 19801.

Division of Revenue, Department of Finance, 820 N French Street, Wilmington, DE 19801.

Central Delaware Chamber of Commerce, PO Box 576, Dover, DE 19903.

Delaware State Chamber of Commerce, One Commerce Center, Suite 200, Wilmington, DE 19801.

District of Columbia

Washington Post, 1150 15th St, NW, Washington, DC 20071.

Washington Times, 3600 New York Ave NE, Washington, DC 20002.

INS District Office, 1025 Vermont Ave NW, Washington, DC 20538.

Washington International School, 3100 Macomb Street NW, Washington, DC 20008.

Economic Development Department, 1350 Pennsylvania NW, Washington, DC 20004.

Department of Education, 415 12th St NW, Washington, DC 20004.

Department of Employment Services, 500 C St NW, Washington, DC 20001.

Department of Finance and Revenue, 300 Indiana Ave NW, Washington, DC 20001.

Chamber of Commerce of the District of Columbia, 1411 K St, NW, Washington, DC 20005.

Florida

Fort Lauderdale News Sun Sentinel, 101 N New River Dr E, Fort Lauderdale, FL 33302.

Miami Herald, 1 Herald Plaza, Miami, FL 33101.

Orlando Sentinel, 633 N Orange Drive, Orlando, FL 32802.

Palm Beach News, Box 1176, Palm Beach, FL 33480.

St Petersburg Times, Box 1121, 490 First Ave S, St Petersburg, FL 33731.

Tampa Tribune, 202 S Parker St, Tampa, FL 33606.

British Consulate, Brickell Bay Office Tower, Suite 2110, 1001 S Bayshore Drive, Miami, FL 33131. Tel: 305 374 1522.

British Florida Chamber of Commerce, Suite 550, 2121 Ponce de Leon Blvd, Coral Gables, FL 33134.

INS District Office, Room 1324, Federal Building, 51 SW First Ave, Miami, FL 33130.

Division of Economic Development, Department of Commerce, 501-B Collins Bldg, Tallahassee, FL 32399. London office: 18–24 Westbourne Grove, London W2 5RH. Tel: (0171) 727 8388. Fax: (0171) 792 8633.

Department of Education, The Capitol, Tallahassee, FL 32399.

Labor and Employment Security Department, 300 Atkins Bldg, Tallahassee, FL 32399.

Public Employee Relations Commission, Koger Executive Centre, Turner Building, 2586 Seagate Dr, Tallahassee, FL 32399-2171.

Department of Revenue, Carlton Bldg, Tallahassee, FL 32399-0100.

Fort Lauderdale Area Chamber of Commerce, 208 3rd Ave SE, Fort Lauderdale, FL 33302-4156.

Jacksonville Chamber of Commerce, PO Box 329, 3 Independent Drive, Jacksonville, FL 32201.

Greater Key West Chamber of Commerce, 402 Wall St, PO Box 984, Key West, FL 33040.

Greater Miami Chamber of Commerce, 1601 Biscayne Blvd, Miami, FL 33132.

Tampa Chamber of Commerce, 801 East J F Kennedy Blvd, Tampa, FL 33602.

Georgia

Atlanta Journal-Constitution, 72 Marietta Ave NW, Atlanta, GA 30302.

British Consulate: Suite 2700, Marquis One Tower, 245 Peach Tree Centre Avenue, Atlanta, GA 30303.

INS District Office, Room 406, 1430 West Peachtree St NW, Atlanta, GA 30309.

Department of Industry and Trade, 230 Peachtree St NW, Atlanta, GA 30301.

Department of Education, 205 Butler St SE, Atlanta, GA 30334.

US Dept of Labor, 1371 Peachtree St NE, Atlanta, GA 30309.

Employment Services Division, Department of Labor, 501 Pulliam St SW, Atlanta, GA 30312.

Department of Labor, 148 International Blvd, Atlanta, GA 30303.
Department of Revenue, 270 Washington St SW, Atlanta, GA 30334.
Georgia State Chamber of Commerce, CCN Center, Atlanta, GA 30303-2705.

Hawaii
Honolulu Advertiser, Box 3080, Honolulu, HI 96802.
INS District Office, PO Box 461, 595 Ala Moana Blvd, Honolulu, HI 96809.
Department of Business and Economic Development, 250 S King St, Honolulu, HI 96813.
Department of Education, 1390 Miller St, Honolulu, HI 96813.
Labor and Industrial Relations Department, 830 Punchbowl St, Honolulu, HI 96814.
Department of Taxation, 425 S Queen St, Honolulu, HI 96813.
Chamber of Commerce of Hawaii, 735 Bishop St, Honolulu, HI 96813.

Idaho
Idaho Statesman, PO Box 40, Boise, ID 83707.
Department of Commerce, Statehouse, Boise, ID 83720.
Department of Education, Len B Jordan Bldg, 650 W St, Boise, ID 83720.
Department of Employment, 317 Main St, Boise, ID 83735.
Labor and Industrial Services Department, 277 N Sixth St, Boise, ID 83720.
State Tax Commission, 700 W State St, Boise, ID 83720.
Boise Area Chamber of Commerce, PO Box 2368, 711 W Bannock, Boise, ID 83701.

Illinois
Chicago Tribune, 435 N Michigan Ave, Chicago IL 60611.
Peoria Journal-Star, 1 News Plaza, Peoria, IL 61643.
Wall Street Journal, 1 S Wacker Drive, 21st Fl, Chicago, IL 60606.
British Consulate, 33 North Dearborn Street, Chicago, IL 60602. Tel: 312 346 0810.
INS District Office, Dirksen Federal Office Building, 219 S Dearbon St, Chicago IL 60604.
Department of Commerce and Community Affairs, 620 E Adams St, 3rd Fl, Springfield, IL 62701.
State Board of Education, 100 N First St, Springfield, IL 62777.
US Dept of Labor, 230 S Dearborn St, Chicago, IL 60604.
Dept of Employment Security, 401 S State St, Chicago, IL 60605.
Department of Labor, #1 W Old State Capitol Plz, Springfield, IL 62702.
Department of Revenue, 101 W Jefferson St, Springfield, IL 62794.
Chicago Association of Commerce and Industry, 200 North Lasalle, Chicago, IL 60601.
Charleston Area Chamber of Commerce, 501 Jackson St, Charleston, IL 61920.

Greater Springfield Chamber of Commerce, 3 South Old State Capital Plaza, Springfield, IL 62701.

Indiana
Indianapolis News-Star, 307 N Pennsylvania Street, Indianapolis, IN 46204.
Business Development and Marketing Group, Department of Commerce, 1 N Capitol, Suite 700, Indianapolis, IN 46204.
Department of Public Instruction, 227 State House, Indianapolis, IN 46204.
Employment Security Division, 10 N Senate Ave, Indianapolis, IN 46204.
Division of Labor, 1013 State Office Bldg, Indianapolis, IN 46204.
Department of Revenue, 202 State Office Bldg, Indianapolis, IN 46204.
Indianapolis Chamber of Commerce, 320 North Meridian St, Indianapolis, IN 46204-1777.

Iowa
Des Moines Register, 715 Locust St, Des Moines, IA 50309.
Department of Economic Development, 299 E Grand, Des Moines, IA 50309.
Department of Education, Grimes State Office Bldg, Des Moines, IA 50319.
Department of Employment Services, 1000 E Grand, Des Moines, IA 50319.
Department of Revenue and Finance, Hoover State Office Building, Des Moines, IA 50319.
Chamber of Commerce of Greater Des Moines, 309 Court Avenue, Ste 300, Des Moines, IA 50309.
Cedar Rapids Chamber of Commerce, 424 First Ave NE, PO Box 4860, Cedar Rapids, IA 52407.

Kansas
Wichita Eagle-Beacon, 825 E Douglas St, Wichita, KS 67201.
Department of Commerce, 400 SW Eighth St, 5th Fl, Topeka, KS 66612.
Department of Education, 120 E 10th St, Topeka, KS 66612.
Department of Human Resources, 401 SW Topeka Blvd, Topeka, KS 66603.
Department of Revenue, 2nd Fl, State Office Bldg, Topeka, KS 66612.
Kansas City Chamber of Commerce, 727 Minnesota Ave, PO Box 171337, KS 66117.
Topeka Chamber of Commerce, 120 E Sixth St, 3 Townsite Plaza, Topeka, KA 66603.
Wichita Area Chamber of Commerce, 350 W Douglas St, Wichita, KA 67202-2970.

Kentucky
Courier Journal, 525 W Broadway, Louisville, KY 40202.
Commerce Cabinet, Capital Plz Tower, Frankfort, KY 40601.
Department of Education, Capital Plz Tower, Frankfort, KY 40601.
Department of Personnel, Capital Annex, Frankfort, KY 40601.
Labor Cabinet, The 127 Bldg, US 127 S, Frankfort, KY 40601.

Revenue Cabinet, Capitol Annex, Frankfort, KY 40601.
Frankfort Chamber of Commerce, 100 Capital Ave, Frankfort, KT 40601.
Louisville Chamber of Commerce, One Riverfront Plaza, Louisville, KT 40202.

Louisiana

New Orleans Times-Picayune, 3800 Howard Ave, New Orleans, LA 70140.
INS District Office, New Federal Building, 701 Loyola Ave, New Orleans, LA 70113.
Department of Economic Development, PO Box 94185, Baton Rouge, LA 70804.
Department of Education, PO Box 94064, Baton Rouge, LA 70804.
Department of Labor, PO Box 94094, Baton Rouge, LA 70804.
Department of Revenue and Taxation, PO Box 201, Baton Rouge, LA 70821.
Baton Rouge Chamber of Commerce, 564 Laurel St, Baton Rouge, LA 70801.
New Orleans and the River Region Chamber of Commerce, 301 Camp St, New Orleans, LA 70190.

Maine

Bangor Daily News, 491 Main St, Bangor, ME 04402-1329.
INS District Office, 76 Pearl St, Portland, ME 04112.
Department of Economic and Community Development, State House Station #59, Augusta, ME 04333.
Department of Educational and Cultural Services, State House Station #23, Augusta, ME 04333.
Department of Labor, State House Station #54, Augusta, ME 04333.
Bureau of Taxation, State House Station #24, Augusta, ME 04333.
Greater Portland Chamber of Commerce, 142 Free St, Portland, ME 04101.

Maryland

Baltimore Sun, 501 N Calvert St, Baltimore, MD 21278.
INS District Office, Room 124, Federal Building, 31 Hopkins Plaza, Baltimore, MD 21201.
Business and Industrial Development Department, 217 E Redwood St, Baltimore, MD 21202.
Department of Education, 200 W Baltimore St, Baltimore, MD 21201.
Department of Economic and Employee Development, 217 E Redwood St, Baltimore, MD 21202.
Division of Labor and Industry, 501 St Paul Pl, Baltimore, MD 21202-2272.
Treasury Department, Goldstein Treasury Bldg, PO Box 466, Annapolis, MD 21404.
Metropolitan Baltimore Chamber of Commerce, Legg Mason Tower, 111 S Calvert St, Suite 1500, Baltimore, MD 21202.
Bethesda-Chevy Chase Chamber of Commerce, Woodmont Ave, Bethesda, MD 20814.

Massachusetts
Boston Globe, PO Box 2378, Boston, MA 02107.
British Consulate, Suite 4740, Prudential Tower, Prudential Centre, Boston MA 02199 Tel: 617 437 7160.
INS District Office, John Fitzgerald Kennedy Federal Building, Government Center, Boston, MA 02203.
Office of Economic Development, State House, Boston, MA 02133.
Department of Education, 1385 Hancock St, Quincey, MA 02169.
Department of Personnel Administration, 1 Ashburton Pl, Boston, MA 02108.
US Dept of Labor, 1 Congress St, 10th Floor, Boston, MA 02114.
Department of Labor and Industries, 100 Cambridge St, Boston, MA 02202.
Department of Revenue, 100 Cambridge St, Boston, MA 02202.
Greater Boston Chamber of Commerce, Federal Reserve Plaza, 13th Floor, 600 Atlantic Ave, Boston, MA 02210-2200.

Michigan
Detroit Free Press, 301 Lafayette Blvd W, Detroit, MI 48231.
Detroit News, 615 Lafayette Blvd W, Detroit, MI 48231.
Grand Rapids Press, 155 Michigan St NW, Grand Rapids, MI 49503.
INS District Office, Federal Building, 333 Mt Elliott St, Detroit, MI 48207.
Department of Commerce, PO Box 30225, Lansing, MI 48909.
Department of Education, S Ottawa Bldg, PO Box 30008, Lansing, MI 48909.
Bureau of Employment Relations, Department of Labor, 1200 Sixth St, Detroit, MI 48226.
Department of Labor, 7310 Woodward Ave, Detroit, MI 48202.
Bureau of Revenue, Treasury Bldg, Lansing, MI 48909.
Greater Detroit Chamber of Commerce, 600 West Lafayette Blvd, Detroit, MI 48226.

Minnesota
Star Tribune, 425 Portland Ave S, Minneapolis, MN 55488-0001.
St Paul Pioneer Press Dispatch, 345 Cedar St, St Paul, MN 55101.
INS District Office, Room 932, New Post Office Bldg, 180 East Kellogg Boulevard, St Paul, MN 55101.
Department of Energy and Economic Development, 150 E Kellogg Boulevard, St Paul, MN 55101. London office: 16 St Helen's Place, London EC3A 6BT. Tel: (0171) 628 4407.
Department of Education, 550 Cedar St, St Paul, MN 55101.
Department of Jobs and Training, 390 N Robert St, St Paul, MN 55101.
Department of Labor and Industry, 443 Lafayette Rd, St Paul, MN 55101.
Department of Revenue, 10 River Park Plz, St Paul, MN 55146.
St Paul Area Chamber of Commerce, 600 North Life Tower, 445 Minnesota St, St Paul, MN 55101.

Greater Minneapolis Chamber of Commerce, 15 S Fifth St, Minneapolis, MN 55402.

Mississippi
Clarion Ledger, 311 E Pearl St, Jackson, MS 39201.
Department of Economic and Community Development, 1201 Sillers Bldg, Jackson, MS 39201.
Department of Education, 501 Sillers Bldg, Jackson, MS 39201.
Employment Security Commission, 1520 W Capitol, Jackson, MS 39203.
State Tax Commission, 102 Woolfolk Bldg, Jackson, MS 39201.
Jackson Chamber of Commerce, PO Box 22548, 201 S President St, Jackson, MS 39225-2548.

Missouri
Kansas City Star-Times, 1729 Grand Ave, Kansas City, MO 64108.
Saint Louis Post Dispatch, 9800 N Tucker Blvd, St Louis, MO 63101.
INS District Office, Room 819, US Courthouse, 811 Grand Ave, Kansas City, MO 64106.
Department of Economic Development, PO Box 1157, Jefferson City, MO 65102.
Department of Elementary and Secondary Education, PO Box 480, 205 Jefferson City, MO 65102.
US Dept of Labor, 911 Walnut St, Kansas City, MO 64106.
Labor and Industrial Relations Dept, 421 E Dunklin St, Box 59, Jefferson City, MO 65104.
Department of Revenue, Truman Bldg, 416 Belai Dr, Jefferson City, MO 65109-0708.
Greater Kansas City Chamber of Commerce, 920 Main St, Suite 600, Kansas City, MO 64105.
St Louis Regional Commerce and Growth Association, 100 South Fourth St, Suite 500, St Louis, MO 63102.

Montana
Billings Gazette, 401 N Broadway, Billings, MT 59107.
INS District Office, Federal Bldg, Helena, MT, 59601.
Business Assistance Division, Department of Commerce, 1424 9th Ave, Helena, MT 59620.
Office of Public Instruction, State Capitol, Helena, MT 59620.
Job Service Division, PO Box 1728, Helena, MT 59624.
Department of Labor and Industry, Capitol Station, Helena, MT 59620.
Department of Revenue, Capitol Station, Box 311, Helena, MT 59620.
Montana State Chamber of Commerce, 11th Ave, PO Box 1730, Helena, MT 59624.

Nebraska
Omaha World-Herald, 14th and Dodge Sts, Omaha, NE 68102.

INS Northern Service Center, PO Box 82521, Lincoln, NE 68501-2521. Tel: 402 437 5218.

INS District Office, Room 8411, 215 N 17th St, Omaha, NE 68102.

Department of Economic Development, 301 Centennial Mall S, PO Box 94666, Lincoln, NE 68509.

Department of Education, 301 Centennial Mall S, PO Box 94987, Lincoln, NE 68509-4987; State Board of Education, 623 Service Life Bldg, Omaha, NE 68102.

Department of Labor, PO Box 94600, Lincoln, NE 68509-4600.

Department of Revenue, 301 Centennial Mall S, PO Box 94818, Lincoln, NE 68509-4818.

Lincoln Chamber of Commerce, 1221 North St, Lincoln, NE 68508.

Greater Omaha Chamber of Commerce, 1301 Harney St, Omaha, NE 68102.

Nevada

Las Vegas Review Journal, 1111 W Bonanza Rd, Las Vegas, NV 89125-0070.

Commission on Economic Development, 600 E William, Suite 203, Carson City, NV 89710.

Department of Education, 400 W King St, Carson City, NV 89710.

Employment Security Department 500 E Third St, Carson City, NV 89710.

Labor Commission, 505 E King St, Carson City, NV 89710.

Department of Taxation, 1340 S Curry St, Carson City, NV 89710.

Carson City Chamber of Commerce, 1191 South Carson St, Carson City, NV 89701.

Las Vegas Chamber of Commerce, 2301 E Sahara Ave, Las Vegas, NV 89104.

New Hampshire

Union Leader, PO Box 780, 35 Amherst St, Manchester, NH 03105.

Department of Resources and Economic Development, PO Box 856, Concord, NH 03301.

Department of Education, State Office, Park S, Concord, NH 03301.

Department of Employment Security, 32 S Main St, Concord, NH 03301.

Department of Labor, 19 Pillsbury St, Concord, NH 03301.

Department of Revenue Administration, PO Box 467, Concord, NH 03301.

Greater Manchester Chamber of Commerce, 889 Elm St, Manchester, NH 03101.

New Jersey

Star Ledger, Court and Plaine Sts, Newark, NJ 07101.

INS District Office, Federal Bldg, 970 Broad St, Newark, NJ 07102.

Commerce and Economic Development Department, 33 W State St, CN 823, Trenton, NJ 08625. UK office: World Trade Centre, St Katherine's Way, London E1 9UN. Tel: (0171) 481 8909.

Department of Education, 225 W State St, Trenton, NJ 08625.

Division of Employment Services, Department of Labor, John Fitch Plz, Trenton, NJ 08625.

Department of Labor, CN 110, Trenton, NJ 08625-0110.
Division of Taxation, CN 240, Trenton, NJ 08625.
Greater Newark Chamber of Commerce, 40 Clinton St, Newark, NJ 07102.
Trenton Chamber of Commerce, 214 West State St, Trenton, NJ 08607.

New Mexico
Albuquerque Journal, 7777 Jefferson St NE, Albuquerque, NM 87103.
Armand Hammer United World College of the American West, PO Box 248, Montezuma, NM 87731.
Department of Economic Development and Tourism, 1100 St Francis Dr, Santa Fe, NM 87501.
Department óf Education, Education Building, Santa Fe, NM 87501-2786.
Department of Labor, 401 Broadway NE, Albuquerque, NM 87102.
Department of Taxation and Revenue, Joseph Montoya Bldg, Santa Fe, NM 87503.
Greater Albuquerque Chamber of Commerce, 401 Second St NW, Albuquerque, NM 87102.

New York State
Times-Union, 645 Albany-Shaker Road, Albany, NY 12210.
Buffalo News, 1 News Plaza, Buffalo, NY 14240-2994.
New York Post, 210 South St, New York, NY 10002.
New York Times, 229 W 43rd St, New York, NY 10036.
Democrat and Chronicle, 55 Exchange Blvd, Rochester NY 14614.
British Consulate, 845 Third Avenue, New York, NY 10022. Tel: 212 593 2258.
INS District Offices: 68 Court St, Buffalo, NY 14202; 26 Federal Plaza, New York, NY 10007.
Anglo-American School, 18 West 89 Street, New York, NY 10024.
United Nations International School, 24-50 East River Drive, New York, NY 10010.
Department of Commerce, 1 Commerce Plz, Albany, NY 12245. London office: 25 Haymarket, London SW1Y 4EN. Tel: (0171) 839 5079.
Department of Education, Education Bldg, Albany, NY 12234.
US Dept of Labor, 201 Varick St, New York, NY 10014.
Department of Labor, Campus, State Office Bldg, Albany, NY 12240.
Department of Taxation and Finance, Campus, Tax and Finance Bldg, Albany, NY 12227.
Empire State Chamber of Commerce, 518 Broadway, Albany, NY 12207.
Greater Buffalo Chamber of Commerce, 107 Delaware Ave, Buffalo, NY 14202.
New York Chamber of Commerce and Industry, 200 Madison Ave, New York, NY 10016.

North Carolina
Charlotte Observer, Box 32188, Charlotte, NC 28232.

Durham Morning Herald, 115-119 Market St, Durham, NC 27701-3222.

News and Observer of Raleigh, 215 S McDowell St, Raleigh, NC 27602.

Business and Industry Development, Department of Commerce, 430 N Salisbury St, Raleigh, NC 27603.

Department of Public Instruction, 116 W Edenton St, Raleigh, NC 27603-1712.

Employment Security Commission, 700 Wade Ave, Raleigh, NC 27605-1167.

Department of Labor, 4 W Edenton St, Raleigh, NC 27601-1092.

Department of Revenue, 2 S Salisbury St, Raleigh, NC 27602-1348.

Charlotte Chamber of Commerce, PO Box 32785, 129 West Trade Center, Charlotte, NC 28232.

Raleigh Chamber of Commerce, 800 South Salisbury St, Raleigh, NC 27601.

North Dakota

Forum, 101 15th St N, Fargo, ND 58102.

Economic Development Commission, 604 E Blvd, State Capitol Grounds, Bismarck, ND 58505.

Department of Public Instruction, 11th Fl, State Capitol, 600 E Blvd, Bismarck, ND 58505.

Job Service ND, PO Box 1537, Bismarck, ND 58502.

Department of Labor, 5th Fl, State Capitol, 600 E Blvd, Bismarck, ND 58505.

Tax Department, 8th Fl, State Capitol, 600 E Blvd, Bismarck, ND 58505.

Fargo Chamber of Commerce, 321 N Fourth St, PO Box 2443, Fargo, ND 58102.

Ohio

Akron Beacon Journal, 44 E Exchange St, Akron, OH 44328.

Cincinnati Enquirer, 617 Vine St, Cincinnati, OH 45201.

Cincinnati Post, 125 E Court St, Cincinnati, OH 45202.

Plain Dealer, 1801 Superior Ave E, Cleveland OH 44114.

Columbus Dispatch, 34 S 3rd St, Columbus, OH 43215.

Dayton Daily News, 4th and Ludlow Sts, Dayton, OH 45401.

INS District Office, Room 1917, Federal Office Bldg, 1240 E 9th St, Cleveland, OH 44199.

Department of Development, 30 E Broad St, Columbus, OH 43266.

Department of Education, 65 S Front St, Columbus, OH 43266-0308.

Bureau of Employment Services, 145 S Front St, Columbus, OH 43266-0308.

Department of Industrial Relations, 2323 W Fifth Ave, Columbus, OH 43266-0567.

Department of Taxation, 30 E Broad St, Columbus, OH 43266-0420.

Greater Cincinatti Chamber of Commerce, 120 W Fifth St, Cincinatti, OH 45202.

Greater Cleveland Growth Association International Trade and Business Development, 690 Huntingdon Building, Cleveland, OH 44115.

Columbus Area Chamber of Commerce, 37 North High St, Columbus, OH 43215.

Toledo Area Chamber of Commerce, 218 Huron St, Toledo, OH 43604.

Oklahoma

Daily Oklahoman, 500 N Broadway, Oklahoma City, OK 73125.

Tulsa World, Box 1770, Tulsa, OK 74103-3401.

Department of Commerce, 6601 Broadway Ext, Oklahoma City, OK 73116.

Department of Education, 2500 N Lincoln Blvd, Oklahoma City, OK 73105.

Office of Personnel Management, B-22 Jim Thorpe Bldg, 2101 N Lincoln Blvd, Oklahoma City, OK 73105.

State Department of Labor, 1315 Broadway Pl, Oklahoma City, OK 73103.

Tax Commission, 2501 N Lincoln Blvd, Oklahoma City, OK 73194.

Oklahoma City Chamber of Commerce, One Santa Fe Plaza, Oklahoma City, OK 73102.

Metropolitan Tulsa Chamber of Commerce, 616 S Boston Ave, Tulsa, OK 74119.

Oregon

The Oregonian, 1320 SW Broadway, Portland, OR 97201.

INS District Office, Room 333, US Courthouse, SW Broadway and Main St, Portland, OR 97205.

Department of Economic Development, 595 Cottage St NE, Salem, OR 97310.

Department of Education, 700 Pringle Pkwy SE, Salem, OR 97310.

Department of Human Resources, 875 Union St NE, Salem, OR 97301.

Bureau of Labor and Industries, 1400 SW Fifth Ave, Portland, OR 97201.

Department of Revenue, 955 Center St NE, Salem, OR 97310.

Portland Chamber of Commerce, 221 NW Second Ave, Portland, OR 97209.

Salem Area Chamber of Commerce, 220 Cottage St NE, Salem, OR 97301.

Pennsylvania

Harrisburg Patriot News, 812 King Boulevard, Harrisburg, PA 17105.

Tribune-Democrat, 425 Locust St, Johnstown, PA 15907.

Philadelphia Daily News/Inquirer, 400 N Broad St, Philadelphia, PA 19101.

Pittsburgh Post-Gazette, 34 Boulevard of the Allies, Pittsburgh, PA 15230.

Pittsburgh Press, 34 Boulevard of the Allies, Pittsburgh, PA 15230.

INS District Office, Room 1321, US Courthouse, Independence Mall W, 601 Market St, Philadelphia, PA 19106.

Department of Commerce, 433 Forum Bldg, Harrisburg, PA 17120.

Department of Education, 10th Fl, Harristown Bldg #2, Harrisburg, PA 17108.

US Dept of Labor, PO Box 8796, Philadelphia, PA 19101.

Employment Security Division, Department of Labor and Industry, 1720 Labor and Industry Bldg, Harrisburg, PA 17120.

Department of Labor and Industry, 1700 Labor and Industry Bldg, Harrisburg, PA 17120.
Department of Revenue, Strawberry Square, 11th Fl, Harrisburg, PA 17101-2290.
Greater Philadelphia Chamber of Commerce, Broad and Chestnut St, Philadelphia, PA 19107.
Greater Pittsburgh Chamber of Commerce, 3 Gateway Center, Pittsburgh, PA 15222.

Rhode Island
Providence Journal Bulletin, 75 Fountain St, Providence, RI 02902.
Department of Economic Development, 7 Jackson Walkway, Providence, RI 02903.
Department of Education, 22 Hayes St, Providence, RI 02908.
Department of Employment Security, 24 Mason St, Providence, RI 02903.
Department of Labor, 220 Elmwood Ave, Providence, RI 02907.
Division of Taxation, 289 Promenade St, Providence, RI 02903.
Providence Chamber of Commerce, 30 Exchange Terrace, Providence, RI 02903.

South Carolina
News and Courier, 134 Columbus St, Charleston, SC 29402.
State-Record, 1401 Shop Rd, Columbia, SC 29201.
State Development Board, PO Box 927, Columbia, SC 29202.
Department of Education, Rutledge Bldg, 1429 Senate St, Columbia, SC 29201.
Employment Security Commission, 1550 Gadsden St, PO Box 995, Columbia, SC 29202.
Department of Labor, 3600 Forest Dr, Landmark Ctr, Columbia, SC 29204 SC.
Tax Commission, 301 Gervais St, Columbia, SC 29201.
Greater Columbia Chamber of Commerce, 1308 Laurel St, Columbia, SC 29201.
Greater Greenville Chamber of Commerce, PO Box 10048, 24 Cleveland St, Greenville, SC 29603.

South Dakota
Argus-Leader, 200 S Minnesota Ave, Sioux Falls, SD 57117.
Office of Economic Development, Capitol Lake Plz, Pierre, SD 57501.
Department of Education, 700 Governor's Drive, Pierre, SD 57501.
Division of Job Services, Department of Labor, 116 W Missouri Ave, Pierre, SD 57501.
Department of Labor, Kneip Bldg, Pierre, SD 57501.
Department of Revenue, 700 Governor's Dr, Pierre, SD 57501-2276.
Sioux Falls Chamber of Commerce, 315 S Phillips, Sioux Falls, SD 57102.

Tennessee
Commercial Appeal, 495 Union Ave, Memphis, TN 38103.
The Tennessean, 1100 Broadway, Nashville, TN 37202.
Department of Economic and Community Development, 320 Sixth Ave N, Nashville, TN 37219.
Department of Education, 100 Cordell Hull Bldg, Nashville, TN 37219.
Department of Employment Security, 504 Cordell Hull Bldg, Nashville, TN 37219.
Department of Labor, 501 Union Boulevard, Nashville, TN 37219.
Department of Revenue, 927 Andrew Jackson Bldg, Nashville, TN 37219.
Memphis Area Chamber of Commerce, 22 N Front St, PO Box 224, Memphis, TN 38101.
Nashville Area Chamber of Commerce, 161 Fourth Ave N, Nashville, TN 37219.

Texas
Austin American-Statesman, 308 Guadelupe St, Austin, TX 78767.
Dallas Morning News, Box 655237, Dallas, TX 75265.
Fort Worth Star-Telegram, 400 W 7th St, Fort Worth, TX 76101.
Houston Chronicle, 801 Texas Ave, Houston, TX 77001.
Houston Post, 4747 SW Freeway, Houston, TX 77001.
San Antonio Express-News, Ave E and 3rd St, San Antonio, TX 78205.
San Antonio Light, 240 Broadway, San Antonio, TX 78291.
Wall Street Journal, 1233 Regal Row, Dallas TX 75247.
British Consulates: 813 Stemmons Tower West, 2730 Stemmons Freeway, Dallas TX 75207. Tel: 214 637 3600; Suite 2250, Dresser Tower, 601 Jefferson, Houston, TX 77002. Tel: 713 659 6270.
INS Southern Service Center, PO Box 568808, Dallas, TX 75356-8808. Tel: 214 767 7769.
INS District Offices: Room IC13, Federal Bldg, 1100 Commerce St, Dallas, TX 75202; Room 343, US Courthouse, PO Box 9398, El Paso, TX 79984; Federal Bldg, US Courthouse, PO Box 61630, 515 Rusk Ave, Houston, TX 77208; US Federal Bldg, Suite A301, 727 Durango, San Antonio, TX 78206.
Department of Commerce, 816 Congress, 12th Fl, Austin, TX 78711.
Texas Education Agency, 1701 N Congress Ave, Austin, TX 78701.
Employment Commission, 101 E 15th St, Austin, TX 78778-0001.
US Dept of Labor, Federal Building, 525 Griffin St, Dallas, TX 75202.
Department of Labor and Standards, Box 12157, Capitol Station, Austin, TX 78711.
Public Accounts, LBJ Bldg, Austin, TX 78774.
Austin Chamber of Commerce, 901 W Riverside Drive, Austin, TX 78704.
Greater Dallas Chamber of Commerce, 1201 Elm St, Suite 2000, Dallas, TX 75270.
El Paso Chamber of Commerce, PO Box 9738, 10 Civic Center Plaza, El Paso, TX 79901.

Greater Houston Chamber of Commerce, 1100 Milam Bldg, 25th Floor, Houston, TX 77002.

Greater Marshall Chamber of Commerce, 213 W Auston St, PO Box 520, Marshall, TX 75670.

Greater San Antonio Chamber of Commerce, 602 East Commerce St, San Antonio, TX 78205.

Utah

Salt Lake City Tribune, 143 S Main St, Salt Lake City, UT 84110.

Salt Lake City Desert News, Box 1257, 30 E First South St, Salt Lake City, UT 84111.

Community and Economic Development Department, 6290 State Off Bldg, Salt Lake City, UT 84114.

Office of Education, 250 E Fifth St S, Salt Lake City, UT 84111.

Department of Employment Security, 174 Social Hall Ave, Salt Lake City, UT 84147.

Industrial Commission, 160 E 300 S, PO Box 45802, Salt Lake City, UT 84145-0802.

Tax Commission, 160 E 300 S, Salt Lake City, UT 84134.

Salt Lake Area Chamber of Commerce, 175 E 400 St, Salt Lake City, UT 84111.

Vermont

Burlington Free Press, 191 College St, Burlington, VT 05401.

INS District Office, Federal Bldg, PO Box 591, St Albans, VT 05478.

INS Eastern Service Center, 75 Lower Weldon St, St Albans, VT 05479-0001. Tel: 802 527 3160.

Agency of Development and Community Affairs, 109 State St, Montpelier, VT 05602.

Department of Education, 120 State St, Montpelier, VT 05602.

Department of Employment and Training, Green Mountain Drive, Montpelier, VT 05602.

Department of Labor and Industry, 7 Court St, Montpelier, VT 05602.

Department of Taxes, 109 State St, Montpelier, VT 05602.

Lake Champlain Regional Chamber of Commerce, PO Box 453, 209 Battery St, Burlington, VT 05402.

Virginia

Times-Dispatch, Box C 32333, Richmond, VA 23293-0001.

Roanoke Times, 201 W Campbell Ave, Roanoke, VA 24010.

Department of Economic Development, 1000 Washington Bldg, Richmond, VA 23219.

Department of Education, PO Box 6-Q, Richmond, VA 23216.

Employment Commission, 703 E Main St, Richmond, VA 23219.

Department of Labor and Industry, PO Box 12064, Richmond, VA 23219.

Department of Taxation, PO Box 6-L, Richmond, VA 23282.

Hampton Roads Chamber of Commerce, 420 Bank St, Norfolk, VA 23510.
Richmond Metropolitan Chamber of Commerce, 201 East Franklin St, Richmond, VA 23219.

Washington State
Seattle Post Intelligencer and *Seattle Times*, 1120 John St, Seattle, WA 98111.
Spokane Chronicle, 999 W Riverside Ave, Spokane, WA 99210-1615.
Morning News Tribune, 1950 S State St, Tacoma, WA 98405.
British Consulate, 820 First Interstate Center, 999 Third Avenue, Seattle, WA 98104. Tel: 206 622 9255.
INS District Office, 815 Airport Way S, Seattle, WA 98134.
Department of Trade and Economic Development, 101 General Administration Building, M/S: AX-13, Olympia, WA 98504.
Department of Public Instruction, Old Capitol Bldg, M/S: FG-11, Olympia, WA 98504.
US Dept of Labor, 909 First Ave, Seattle, WA 98174.
Department of Employment Security, 212 Maple Park, M/S: KG-11, Olympia, WA 98504.
Department of Labor and Industries, General Administration Bldg, M/S: HC-901, Olympia, WA 98504.
Department of Revenue, General Administration Bldg, M/S: AX-02, Olympia, WA 98504.
Greater Seattle Chamber of Commerce, 600 University St, Suite 1200, Seattle, WA 98101.

West Virginia
Charleston Gazette/Daily Mail, 1001 Virginia St E, Charleston WV 25301.
Governor's Office of Community and Industrial Development, Rm 146, State Capitol, Charleston, WV 25305.
Department of Education, 1800 Washington St E, Bldg 6, Charleston, WV 25305.
Division of Employment Security, 112 California Ave, Charleston, WV 23505.
Division of Labor, State Capitol Complex, Bldg 3, Charleston, WV 25305.
Department of Revenue, State Capitol Complex, Bldg 1, Charleston, WV 25305.
Charleston Chamber of Commerce, 106 Capitol St, Suite 100, Charleston, WV 25301-2610.
Huntington Area Chamber of Commerce, 522 Ninth St, PO Box 1509, Huntington, WV 25716.

Wisconsin
Milwaukee Journal, PO Box 661, 333 State St, Milwaukee, WI 53201.
Milwaukee Sentinel, Box 371, Milwaukee, WI 53201.
Bureau of Business Expansion and Recruitment, Department of Development, PO Box 7970, Madison, WI 53707.

Department of Public Instruction, 125 S Webster St, PO Box 7841, Madison, WI 53707.

Job Service Division, Department of Industry, Labor and Human Relations, PO Box 7903, Madison, WI 53707.

Department of Industry, Labor and Human Relations, 201 E Washington Ave, PO Box 7946, Madison, WI 53707.

Department of Revenue, 125 S Webster, Madison, WI 5302.

Greater Madison Chamber of Commerce, 615 E Washington Ave, Madison, WI 53701.

Metropolitan Milwaukee Chamber of Commerce, 756 N Milwaukee St, 4th Floor, Milwaukee, WI 53202.

Wyoming

Casper Star-Tribune, PO Box 80, Casper, WY 82602.

Economic Development Stabilization Board, Herschler Bldg, Cheyenne, WY 82002.

Department of Education, Hathaway Bldg, Cheyenne, WY 82002.

Employment Security Commission, PO Box 2760, Casper, WY 82602.

Department of Labor and Statistics, Herschler Bldg, Cheyenne, WY 82002.

Department of Revenue and Taxation, Herschler Bldg, Cheyenne, WY 82002.

Cheyenne Chamber of Commerce, 301 W 16th St, Cheyenne, WY 82001.

Note

Where two branches of a state department of labour are listed the first is likely to provide a placement service and job advice while the second administers and enforces the state's labour laws.

Appendix H
Bibliography

Reference books
(UK publications are asterisked)

Allied Dunbar Expatriate Tax Guide (Longman).★

The American Almanac of Jobs and Salaries, J. W. Wright (ed) (Avon Books).

Anglo-American Trade Directory (Kogan Page).

Career Guide to Professional Associations–A Directory of Organisations by Occupational Field, C. N. Shrameck (Sulzberger & Graham).

The Career Guide (Dun & Bradstreet).

CEPEC Recruitment Guide (Centre for Professional Employment Counselling, Kent House, 41 East Street, Bromley, Kent BR1 1QQ).★

Cities of the United States, Diane L. Dupuis (ed) 4 vols. (Gale Research).

Computer Industry Almanac, Karen Jullussen (ed) (8111 LBJ Freeway, 13th Floor, Dallas, TX 75251).

Consultants and Consulting Organisations M. and Karin Koek (Gale Research).

Directory of Executive Recruiters, James H. Kennedy (ed) (Kennedy Publications).

Directory of Franchising Organisations (Pilot Books).

Directory of US Subsidiaries of British Companies (British-American Chamber of Commerce, New York).

Dun & Bradstreet's Million Dollar Directory (Dun & Bradstreet).

Dun & Bradstreet's Middle Market Directory (Dun & Bradstreet).

Dun's Directory of Service Companies (Dun & Bradstreet).

Employment Directory for the Americas and Canada (Maple Marketing. Tel: (0181) 813 9868).

The Economist Business Travel Guide: United States (Economist Publications Ltd).★

Employment and Earnings (US Department of Labor).

Encyclopedia of Associations (Gale Research).

Encyclopedia of Careers and Vocational Guidance, William Stopke (Ferguson). Also on CD-Rom.

Encyclopedia of Medical Organisations and Agencies (Gale Research).

Encyclopedia of Second Careers, G. R. Hawes (Facts on File, 1984) 0-87196-692-1.

Executive Employment Guide (The American Management Association, Inc., 135 W 50th Street, New York, NY 10020).

Executive Grapevine Vol. I: The Directory of Executive Recruitment Consultants (UK edition); Vol. II: The International Directory of Executive Recruitment Consultants (Executive Grapevine, 2nd Floor, Cottonmill Lane, St Albans AL1 2HA. Fax: (01727) 844779).*

Expatriate Compensation Reports (Business International, 40 Duke Street, London W1A 1DW).*

The Fourth of July Guide to Careers, Internships and Volunteer Opportunities in the Non-Profit Sector, D. C. Smith (ed) (Garrett Park Press).

Franchise Opportunities Handbook (Sterling).

Guide to American Directories (Todd Publications).

Handbook of Private Schools (Porter Sargent Publishers).

Handbook of Trade and Technical Careers (National Association of Trade & Technical Schools, 2021 K St NW, Washington, DC 20006).

Harvard Guide to Careers, M. P. Leape and S. M. Vacca (Harvard University Press).

Independent and Boarding Schools World Yearbook (Nexus Business Publications).*

Information Please Almanac (Houghton Mifflin).

International Pay and Benefits Survey (PA Personnel Services, Hyde Park House, 60A Knightsbridge, London SW1X 7LE).*

Job Hunters' Yellow Pages: The National Directory of Employment Services, Steven A. Wood (Career Communications).

Job Seekers' Guide to Private–Public Companies, Charity A. Dorgan (Gale). Four Volumes.

MacMillan Directory of Leading Private Companies (National Register Publishing).

National Directory of Addresses and Telephone Numbers (Omnigraphics Inc).

National Directory of State Agencies (Cambridge Information Group).

National Jobline Directory, Robert Schmidt (Adams Publishing).

National Trade & Professional Associations of the United States (Columbia Books).

Occupational Outlook Handbook, US Department of Labor (VGM Career Books) 0-8442-8562-5.

Offbeat Careers–The Directory of Unusual Work, Sacharov A (Ten Speed Press).

Professional & Trade Association Job Finder–A Directory of Employment Resources Offered by Associations and Other Organisations, S. N. Feingold and A. Nicholson (Garrett Park Press).

Summer Employment Directory of the United States (Writer's Digest Books).

The Traveller's Handbook, S. Gorman (ed) (WEXAS, 45 Brompton Road, London SW3 1DE).*

Thomas Register of American Manufacturers (Thomas Publishing).

Ulrich's International Periodicals Directory (R. R. Bowker).

US Government Jobs (US Office of Personnel Management, 1900 E Street NW, Washington DC 20415).

US Government Manual (Office of Federal Register, National Archives and Record Administration, Washington DC 20408).

The World Almanac and Book of Facts (Funk & Wagnall).

When Can You Start? The Complete Job Search Guide for Women of All Ages, Catalyst (Macmillan, 1981).

Working Abroad, J. Golding (International Venture Handbooks.)*

Yearbook of American and Canadian Churches (Abingdon Press).

Yearbook of Recruitment and Employment Services (Federation of Recruitment & Employment Services) (AP Information Services Ltd, 33 Ashbourne Avenue, London NW11 0DU).*

40 + Job Hunting Guide, P. Birsner (Simon & Schuster 1987).

General books
(UK titles are asterisked)

America's Fifty Fastest Growing Jobs (JIST, 1995).

Best Jobs for the 1990s and into the 21st Century, Ronald and Caryl Rae Krannich (Garrett Park, 1995).

Applying for a United States Visa, R. Fleischer (International Venture Handbooks, 1993).*

Career Guide to America's Top Industries (JIST).

Career Makers: America's Top 150 Executive Recruiters, John Sibbald (Harper Business).

The Complete Job and Career Handbook, S. Norman and Marilyn Feingold (Ferguson, 1993).

Coping with America, Peter Trudgill (Blackwell, 1985).

Culture Shock: USA, Esther Wanning (Kuperard).

Destination USA, K. K. Singh (Park Publications, 1 Park Close, London NW2 6RQ).

Doing Business in the USA, R.Starr and R.B.Donin (Oyez Publishing).*

Emerging Careers–New Occupations for the Year 2000 and Beyond, S. N. Feingold and N. R. Taylor (Garrett Park Press).

Finding a Job in the USA (Overseas Jobs Express).*

Finding the Right Job at Mid-life, J. F. Allen and J. Gorkin (Fireside Books).

Handbook for Foreign Students and Professionals (Office of International Education and Services, University of Iowa, 200 Jefferson Building, Iowa City, IA 52242).

How to Emigrate, R. Jones (How To Books, 1994).*

How to Get a Job Abroad, R. Jones (How To Books, 1994).*

How to Live and Work in America, S. Mills (How To Books, 1992).*

How to Manage Your Career, R. Jones (How To Books, 1994.)*

How to Teach Abroad, R. Jones (How To Books, 1994).*

Internships (Writer's Digest Books).

The Job Hunters' Guide to 100 Great American Cities A. Kuman and R. Salmon (Brattle Publishing).

Jobhunting after 50, Samuel N. Ray (Wiley, 1991).

Job Hunting with Employment Agencies, E.Gowdy (Barron).

Jobs and How To Get Them, H.W.Koch (Ken Books).
Jobs–What They Are, Where They Are, What They Pay, R. O. and A. M. Snelling (Simon & Schuster).
Living and Working in the USA, D. Hampshire (Survival Books).*
Live and Work in the USA, A. Harper (Grant Dawson).*
Live and Work in the USA and Canada, V. Pybus (Vacation Work, 1995).*
Long Stays in America: R. W. Hicks and F. Schulz (David & Charles/Hippocrene, 1986).*
Newcomers' Guide to Living in the USA, Leon I Snaid (International Business Seminars).
Planning Your Career of Tomorrow, A. Paradis (Passport Books).
Predeparture Orientation Handbook for Foreign Students and Scholars Planning to Study in the USA, M. Ernst (ed) (Bureau of Education and Cultural Affairs, USIA, Washington, DC 20547).
Telesearch—Direct Dial to the Best Job in Your Life, J. Truitt (Facts on File, 1983).
US Business Visas, Richard S. Goldstein (Department of Trade & Industry, London).*
Using the Internet in your Job Search, Fred E. Jandt and Mary Nemnich (JIST, 1995).*
What Color is Your Parachute?, R. N. Bolles (Ten Speed Press).

For a more extensive bibliography of American careers and employment titles, consult:
Where to Start Career Planning: Essential Resource Guide for Career Planning and Job Hunting, Carolyn Lloyd Lindquist (Cornell University Career Center: distributed by Peterson's Guides).

US publishers
The following list includes publishers which publish careers books aimed at Americans, particularly young Americans, yet offer insights into different careers in the US and give useful contact addresses. Where no distributor is stated, your local bookseller should be able to obtain any North American book through the specialist US wholesalers Baker & Taylor International, Northdale House, North Circular Road, London NW10 7UH. Tel: (0181) 453 3627.

Abingdon Press, 201 Eighth Ave S, Nashville, TN 37202.
Adams Publihsing, 260 Center Street, Holbrook, MA 02343. Publisher of the *Job Bank* series.
Arco Publishing, 1230 Ave of the Americas, New York, NY 10020. Publishers of a series of careers guidance books entitled *Your Career In . . .* Designed principally for high school students. A subsidiary of Simon & Schuster.
Avon Books, Hearst Corporation, 105 Madison Avenue, New York, NY 10016.

Barron Educational Series, 250 Wireless Boulevard, Happauge, NY 11788; UK rep: D Services, Euston Street, Freeman's Common, Leicester LE2 7SS. Tel: (01533) 547671.

R.R.Bowker Co, 245 W 17th St, New York, NY 10011; Borough Green, Sevenoaks, Kent TN15 8PJ. Tel: (01732) 884567.

Brattle Communications, 24 Computer Drive W, Albany, NY 12205. Publishers of *The Job Hunters' Guide* series.

Cambridge Information Group Directories Inc, 7200 Wisconsin Avenue, Bethesda, MD 20814.

Columbia Books, 1212 New York Ave NW, Suite 330, Washington, DC 20005.

Contemporary Books Inc, 2 Prudential Plaza, Suite 1200, Chicago, IL 60601. UK rep: Gazelle Book Services, Lancaster.

Dun & Bradstreet, 299 Park Ave, New York, NY 10171; Holmers Farm Way, High Wycombe, Bucks HP12 4UL. Tel: (01949) 423698.

Facts on File, 460 Park Avenue South, New York, NY 10016, USA. Tel: 212 683 2244; Collins Street, Oxford OX4 1XJ. Tel: (01865) 728399. Fax: (01865) 244839. Publisher of the *Career Opportunities* series which includes writing, music, TV, cable and video, advertising and PR, art, robotics.

Ferguson Publishing Co, 200 W Madison St, Suite 300, Chicago, IL 60606.

Fireside Books, 8356 Olive Blvd, St Louis, MO 63132.

Gale Research Inc, 835 Penobscot Building, Detroit, MI 48226; North Way, Walworth Industrial Estate, Andover, Hants SP10 5YE. Tel: (01264) 334446.

Garrett Park Press, Box 190, Garrett Park, MD 20896.

General Information Co, 11805 North Creek Parkway S, No. 101, Bothell, WA 98011.

Houghton Mifflin Co, 215 Park Ave S, New York, NY 10003.

JIST Works Inc, 720 N Park Ave, Indianapolis, IN 46202-3431.

Ken Books, 56 Midcrest Way, San Francisco, CA 94131.

Kendall Hunt Publishing, 4050 Westmark Drive, Dubuque, IA 52004.

Klein Publications, PO Box 8503, Coral Springs, FL 33075.

Lerner Publishing, 241 First Avenue, N Minneapolis, MN 55401. UK rep: Ruskin Book Services. Publishers of the *Careers In . . .* series.

Macmillan Inc, 866 Third Avenue, New York, NY 1002.

McGraw-Hill Book Co, 1221 Avenue of the Americas, New York, NY 10020. Tel: 212 512 2000; McGraw-Hill House, Shopenhangers Road, Maidenhead, Berks SL5 2QL. Tel: (01628) 23432. Distributes *Harvard Business School Career Guides* in Management Consulting, Marketing and Investment Banking (Harvard Business School Press).

National Register Publishing, 3004 Glenview Road, Wilmette, IL 60091. Subsidiary of Reed Elsevier.

National Textbook Co, 4255 W Touhy Avenue, Lincolnswood, IL 60646. Publishes under the VGM imprint the *Opportunities In . . .* series, the *Careers for You* series, the *Professional Résumés* series, the *Professional*

Careers series, a *Careers Encyclopedia* and the comprehensive *Occupational Outlook Handbook* compiled by the US Department of Labor. Publishes under the Passport Books imprint *Finding a Job in the United States*.

Peterson's Guides, PO Box 2123, Princeton, NJ 08543.

Raintree Publications, PO Box 26015, Austin, TX 78755. Publishers of the *Careers In . . .* series.

Random House Inc, 201 E 50th St, New York, NY 10022; 30-32 Bedford Square, London WC1B 3SG. Tel: (0171) 255 2393.

Rosen Publishing, 29 East 21st Street, New York, NY 10010. Publishes around 100 careers titles.

Self-Counsel Press Inc, 1704 N State St, Bellingham, WA 98225.

Simon & Schuster, 1230 Ave of the Americas, New York, NY 10020; 66 Wood Lane End, Hemel Hempstead, Herts HP2 4RG. Tel: (01442) 23155. Simon & Schuster subsidiaries Cambridge Books, Julian Messner, Prentice Hall all publish a number of careers titles.

Sulzberger & Graham, 165 West 91st Street, New York, NY 10024.

Surrey Books, 230 E Ohio Street, Suite 120, Chicago, IL 60611. Publishes a *How To Get a Job In . . .* series for various cities.

Ten Speed Press, Box 7123. Berkeley, CA 94707. UK rep: Airlift Book Co, 26-28 Eden Grove, London N7 8EF. Tel: (0171) 607 5792. Publishers of *Who's Hiring Who?; Offbeat Careers—The Directory of Unusual Work; What Color is Your Parachute?*.

Thomas Publishing, 5 Penn Plaza, New York, NY 10001.

VGM Careers Books (see National Textbook Co).

Walker & Co, 435 Hudson Street, New York, NY 10014. Publishers of *Career Choices for the Nineties*, a series of career guides for students arranged according to different fields of study.

Franklin Watts, Sherman Turnpike, Danbury, CT 06816; 96 Leonard St, London EC2A 4RH. Tel: (0171) 739 32929. Publishers of the *Career Concise Guide* series of some 50 titles.

John Wiley & Sons Ltd, 605 3rd Avenue, New York, NY 10158; Baffins Lane, Chichester, West Sussex PO19 1UD. Tel: (01243) 779777. Publishes a number of careers books including *The Job Finder's Library*.

Writer's Digest Books, 1507 Dana Ave, Cincinnati, OH 45207; UK rep: Vacation Work Publications, 9 Park End St, Oxford OX1 1HJ. Tel: (01865) 241987.

Index